Practical Information Engineering
the management challenge

Practical Information Engineering

the management challenge

Alex Davids

Pitman

PITMAN PUBLISHING
128 Long Acre, London WC2E 9AN

A Division of Longman Group UK Limited

© A. Davids & Data Logic Ltd. 1992

First published in Great Britain 1992

British Library Cataloguing-in-Publication Data
A catalogue record for this book is available
from the British Library

ISBN 0 273 03692 0

Printed and bound in Great Britain

Table of Contents

Preface

The ideas that are consolidated in *Practical Information Engineering* have arisen not only from my experiences in applying Information Engineering principles, but flow from the totality of my experience in computing. As I look back over that length of time, I recognise that there are a number of people whose attitudes and practices have strongly influenced me and to whom I owe a debt of gratitude. Often unbeknown to themselves, they have shown me, simply through their professionalism and dedication, that it is possible to achieve results that truly meet the needs of the users of the systems we have built together.

To my earliest colleagues on the DAP team, Inge Kristofferson and Margaret Sutton, you showed me how important the need was to communicate at all times among a team, and how to be generous in sharing knowledge, for it was of benefit to all in the long run. To Madinie Abrahams, Deon van Rooyen, and Marilyn Hawkins, you showed me that it was possible easily to co-ordinate an effort across very different technical environments by being willing to talk openly about the problems we were sharing, and by treating one another with professional respect. You all taught me that team spirit is intrinsic to success and imbued that spirit strongly in me. To Len van der Westhuizen and his team of co-ordinators, you showed me that a user-driven project can work, and, moreover, you showed me how to make it work by owning the complex system and making sure that we were always driven by your business needs.

To my colleague on the PCO team, Ana van Aardt, you showed me how to achieve astonishing productivity by doing it right the first time, how to clone reusable modules, though at the time we would never have called them that, and how critical user training was to the success of any system. To Peter Wilkins, your straightforward, honest management style, whether we were developing new systems or picking up old ones, has helped me to realise the strength that can come from managing people, not projects, and from empowering them to the fullest extent of their capabilities.

A particular debt of gratitude goes to the extraordinary team that worked with me on the first full IE project I undertook. Rarely have I encountered such a pool of talent in one place, and I am aware that many of you, too, believe that the project was a great learning experience. To Keith Downes, who pushed all of us screaming up a steep learning curve, your commitment to the project never faded, even at the most trying of times. To Ray Julian, Paul Hollingsworth, and Dave O'Keeffe, who turned IE concepts into reality against extraordinary odds, and Steve Olding, Steve Davies, Steve Mander, and Wendy Malcyk who got the most complex data captured into the right places, your belief in what we were doing, and perseverance in a complex and untried technical environment helped us to reap success against all odds: often the real heroes go unmarked, but not on this occasion. To my team members on the next BAA, Colin

Franklin, Anne McKnight, Mark Wightman and John Horne, you applied IE principles to regain user confidence and meet their needs, even where those needs spanned boundaries of language and territory. You proved that IE could be made to work efficiently and effectively.

To my colleagues, both past and present, in the Software Engineering Centre, Neville Boxer, Mike Payton, Martin Creedy, Jane Forster, Chris Leitzell, Chris Paris, Steve McGee, Steve Ellingham, and Gwen Baker: your broad array of experience has helped me to test out ideas and stimulated my thinking about matters related to IE. You will recognise many of the ideas in this book because you helped to form them.

To Graham Jackson and Bas Kadam, your ideas on the assessment of packages, and the BSD end of the life cycle in a complex array of technical environments have left an obvious mark on the book.

To John Wilson, your willingness to facilitate the production of the book, and interest and encouragement throughout are greatly appreciated. To Robert Burford, thank you for your comments on the early drafts, and willingness to plough through it at short notice.

To my editor, John Cushion, your easy-going encouragement, personal touch, and belief in the book have enabled me to turn an idea into reality.

To my wife, Jenny, who has, at times, wondered where I have disappeared to: it *is* finished. Thank you for providing the environment in which creative endeavour was possible, and for believing in what I was doing. To my parents, your encouragement from a great distance has given added impetus to my work. To Leon, your empathy over the past year is greatly appreciated. To Manfred, your friendship has always helped me through the good times and the tough ones.

The idea for this book came during an early morning walk in the hills beside Newfound Lake in central New Hampshire. My only companion was a dog called Abigaile, whose role in this book, though totally inexplicable, was significant. The conviviality of our hosts, Peter and Lee Fortescue of Six Chimneys, greatly facilitated the flow of ideas.

I would like to dedicate the book to B.S. and J.R. - good midwives, both.

Chapter 1 Introduction

During the second half of the 1980s, the Information Engineering approach to the development of software systems had become known and increasingly used among computer professionals throughout the world. Its growing acceptance in the United Kingdom has been signalled by the emergence of a fully fledged Information Engineering Certification Board under the auspices of the British Computer Society, which has drawn up a syllabus for a formal Certification in Information Engineering, and held the first such examinations in 1991.

Throughout the past decade, the concepts and theory underlying Information Engineering (IE) have gradually become known and are being applied in a commercial context. In most cases, IE principles were introduced to organisations in conjunction with the emerging Computer Assisted Software Engineering (CASE) tools that have enabled IE to work in practice. A large and complex learning curve resulted during which techniques, often familiar to the computer professional, were applied with a different emphasis in an unfamiliar context using automated software. Focus on the goal - the faster, more efficient development of software systems to meet business needs better - wavered as initial emphasis on the part of vendors and consultants lay in proving that the tools and methods worked. Often business users and computing professionals who were caught up in the learning curve found themselves unable to apply IE principles pragmatically and to good effect because they were unable to grasp an overall picture of the complex process that they were involved in.

1.1 Scope of the Book

Practical Information Engineering is aimed at both managers and doers who have to make IE work in practice. A significant part of this target audience consists of the managers from both the computing and the business communities, who will be responsible for some phase of the development of computerised systems using IE, or will be involved in such development either actively, or as reviewers of its output. There is a strong need not only for them to understand the IE context and process, but also the techniques involved and deliverables produced. Computer professionals, whose emphasis is on how to do IE effectively, will also find this book of relevance, for its primary emphasis is on making IE work in practice.

The pioneering days of IE have seen a number of modest successes being achieved, but what has loomed more ominously for IT professionals in particular has been those projects where vast resources were allocated but meaningful results were slow in coming. It is an aim of this book to assist IE practitioners to avoid the painful paralysis-through-analysis syndrome, to recognise the symptoms of a project going wrong, and to take effective remedial action. Equally important is the book's aim of assisting Information Engineers to recognise and achieve realistic quick, effective wins using IE. IE is not a panacea, nor are there simple paths to understanding it. It is not the author's intention to oversimplify complex issues; but it is his hope to avoid the air of mystification that some IE consultants have thrown over the process and the underlying concepts.

In an ideal world, the principles behind IE would be applied with great effectiveness to a green-field site. In most cases, however, any computerisation project is faced with the technical and application legacy that is the result of the history of automation in that organisation. In such cases, it is not possible to be idealistic or dogmatic about principles. Business realities require solutions that are achievable, and where IE is applied in these contexts, a great dose of pragmatism needs to accompany it. This does not, however, mean that quality need be compromised, or that the real requirements of users be swept under the carpet. In the context of this book, the pragmatic application of IE principles requires an understanding both of the problem to be solved, and the means of solving it that IE presents. This book hopes to encourage the use of IE in a manner best calculated to achieve the results that the business requires. This implies a strong partnership between computer professionals and end-users in the process of building computer systems. The business users know and understand their business; computer professionals understand the process of computerisation. In this alliance, IE can facilitate the joint definition and understanding of the problem - an aspect of the business that requires computerised support - in terms of information and the processing thereof, as well as the constructing of systems that solve the problem by providing adequate computerised support to the business.

IE can be seen in terms of clear stages: first the gross sizing and scoping of computerised support for the whole business needs to be undertaken. During this stage, the nature of the overall business is understood and its priorities are translated into manageable projects. Many organisations have undertaken such Information Strategy Studies, and often find themselves unable to proceed effectively from this necessarily high-level view of the business into anything meaningful in terms of computerisation and eventual systems. The second stage in the IE process involves the rigorous definition of the problem: the building of a model of a cohesive part of the business that will serve as the basis for the further development of computerised systems. This stage is central to the IE approach. Any computerised system based upon such a model necessarily represents a single solution to some or all of the problem defined, and will always be constrained by factors such as time, resources, and technology. The model itself can provide a relatively stable basis from which to bridge from what the business does, into systems that support it in its operation. Different systems that operate on different platforms (and include application packages) could be designed and implemented using the same business model as a basis. The primary emphasis of this book is, therefore, on defining the problem that computerisation assists in solving. This requires a strong understanding of how an effective business model is built, and what can be done with it subsequently. The third stage of IE involves the designing and construction of a system solution to the problem. In this stage, IE can provide assistance on the path forward, but more and more technical considerations come into play as the nature and structure of software and hardware platforms begin to impose their own constraints upon any system solution. For this reason, this book will deal more generally with how the business model can be effectively used in going ahead either with selecting packages, or with building systems. Throughout this process, the application of IE principles ensures that the business itself is the major driving factor behind any decisions made.

Any manager of an IE project should be aware that in applying business modelling skills to understanding the business, the users themselves may gain new or enhanced insights into the business processes and practices that they have hitherto taken for granted. This can result in some serious reconsideration of these issues, and the impact of this on the business and its possible political reverberations cannot be understated. If, in such a case, the users have not been involved in the evolution of the understanding of these potential changes, then the computing department stands in danger of being seen as a group of technical people who think they understand the business better than the business people themselves, and such an IE initiative is bound to fail.

1.2   Main Topics and Structure

It is hoped that this book will provide readers with a way in which to harness the vast potential power that an Information Engineering approach brings to the process of building application systems that meet the needs of business users. It may be useful to make a few observations about the main topics covered by the book in order that the reader's objectives can most effectively be met.

Chapters 2 and 3 introduce IE and CASE tools respectively, and provide useful overview material to assist in understanding the rest of the book. Chapter 4 deals with the linking of business and information issues at a high-level so that business priorities can be brought to bear upon the planning and development of computerised solutions. The heart of the book can be found in Chapters 5 to 11 where the topic of defining the problem is directly and fully addressed. Of these chapters, the most technical are Chapters 8 to 10. A manager wishing to understand the process may chose to skip these chapters in an initial reading, but will probably dip into it later as each technique begins to be applied formally in an IE project. On the other hand, any team member applying the techniques described, or reviewing their output, will probably want to refer to this chapter in more depth as it is relevant to them from the outset.

Chapters 12 and 13 address the design and construction of computerised systems in an IE context. Many of the problems experienced at this stage are familiar to computer professionals, and the emphasis in these chapters is therefore on the new challenges and opportunities that IE brings to this end of the development life cycle. Lastly, Chapter 14 looks into the not too distant future to conjecture as to where IE might lead. It is intended as a coda to the main body of the book which emphasises the practical and effective application of IE principles in the here and now.

The ultimate challenge to all IE practitioners is to "make it work." It is hoped that this book will facilitate that task.

Chapter 2 What is Information Engineering (IE)?

A way of approaching IE, with a view to understanding better what it is, is by briefly examining where it comes from. To do so, one has to look back to the earliest years of commercial computing and briefly trace the growth of what today are recognised and accepted as "structured" approaches to the analysis and design of computer systems. It is interesting to note in such a survey, how structured analysis and design have grown out of a number of parallel needs that drive commercial computing ever forwards. These can be broadly classified as technical and business needs. On the one hand there have been the technicians, constantly looking for approaches to their job that will simplify the tasks at hand; on the other there have been the businessmen who have invested vast sums of money to automate processes with a view to improving business, and, frankly, making more money.

2.1   The Growth of Structured Approaches to Analysis and Design

The earliest commercial computer systems were extremely primitive by today's standards. They were severely limited by the power of the computers themselves and, in effect, consisted of programs to solve clearly structured problems. The first real systems consisted of a suite of sequential programs that together mechanised a number of business processes that were often tedious and repetitive, or required a large amount of calculation. Payrolls were among the first parts of the business to be supported in this way. But these earliest systems were plagued by a fundamental problem which still haunts IT managers: they needed to be updated - **maintained** - on a regular basis to keep up with the demanding needs of users.[1] The maintenance problem was initially addressed by the IT community at the program level. "Ban the GOTO statement!" became the rallying cry of many a Data Processing (DP) department (and remains so in many to this day!). What was the real problem that they were trying to address? Fundamentally it all boiled down to a lack of formal structure, or what is termed "spaghetti code". A programmer called in to make amendments to another programmer's code could not recognise any familiar pattern in it. This was especially compounded when early, "primitive" or low-level languages were used for coding. Technical *whiz* kids did wonderful things with complex logic, but no-one else could understand the code. Third generation languages that were higher-level and so utilised more English-like words and structures were seen as one means of addressing the

---

[1] Maintaining code produced by other programmers according to their whims has always proved difficult - particularly when that code lacks documentation and obvious structure.

problem, but it was soon found that spaghetti code was just as easy to produce in say, COBOL, as it had been in ASSEMBLER. The programs being produced often lacked any sense of structure, and this problem was often compounded by the real commercial pressure to bring systems on stream within budgeted costs and time scales.

The problem is, no doubt, a familiar one. "How little times change," you may be muttering.

How was the abolition of the GOTO statement to solve this problem? Well, the implication was that programmers would be forced to understand the structure of the logic behind the process that they were attempting to automate, and use *this* to drive their program design. In the early sixties, it became recognised that the logical structure of a program could effectively be represented by means of the three basic structures illustrated in Figure 2.1: sequence, selection, and iteration. This

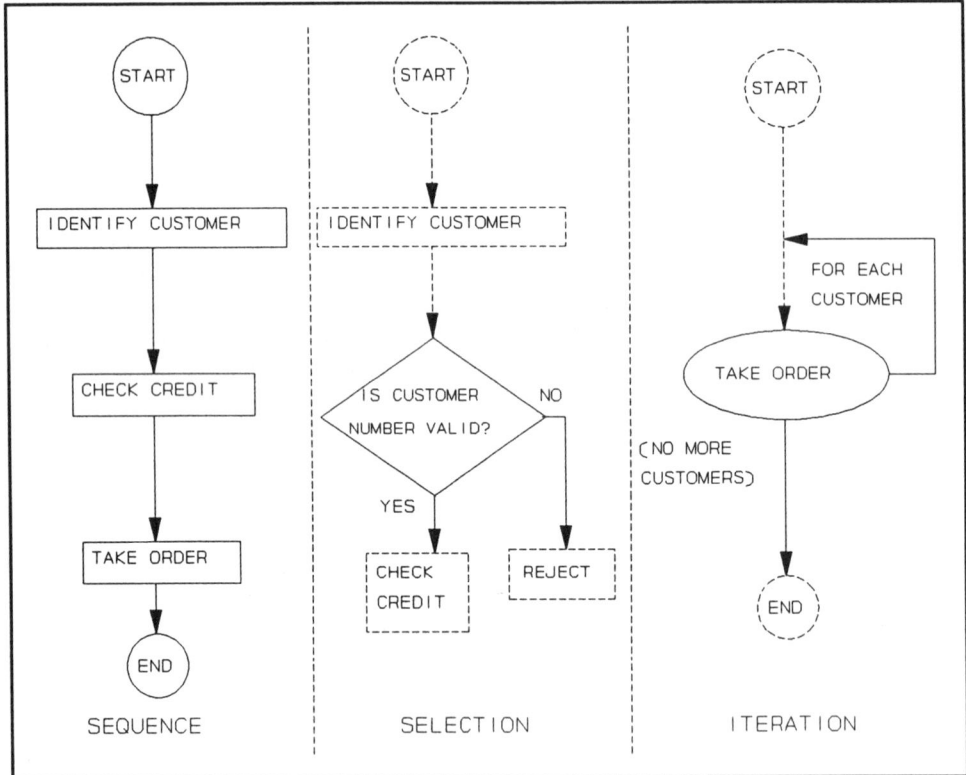

Figure 2.1 The Three Basic Programming Structures

recognition gave programmers the rules and structures for representing the logic of any program, and for communicating it at a high level to their peers. Furthermore, the principles underlying structured programming could be applied to any language that was based on the premise of a sequential flow of logic. Thus it could be retroactively applied to languages like ASSEMBLER, FORTRAN, COBOL, and BASIC, and could also be used in the formulation of present and future standards for the use of those languages in any organisation. Again, let it be said, the main impetus behind this was the need to be able to pick up a program someone else had written and "run with it." Whether you approached this need as a programmer called upon to maintain someone else's code, or as a user who needed a quick change to be made to a program, the end result was the same: productivity was increased through fundamentally structured code based upon recognised principles of organisation.

But, by the late sixties and early seventies, the problem had already shifted to some extent: no longer were programs the main focus and locus of attention. The system had come of age, and business users recognised that in computerising their business problems a series or suite of programs that constituted a computer system was needed. Again the shift had occurred through a varied number of changes, some technical, some competitive in nature. The actual computers that were running systems were larger and had much greater capacities. Efficient compilers meant that third generation languages had become the norm, and they were well suited to exploiting the new disk technologies, and their random access technique. No longer was it necessary to constrain business systems to what could be processed sequentially. On-line systems were becoming a possibility and a reality.

The response on the part of theorists and practitioners was the natural extension of the concept of "structured programming" into the concept of "structured systems analysis and design." The techniques and process involved in this evolution had a great deal to do with understanding the real needs of users (not their perceived ones). Many of these techniques were directed at bridging the gap between the real business users, and the technocrats in the Data Processing (DP) department. A variety of methods arose, mostly driven by an understanding of what business needs were, which amounted to understanding how the business operated within a given context and scope.

With the rise of database management systems (DBMS), the concept of "corporate data" was increasingly recognised by both the business community and by the DP department. There became an increased need to understand the way in which data supported an organisation and met its business needs. One of the myths that DBMS led to, certainly in the mind of many a business user of computer systems, was that all the data in an organisation would be consolidated in one place and be easily accessible to them. (Well, did we not also believe it at the time, and build up user hopes and aspirations in parallel with our own?) This certainly seemed like yet another in the large series of panaceas that has dogged computing since its infancy. A problem that this "panacea" would solve is one recognisable to many a user and customer to this day: users "knew" that the data they wanted was "in the computer," for they had seen it in various reports; they just could never get at it when and how they wanted to.

The reason for this is that computerised systems across an organisation had been designed in isolation from one another. Moreover, the islands of systems within an organisation very often required the construction of other systems, sometimes extremely complex ones, to act as interfaces between them. This, of course, added to the number and complexity of systems that had to be run and supported, and, rather obviously, added to the overall costs of computing in an organisation.

During the seventies, but particularly through the eighties, a number of structured methods or "methodologies" for the development of computerised systems became formalised. These were designed to ensure that the communication gap between the business users' and system developers' understanding of what was required from the system was bridged, and that, from a developer's point of view, all information required to build the system was gathered and formally recorded. Many of the established "methodologies" are often compendiums of the tasks and associated deliverables that are perceived to be necessary for building a system. What they often require is the exercise of some discretion if they are not to become nothing more than a bureaucratic means for producing voluminous amounts of paper which are seldom effectively reviewed or understood by business users. Such "methodologies" are excellent at placing a tight umbrella of control over a project, but the production of paper, not a system, can become an end in itself, and the real **business information processing** nature of the project can become obscured.

Not surprisingly, many of these methods are process-driven: they start with an attempt at understanding how the business processes they wish to computerise work, and from this they build up an understanding of the data required to make the system work. Implicit in such an approach is that **each system will redefine data needs anew**. A changing emphasis was forced onto such structured approaches by the growth of Data Base Management Systems (DBMS), because these implied that a single unified corporate view of data is required across an organisation. As a result, data-driven analysis techniques have grown and been incorporated to varying degrees into a number of methodological approaches. It is such a data-driven emphasis that underlies the IE approach to developing computerised systems.

While this overview of the background to the growth of structured approaches to the analysis and design of computer systems has necessarily been brief and cursory, it forms a useful backdrop against which to understand and view IE, for IE grows directly out of the same series of difficulties and concerns on the part of (now) Information Technology (IT) managers and staff. It also arises directly out of the technological push with which a variety of technical advances in computing have challenged both developers and users. These include: relational database systems, where data can be stored and interrelated in ways that are closer to their real logical structures than ever before; personal computers (PCs) and the massive growth in computer literacy and user expectations they have spawned; Computer Assisted Software Engineering (CASE) tools (see chapter 3), which allow IT professionals to perform a great number of the planning, analysis, design, and construction tasks they had previously done manually with the aid of a computer, more often than not a PC. These great advances, however, still exist against the backdrop of poor development productivity; systems that do not adequately meet user needs; overruns of computer projects both in terms of time and money; and massive proportions of computing budgets being spent on maintaining old, cumbersome, but critical systems.

2.2   Business Impetus for Structured Approaches to the Development of Systems

Against this essentially technical view of the challenges systems developers are faced with, it is possible to juxtapose some of the critical threats and challenges facing any serious business manager as we enter the 1990s. Many of these can be summed up as an **acceleration in the pace of change** that businesses are having to cope with. We are familiar, for example, with some of the challenges in dealing in a global marketplace where events in remote places have immediate implications on all aspects of business. This is partially a direct result of a series of accelerations in the technology surrounding communications in the broadest senses of the term: air travel is commonplace, satellite communications facilitate the transfer of data on a massive scale - and that transfer involves information, voice, pictures and sound. Computerisation has had no small part to play in the pressures placed on running a competitive business today. When we look purely at the cost/performance ratio of computer hardware, we have seen a million-fold increase **every twenty years** since the inception of computers in the 1940s. This increase in MIPS[2] per currency unit is likely to continue at the same rate. It means that, in the years ahead, more and more complex problems can potentially be tackled effectively by computers. This will immediately challenge us on two fronts: the developers of computer systems will not be able to resort to essentially manual and often seat-of-the-pants ways of constructing and delivering systems. Their "art" will have to become subject to the rigours that face all major construction tasks. They will have to adopt the appropriate techniques, tools, and methods in order to build systems that are fully responsive to business needs.

But the challenge to business is likely to be just as great, and as such must bring the users and the developers into an alliance if any future systems are to meet and fulfil the vital requirements that a fast-changing business environment will impose upon them.

Up until recently, business users and developers have shared a fundamentally simplistic view of the information needs and flows of a business. We initially viewed businesses as allied to closed systems, believing that businesses responded as integrated units to challenges in the outside world. Perhaps we never recognised the obvious: that those responses required a similar flexibility and resilience to be built

---

[2] Million Instructions Per Second.

into the systems we constructed to support the business. From a computerisation point of view, we were driven by a very functional view of the business. We always were asked to produce systems based on "Functional Specifications." The result has been a series of islands of systems many of which perform the **function** that was originally envisaged (to some or other extent), but that are "incompatible" with one another. Often the issue of incompatibility is wrongly reduced to hardware differences: system A runs on a yellow box, system B on a green one, and we cannot get them talking to one another. Although this may indeed be part of the problem, it is only a symptom, not a cause. Even if the two machines could communicate physically with one another, for the two systems to do so effectively, they require some common ground to be established between them. This is often precisely what an interface system between them achieves in reality: it translates the data format from one system to another, but in so doing it also translates the meaning and often the context in which that data operates when seen from each system's differing perspective. All of this though is very *ad hoc*: an interface allows two specific systems to exchange data, but what about many more systems, all of which need to be talking to one another? "Ah," I hear you exclaim, "An integrated operational corporate database!" Well, yes, that would be the ultimate conceptual goal, but we all know it is impossible to achieve in practice.

Let us step back for a moment and look again at what we have been talking about, for it is a focus that we as purveyors of information, or at least of raw data, have failed to recognise. **Our primary responsibility as developers of computer systems is not with what the business does, nor how it achieves its objectives, but rather with providing the information it requires to do so.** In building systems based upon functional specifications, we have failed to understand the nature of the basic building blocks upon which information systems must be built: the structure of the data itself. The ways in which a business may chose to operate (its functions, if you like) definitely will change over a period of time - they must if the business is to continue operating effectively within a changing environment. However, the data entities (things that it needs to keep information about) and their relationships to one another tend to remain fundamentally unchanging over time. A Victorian banker would have recognised concepts such as "Customer," "Account," "Ledger Entry," etc. just as a modern day banker will. Our nineteenth century counterpart, however, would not know what we are talking about when it comes to some of the "hows" of today's banking operation: plastic cards, automatic teller machines, electronic fund transfers, etc.

By recognising that the data that underpins any business operation remains fundamentally unchanging over time, we have in our hands a powerful means for building stability into the ways in which we construct systems to meet **changing** business needs. What is even more attractive to our users - the business community itself - is that we can adequately capture and model some of these unchanging aspects of their businesses as a solid basis for the future construction of computerised systems. Furthermore, in combining them, in a model, with a view of what the business does, we can provide managers with a business model that provides a stable baseline against which to manage the processes of change and structural re-organisation that they are being forced to encounter in their everyday working environment.

2.3   The Information Engineering Approach

The Information Engineering (IE) approach attempts to bring the business and its inherent underlying structures into the process of information systems development. At its heart it is an architectured approach. It implies that behind every major systems development project undertaken within an organisation, there lies a blueprint or master plan into which that project fits. Such a master plan is derived directly from the business itself: from its objectives, goals, and critical success factors; and it is *these* factors that drive every development or maintenance project, not an organisation's perceived view of itself at a given point in time.

IE allows for the setting up of a series of business architectures - Information Architecture, Systems Architecture, and Technical Architecture - that are derived from, and driven by, the business. Within these architectures, systems are developed based on refined **models** of a Business Area. It is these two basic elements of IE that distinguish it from all other systems development approaches:

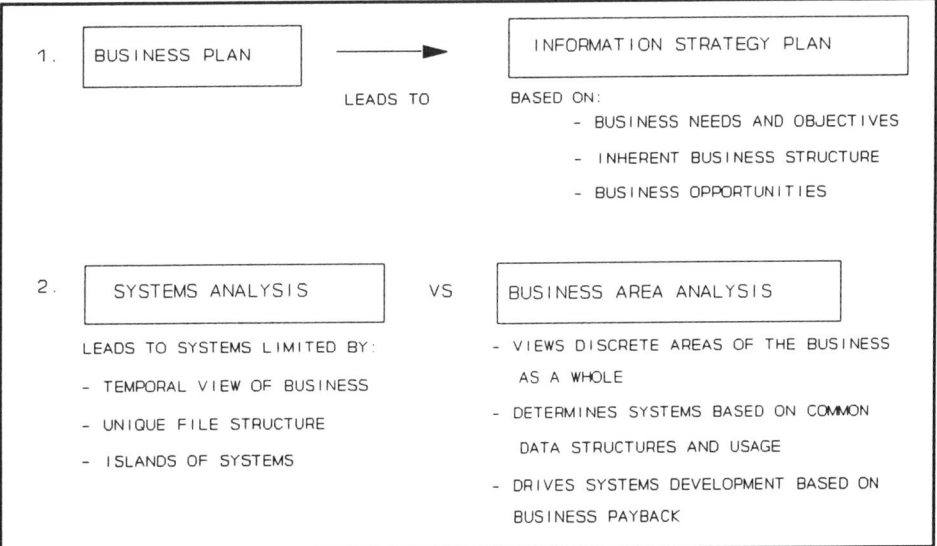

Figure 2.2 Basic Elements of IE

- It advocates the development of an Information Strategy Plan that **flows out of and is closely aligned with the organisation's Business Plan** and that forms the basis for all future computerised systems development.
- It views and analyses a discrete area of the business in the development of a series of logical **Business Models** that form the basis of any future systems

development. The discrete Business Areas are based not upon the whims of a single person, or a (static) view of the business at a given time, but upon the **information usage** that functional pieces of the business share with one another.

To understand the overall IE process better, it will be useful at this stage to give a brief overview of the IE development life cycle and to summarise the main tasks and objectives of each IE phase. The paths through this life cycle framework are the topics of Chapters 4 to 12.

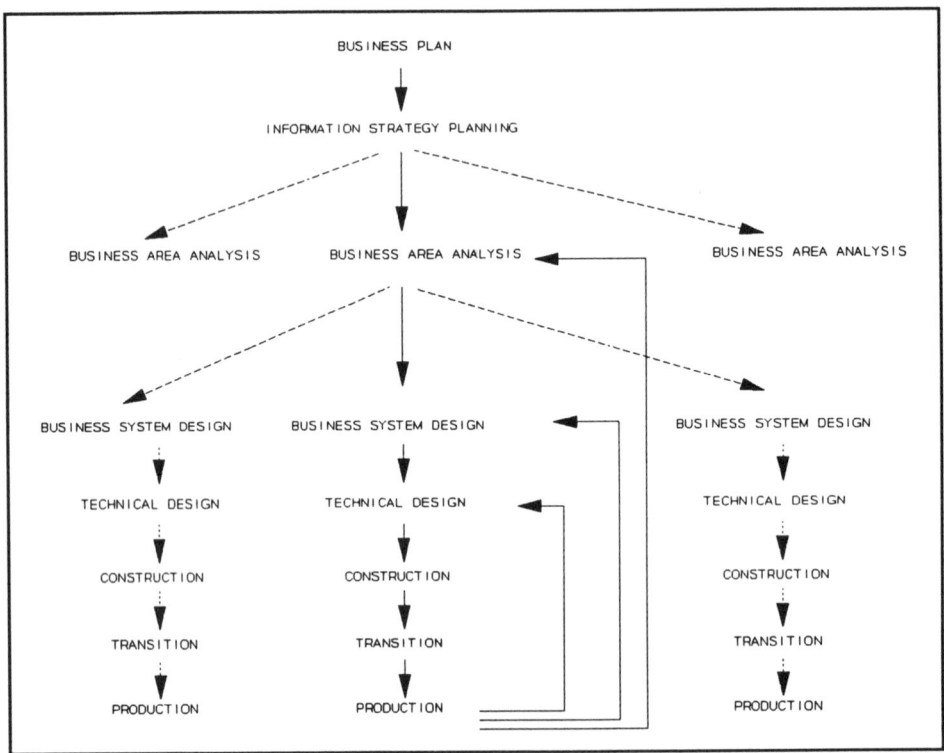

Figure 2.3 The Information Engineering Life Cycle

2.3.1   Phase 1 - Information Strategy Planning (ISP)

The ISP phase of IE is discussed more fully in Chapter 4.

Objectives

●   To provide an organisation with an objective basis for making Information

Technology (IT) investment decisions.

- To link an organisation's mission, objectives, and the critical success factors it recognises for achieving them to an Information Strategy that supports the organisation in realising its goals.

- To ensure that future systems developers (analysts and designers) have a clear understanding of the underlying business information structure into which their project fits, and the business issues that are driving IT investment decisions.

- To obtain senior management commitment to the Information Plan.

Main Tasks

- Plan the project.

- Determine the organisation's mission, its objectives, and the main critical success factors for achieving them.

- Determine, at a broad level, the main categories of information or "subject areas" that the organisation requires in order to function effectively.

- Determine what the main activities of the organisation are. This means understanding at a high, functional level what the organisation does.

- Group the main functions, based on their usage of the main categories of information identified. This grouping of functions determines the Business Areas that the organisation covers.

- Determine within each Business Area a set of Conceptual Systems that the business requires to operate effectively.

- Evaluate the organisation's current systems in terms of their applicability to the business and their effectiveness.

- Use the broad understanding of the underlying business structure to determine a technological strategy that will support the business. This will take into account the categories of hardware and software the business will require to meet its objectives.

- Evaluate where the potential business investment opportunities lie in terms of potential systems that meet business objectives and provide a competitive advantage.

- Present the Information Plan to senior management and obtain permission to proceed.

An ISP project is likely to lead to one or more Business Area Analysis projects and the Information Strategy Plan should be reviewed and updated as part of an organisation's annual business planning cycle.

2.3.2   Phase 2 - Business Area Analysis (BAA)

A fuller overview of the BAA phase is presented in Chapter 5, and the analysis process is discussed in detail in Chapters 6 to 11.

Objectives

- To build a model of the Business Area in terms of:
  - its information requirements (data entities);
  - its business processes;
  - the interaction between elementary business processes and data entities.

- To identify potential system solutions based on a better understanding of the data usage within a Business Area.

- To propose System Design Projects that relate potential system solutions to the organisation's mission, objectives, and main critical success factors. This confirms the areas for potential business investment opportunities identified in the ISP phase.

Main Tasks

- Prepare for the Analysis project by ensuring that a project plan, together with the necessary support and control structures, is in place.

- Confirm or Construct the high level model. This task is fundamentally a formal confirmation of the project scope in terms of IE conventions, and the ISP deliverables (where they exist). The issues addressed in this task and the previous one are fully discussed in Chapter 6.

- Gather information (discussed in section 8.1).

- Model the Business Area (discussed in sections 8.2.1, 9.1, and 10.1).

- Analyze, and where appropriate, derive a business model from current systems (discussed in sections 5.2, 6.7, and 8.2.2).

●   Confirm and check the Business Area Model (discussed in section 10.2).

●   Plan for design (discussed in Chapter 11).

●   Present and obtain authorization (discussed in section 11.5).

2.3.3   Phase 3 - System Design

This phase is often divided into a logical design stage, known as **Business Systems Design (BSD)**, and a physical design stage, known as **Technical Design (TD)**. Where it is not intended to use the code generators that are integral to an Integrated CASE (I-CASE) tool, these phases tend to be more closely coupled and targeted towards a specific hardware and software platform. The design phase is discussed fully in Chapter 12.

Objectives

●   To ensure that the designed system both supports the business enterprise's stated goals, and its current and/or intended business practices.

●   To transform a subset of the Business Model into a design specification.

●   To ensure that the system design meets user requirements.

●   To establish test design and user acceptance criteria.

●   To detail the procedures required to load data into the system and to convert from existing systems to the designed one.

●   To define the construction tasks.

Main Tasks

●   Plan and allocate time and resources.

●   Review the results of the Business Area Analysis project and confirm the scope of the design project.

Business Systems Design (BSD) Tasks

●   Design the preliminary data structure.

●   Map elementary business procedures to procedures.

●   Design the overall system structure.

- Design procedural dialogue flows.

- Design screens and report layouts.

- Design the procedure logic and detailed data access.

- Confirm the design.

Technical Design (TD) Tasks

- Design implementable procedures.

- Design run control procedures for the overall system.

- Design and issue standards for the chosen hardware and software platform.

- Design standards and procedures for acceptance testing.

- Define plan for the construction stage of the project.

2.3.4   Phase 4 - Construction

Where a code generator is used that is part of an Integrated CASE (I-CASE) tool, this phase tends to be more closely linked in with the design phase. In this case, the rapid building of systems can be facilitated through the use of prototyping in Joint Application Development sessions that lead directly to the generation of systems. Where a separate code generator or 4GL is used for construction, this is more likely to conflate the Technical Design and Construction phases, and separate BSD from them.[3] The exact relationship between what we have called phases 3 and 4 will be very dependent on the tools chosen for the task. The construction phase is more fully discussed in Chapter 13.

Objectives

- To construct and test the specified system.

- To meet company audit, security, and archiving requirements.

- To develop procedures for the day-to-day operation of the system in a production environment.

---

[3] This is fully discussed in section 12.1.

Main Tasks

- Plan for construction.

- Prepare the construction and test environments.

- Code and test the system using a 3GL and/or 4GL and/or a code generator. (In practice, the final overall system is likely to involve a combination of these software platforms.)

- Develop and test the operating procedures.

- Build and test the complete system.

- Produce operating instructions and user documentation.

2.3.5   Phase 5 - Transition

Phases 5 and 6 are familiar to any systems development manager, and procedures that are adopted to effect them will vary widely from organisation to organisation. For this reason it is not intended to detail the tasks involved. Chapter 13 discusses different ways in which IE potentially deals with the issues of production systems and the question of maintenance.

Objectives

- To verify system performance levels.

- To verify that the system functions as users require it to.

- To train users in the use and operation of the system.

- To load and/or convert data.

2.3.6   Phase 6 - Production

Objectives

- To bring the system into the production environment.

- To maintain the required levels of performance and functionality.

- To monitor the system's performance against ongoing business needs.

- To ensure that the system continues to meet current business needs.

***

Before going on to discuss the IE phases in detail, it is necessary to examine briefly the tools that can be used to simplify the path ahead.   Chapter 3 deals with the use of CASE tools, particularly in an IE environment.

Chapter 3 The Use of CASE Tools

The term, Computer Aided (or Assisted) Software Engineering, or more simply, CASE, refers to a wide variety of software based tools that assist in various aspects of the system development life cycle. The use of the term became common in the 1980s, and is applied to a wide variety of software products. As a result, almost *any* software product that assists in any way in the development of computerised systems today lays claim to the label CASE.

In an IE context we are interested in certain types of CASE tools only, because of the way in which they allow the practical implementation of the concepts and practices that underlie IE. In fact, IE and CASE go hand in hand: an IE-based method provides a solid framework for the use of CASE tools, while IE itself could not be practised effectively without CASE tool support.

Before examining each of these points in more depth in section 3.2, it is necessary to consider what it is that we mean by CASE tools in an IE context.

3.1   What is CASE?

A CASE tool that is of relevance in an IE context is one that allows business users and computer professionals together to interact with information about the business, contained in a single dictionary, via graphical and/or pictorial representations of that information. Furthermore, the dictionary containing the information should in itself contain and enforce rules about the complex interrelationships between the elements of information that it contains.[1] In order to support IE, the CASE tool should, by definition, provide full life cycle coverage from ISP through Construction into Production support. As such, it should have the following characteristics:

- Seamless transition from phase to phase, with the same model being used throughout the development life cycle.

- An ability to generate a system automatically from the information contained in the central encyclopedia.

Such a CASE tool is generally referred to as an integrated or I-CASE tool.

By contrast, an approach to CASE that is currently gaining momentum takes the approach that the central repository is the key to a CASE (and, indeed, an engineered)

---

[1] Such a dictionary is variously referred to as a "Repository" or an "Encyclopedia".

approach to system development. Various CASE tools can provide the pieces of functionality needed for full life cycle coverage, with the repository providing the means of co-ordination as the models are passed from CASE tool to CASE tool. This approach, known as Component-CASE, or C-CASE, relies on a fully functioning central repository and standard definitions for the interfaces to and from it, and some of its future focus and impetus is briefly discussed in section 14.2. A C-CASE approach is not at odds with IE as long as integration between the components can be achieved. In current practice, the moving of a model from one environment to another may not be as smooth or as simple as suppliers claim, and significant information can get lost or may need to be re-entered.[2]

In addition to the characteristics described above, for a CASE tool to be suitable in an IE context, it must also provide support for the basic modelling techniques that are appropriate to each specific IE phase.[3]

3.2   The Relationship between IE and CASE

Initially the I-CASE approach was seen to be the only way in which IE could be practised because it was the only context in which consistency of approach could be applied to an evolving set of models throughout the development life cycle. In practice though, any I-CASE tool imposes its own approach to IE upon its users. It is important that this is fully understood by would-be IE practitioners for in reality, unless they have a clear view of **what it is they are doing or wish to do by applying IE, the I-CASE tool can become an end in itself, and an off-the-shelf method, closely tied in to the CASE tool, can shackle them.** The primary focus of this book aims at presenting IE practitioners with a clear understanding of the principles and techniques underlying IE. This will enable them to apply the principles and techniques within the constraints that **any** I-CASE tool will impose upon them. In doing so, the practitioner is better able to exercise judgement, and keep an eye on the final target that the implementation of IE aims at: systems that better meet user needs. This is the ultimate goal, even if theoretical considerations need to be compromised to reach it. The approach to IE taken in this book is thus an entirely pragmatic one. In order for the practitioner to apply IE well there are two things that need to be known and understood:
- What it is that is being attempted (the IE framework); and
- The limitations imposed upon that framework by the tools being used (whether I-CASE or C-CASE).

The emphasis of this book is upon the former. Armed with an overview and

---

[2] This both introduces potential errors and requires additional work.

[3] The full significance of this statement can only be understood if the relevant techniques described in Chapters 4 to 12, and the relationship between them, are fully understood.

understanding of IE principles in theory and in practice, it is then up to the project manager to exercise judgement and experience based on practical knowledge gained and a thorough understanding of the tools being used to do the job.

It is clear that CASE tools in general have not provided many of the productivity benefits that were originally claimed or hoped for from them. In some cases, this is because the tools themselves have been used as no more than sophisticated drawing aids without the full exploitation of their potential being effected. Used as a framework, not as a doctrine, IE can provide an effective framework for the use of the CASE tools that meet the basic requirements discussed in section 3.1. In so doing, IE helps to minimise the risk of failure, and will assist, once an initial learning curve has been overcome, in increasing productivity and enhancing system quality. This is partially because the framework given by the method provides a means for guiding the overall project direction, and for measuring both its achievement and quality. IE on its own cannot make up for a whole series of other deficiencies that may threaten the progress of any project. Many of the Critical Success Factors that have been identified for a BAA project[4] apply throughout the life cycle of any IE endeavour, and their applicability should be considered carefully.

While IE provides a good framework for the use of CASE tools, it is equally true to point out that it would be impossible to practise IE effectively without CASE tool support. The models that are developed in IE are complex: the rules by which elements in the model are associated need to be recorded and enforced. The CASE tool becomes the primary means for doing so. By presenting aspects of the model to users of the tool, very often by means of a diagrammatic representation, the CASE tool facilitates communication between business users and IT professionals, and concentrates attention upon a single part of the problem being analyzed. Complexity is thereby effectively reduced through segmentation.

The CASE tool can also provide support for a wide variety of analysis and design techniques: it facilitates their use by automating many aspects of their application. This is most apparent when it comes to the construction and maintenance of diagrams: a CASE tool can make the changing of diagrams an easy task, while at the same time ensuring that consistency is maintained throughout the underlying model. Containing, as it does, all the relevant information about the model, an effective CASE tool will also provide support for the production of deliverables that are based on aspects of the model it contains. A major productivity factor in the use of a good CASE tool will be its ability to check the model for completeness and correctness, or to facilitate such checking. This often takes the form of consistency reporting, and of listings of aspects of the model based on predetermined criteria. The ultimate aim of an effective IE CASE tool is the automatic generation of a system from the models that it contains: it is at this end of the life cycle that the most potential productivity gains are to be

---

[4] See section 6.8.

made. However, it is clear that effective code or system generation is dependent on the quality of the models that they are generated from, and so the spotlight falls strongly on, particularly, the BAA and BSD phases of IE - those most emphasised in the rest of this book.

3.3   Current Problems with CASE

In the current implementation of many CASE tools that span some or all of the IE development life cycle, a series of problems arise that may present challenges to the would-be CASE user. Many of the CASE tools are PC-based in order best to capitalise on the graphic capabilities of such a platform. However, in attempting to increase functionality and provide full I-CASE support, they are often pushing PC technology close to its limits: in order to run some CASE tools very large extended memory and disk storage is a prerequisite. In this trend, CASE tools are no different from other software products. However, a user should be careful to determine exactly what sort of hardware configuration is minimum and/or recommended for adequate performance of the product being considered.

In both I-CASE and C-CASE implementations, the reality of the hardware architectures of most of the current tools means that work on a subset of a model is effectively restricted to a single user at a time, and that the models are not secure. Careful manual (supplemented sometimes by automated) controls need to be put into place in order to control the transfer of models between PCs, to control the consolidation of models into a single encyclopedia, and for recovery and backup of models. The nature and extent of these problems will differ depending on the software tool itself, but, though they are improving over time, they should not be underestimated or trivialised.

***

It is time now to turn to the IE process itself, beginning, in the next chapter with the first phase of IE - Information Strategy Planning.

Chapter 4 Information Strategy Planning (ISP)

Many organisations have begun to understand the need to align their development of computerised systems with the needs and priorities of the business itself. In practice, this often takes the form of a prioritisation of the requests for systems that business users perceive that they need, and then the allocation of the appropriate resources to the project when it reaches the top of the pile. There is often a substantial time delay involved in this process that business users find frustrating - so much so that in the era of desktop computers, it is not uncommon to find that computer literate users have gone ahead and developed make-shift systems which, with time, become the key to the way they do business, and the provision of their information needs. As long as they use information, or create information that is strictly of local use, this sort of development poses no real problems to an organisation. It is when information used by various parts of the corporation is collected and/or manipulated by such unco-ordinated systems that problems begin to arise. At worst, there is a duplication and proliferation of critical information throughout the organisation: no-one knows which system's view of the information is current or correct, and it is often difficult to collate information from such systems. Often, definitions of the information differ, and attempts at blending or importing information highlight the fact that dissimilar things are being used as the basis for comparison and co-ordination.

Within the Information Engineering life cycle, the first issue that is tackled is the development of a plan for exploiting information that **grows out of, and is aligned with, the overall business plan of the organisation**. This chapter deals with the development of such an Information Strategy Plan and concentrates on the first IE phase in the development life cycle - Information Strategy Planning (ISP).

The actual development of the Information Strategy Plan, discussed in section 4.4, is dependent on a number of specific links being made between business issues and information issues. In order to do this, it is necessary to identify formally those aspects of the business that are relevant to driving the creation of an Information Strategy Plan - the key business goals, objectives, and critical success factors that have to be addressed by information systems. These business issues and their formulation in terms that can be used in the ISP process - and indeed beyond - are addressed in section 4.1.

Similarly, a helicopter view has to be developed of the information issues that underpin the business. These aspects of developing the ISP include the identification and modelling of key information needs, an understanding of the main business functions, and an assessment of the current systems, and are discussed further in section 4.2.

At the core of any work undertaken as a result of the ISP lies the corporate

Information Architectures. These will form the framework within which any future systems development takes place and are key to the development of any Information Strategy Plan. The architectures themselves are the subject of section 4.3.

Lastly the main features of the Information Strategy Plan itself are examined in section 4.4.

It is not the intention of this chapter to make the reader proficient in performing an ISP. Its main purpose is to ensure that the issues underlying the Information Strategy Plan are understood so that its components can be fully utilised in the subsequent IE phases - particularly the BAA and the BSD.

4.1   Identifying the Business Issues

The starting point for any ISP work is the company business plan itself. The format and content of this may differ widely from company to company, and the first activities of the ISP are involved in transforming that plan into a series of clearly defined sets of goals and objectives. These are then captured in the format of spreadsheets which can be easily manipulated and analyzed further, and, in this process, further aspects of the business, such as the critical success factors related to any business goal, are analyzed and documented.

It is important to note that the undertaking of an ISP presupposes the existence of a business plan. In reality, for many organisations, the format of the business plan may obscure or only indirectly address the issues that need to be brought to the fore in order to develop an Information Strategy Plan. **Even where no formal business plan appears to exist, the highest level of management in the company will have a view on where they believe the company is going, and by what path.** It is this information that will be formally captured and analyzed at the beginning of an ISP. The less formal the business plan is, the more up-front work may be required, and this will inevitably extend the length of the ISP. As with any IE activity, the users - in this case the highest level of management in the company - need to understand what is being done, and need to be informed of potential limitations with the basic input to the ISP process that may impact upon the project timescales.

A particularly effective way of gathering the base information required, and at the same time securing the agreement of senior management as to how the issues that emerge are resolved and documented, is to use User Intensive Analysis sessions.[1] At

---

[1] At an ISP level these are sometimes referred to as Joint Requirement Planning sessions. These are similar in structure to the sessions that can be held at the beginning of a BAA, particularly when speed is essential, and to the Joint Application Development sessions that can form part of the transition from BAA to BSD. (See section 8.1.2, page 118.)

these, the key directors and senior managers are brought together, and, as the main business issues are aired and documented, initial information models are also developed.[2] In many ways, this approach is preferable when operating at the top level in a company: the senior managers, whose input and commitment to the process is crucial, are used to working under pressure and making high-level decisions. The alternative approach of structured interviews where two analysts interview individual managers[3] does not facilitate the resolution of conflicting ideas and attitudes. Where these conflicts are either based on the personalities involved, or have to do with the internal company politics, it will be extremely difficult for such issues to be adequately resolved, or even brought out into the open, and such an open forum can facilitate this.

It is **absolutely essential** for the top echelons of management to be involved in the ISP process, for the ultimate success of an ISP exercise will depend upon the quality of the steering, information and commitment gained from them.

The key business issues that need to be analyzed and recorded are often formally recognised for the first time during the ISP process. This does not mean that management are not aware of them, only that they are forced to consider and formulate them unambiguously.

A high-level understanding of the business usually begins with its purpose or mission which is sometimes formally recorded in a **Mission Statement**. From the mission, the company's **strategy** expressed as **aims and objectives** flows, and it is the task of the ISP to record each of these formally and unambiguously. The aims and objectives are the broad, medium to long term results that the organisation wishes to achieve; the strategies are approaches to achieving them.

The formulation of the business objectives allows the analysts to begin to isolate the **Critical Success Factors (CSFs)** which describe the essential conditions the business requires to meet if it is to achieve its objectives. CSFs do not depend only on internal factors: what the competition and the market are doing will certainly affect both strategies and objectives. CSFs may also be expressed negatively as **Risks**.

The CSFs relating to each objective are recorded and co-ordinated in the form of a matrix such as is illustrated in Figure 4.1.

Whilst aims and objectives are generally medium- to long-term, **Goals** are the translation of those aims into measurable targets to be achieved at a specific point in time. They must be formulated in such a way that they can be measured. A long term strategic aim might be, "To expand the business into Europe," but it is too

---

[2] The information models are discussed further in section 4.2.

[3] See section 8.1.

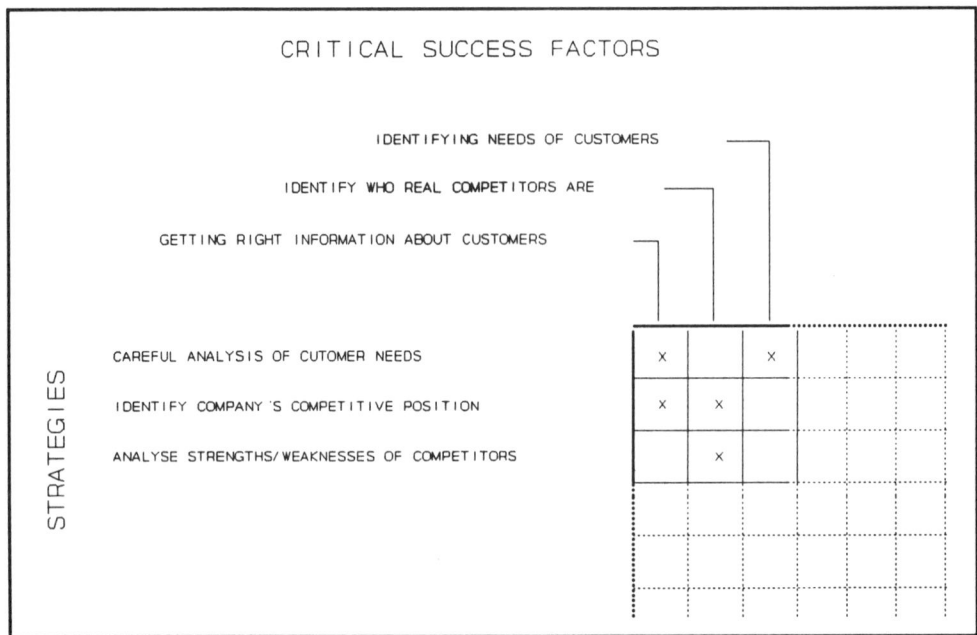

Figure 4.1 Objectives/Critical Success Factors Matrix

vaguely formulated for one to measure and monitor its achievement. The strategic aim may be supported by a series of shorter term goals such as, "To open five wholesale outlets in at least two European countries within the next twelve months." These will permit progress to be measured against the business action plan. It is important that clear **Performance Measures** are identified for each goal. The goals can then be recorded as an axis of a matrix, and can be related back to particular aims and also to specific CSFs as the business analysts and users begin to share an understanding of the key needs and priorities for the business. As that understanding grows, the priorities to be assigned to aims, CSFs, and supporting goals are formally agreed.

The identification of the key business issues described above are the minimum, basic building blocks for the development of an Information Strategy Plan. They also provide the basis, as shall become clearer in chapters 7 and 11, for directing the analysis and design work undertaken later in the BAA and BSD phases of IE.

In addition to the understanding of such key business issues, the final ISP plan needs to take cognisance of the current organisational structure, and will be affected by any planned changes to this. The ISP team needs also to explore future scenarios with the senior management team in order to ensure that the final plan it produces has taken the most important and likely of these into account. These considerations feed directly into scoping considerations at the beginning of a BAA project, and into the stability analysis that is formally undertaken at its end (see section 10.2.3).

4.2   Defining the Information Issues

The ISP is directed at producing a plan for the development of information systems that directly relate to, and grow out of, the business issues described in section 4.1. In order to do that, the business itself needs to be described, and ultimately modelled, in terms that permit such direct relationships to be made. The key elements of such a description relate to bridging a gap between business people's perceptions of the business itself, and the perception that IT developers will have of the business. IT developers are concerned with gaining a particular perspective on the business: they are interested in how it uses information to do whatever it is it is doing. This perspective has two sides that need to be understood and, ultimately, formally and rigorously interrelated:

● There is the information itself, of which the following questions need to be asked:

- What information does the business require in order to operate?

- How do the constituent parts of this information interrelate to one another? Another way of formulating the same question is: What is the underlying structure of the information that underpins the whole organisation?

At an ISP level, the aim will be to answer these questions in outline by establishing the basic "things" (sometimes called "high-level data entities") that an organisation needs to know about. These will be defined - sometimes grossly, for their refinement is part of the BAA process - and their relationship with one another will be documented. Broad constellations of these high-level entities may be grouped along business lines for the purposes of aiding comprehension, and these business groupings are called Data Subject Areas. The broad definition of the overall business data needs is further discussed in section 4.2.1.

● There is what the business does with the information it requires. Initially though there is simply the need to understand what it is that the corporation does in broad terms (its main functional areas) independently of how it is currently organised in performing its activities. This involves a careful top-down analysis of the corporate business functionality in order to determine the overall gross business activities that the business is involved in. In this analysis, the ISP team will be looking at both true business functions, and those that are strictly speaking supportive to the overall business operation. The analysis and modelling of business activities is discussed in section 4.2.2.

The understanding of how these two perspectives of the business interact is used as a basis for defining and describing the Business Information Architecture, a topic that is tackled in section 4.3.1 as part of an overall discussion of the Corporate Information Architectures.

A further aspect of information that needs to be considered is how the business information needs are currently being addressed. Existing information systems will affect the building of an Information Strategy Plan, and their current status needs to be understood. This will require an assessment of all current information systems in terms of their applicability to the business, and the extent to which they address business needs, a topic which is further explored in section 4.2.3.

4.2.1   Information Needs - High-level Entities and Data Subject Areas

An ISP needs to discover and model the main information needs of the overall organisation as they are perceived when taking a helicopter view of the business. The objective at this stage is to identify the "things" (or Entity Types) that the business needs to know about in order to operate. This initial view of the business information needs is, necessarily, gross and lacking in fine detail. The main aim is to identify what the business needs to know about: it becomes the task of the BAA phase to refine the understanding of the particular information needs of a specific business area.[4] Very often, an entity type that is identified and defined in ISP becomes several entity types at the BAA stage. Board level managers may feel comfortable with identifying PRODUCT as an entity type, but as Figure 4.2 illustrates, product developers may need to see a more complex picture. For this reason, entity types identified and defined at the ISP stage are often loosely referred to as "high-level entity types," or, more simply, "high-level entities."

The business relationships that are seen to exist between the high-level entities are shown and labelled, and the emerging high-level Entity Relationship Model[5] forms both the basis for a Corporate Data Model, and the starting point for further data modelling in the BAA phase.

It is often simpler for top-level management to think of their information needs as they relate directly to the aspects of the business that they are responsible for. Thus entity types are often grouped together around a key business concept (for example, Purchasing, Accounting, Product Distribution). Such groupings of data are known as Data Subject Areas, and an example of a Subject Area Diagram is shown in Figure 4.3. Quite clearly, such subject areas may share one or more entities with one another: Purchasing and Accounting will want to know about the entity SUPPLIER; exactly what they will need to know may differ in fine content. It becomes clear from an

---

[4]   This topic is fully treated in section 8.2.1 where the basic concepts of data modelling are introduced and discussed.

[5]   *ibid.*

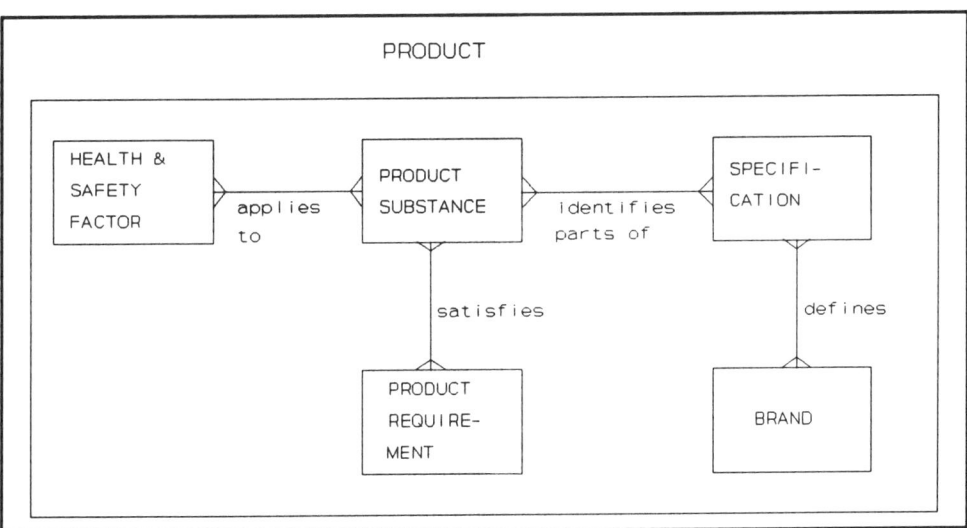

Figure 4.2 PRODUCT as a High-Level Entity Type

analysis of Subject Area Diagrams what entities are "owned" by a particular subject area and which are shared more widely throughout the business. A corporate data management function can use the subject area diagrams as a basis for determining ownership of entity types as BAA projects commence and progress. Subject Area Diagrams can also help in the formulation of the Technical Architecture (see section 4.3.3) where conceptual databases and their content are defined.

4.2.2   Business Functions

During the ISP it is essential to discover and model, from a helicopter perspective, what the overall business activities are. The way in which this is done is to attempt to isolate the main business function areas and to attach firm definitions to them. Then each top-level function is formally decomposed into a number of sub-functions that, together, completely contain the functionality of the top-level activity. Each function is further decomposed until its main high-level business processes have been identified. The technique of functional decomposition is more fully discussed in section 9.1.1 where the formal differences between Functions and Processes are described.

The Functional Hierarchy Diagram that results from this decomposition is unlikely to represent the current organisational structure of the business. Indeed, it should not be determined by the structure of the organisation at any given point in time, for it is intended to give a snapshot of the business activities undertaken in order for the organisation to operate. It is possible to link each business function identified to the organisational unit (or units) responsible for it by means of a matrix such as is shown in Figure 4.4. In such a case, the axis of the matrix that represents the current organisational units is taken from a current organagram or, where none is available,

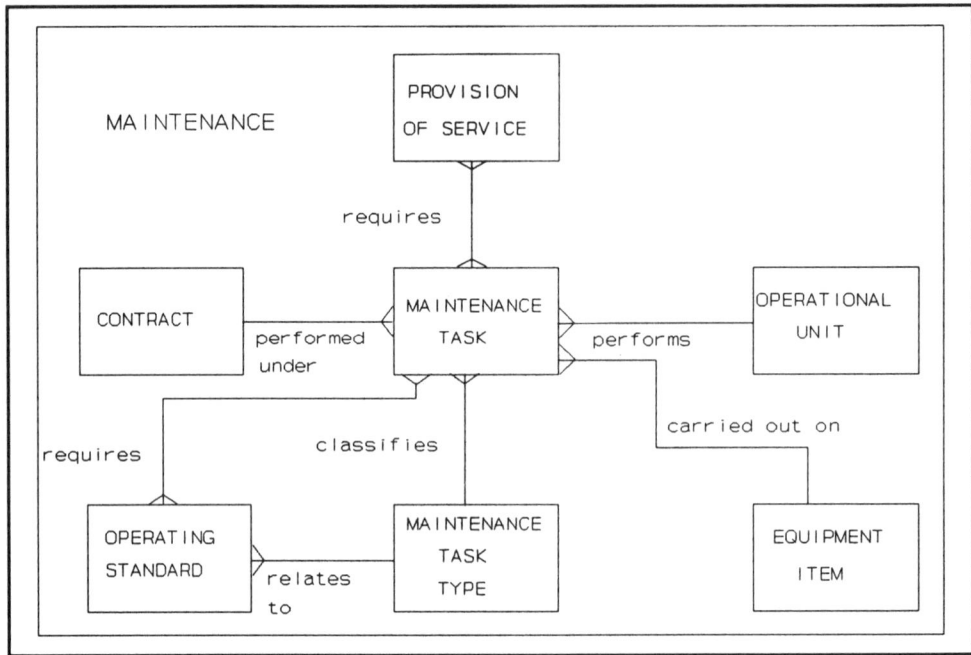

Figure 4.3 A Subject Area Diagram

could be drawn up by the ISP team itself. This matrix can help the ISP team and future BAA project teams to determine who to interview when a particular aspect of the business is being investigated.

4.2.3   Assessing Existing Systems

All currently used computerised systems need to be identified and assessed. These will include all those systems that are formally acknowledged as part of the overall business operation, as well as, to the extent that this is possible, all private systems running on PCs that have become essential to the operation of the business.

For all systems that have been identified, it is necessary to discover what it is that the system does. This can then be expressed via a matrix that maps each system to the business functions, defined in section 4.2.2, that it covers. At the same time, it is also necessary to get a formal assessment **from the users of each system** as to the extent to which the system covers their business needs, and the effectiveness of the system in meeting them. Users should also be given the opportunity to comment on known and/or perceived deficiencies with each system. This information is usually gathered by means of focussed questionnaires that are sent to all users of systems, or to a representative sample of them. The replies are analyzed and summarised (very often in a spreadsheet), and are used in building up the Technical Architecture (section 4.3.3) and in prioritising the investigation of Business Areas (section 4.4). The information

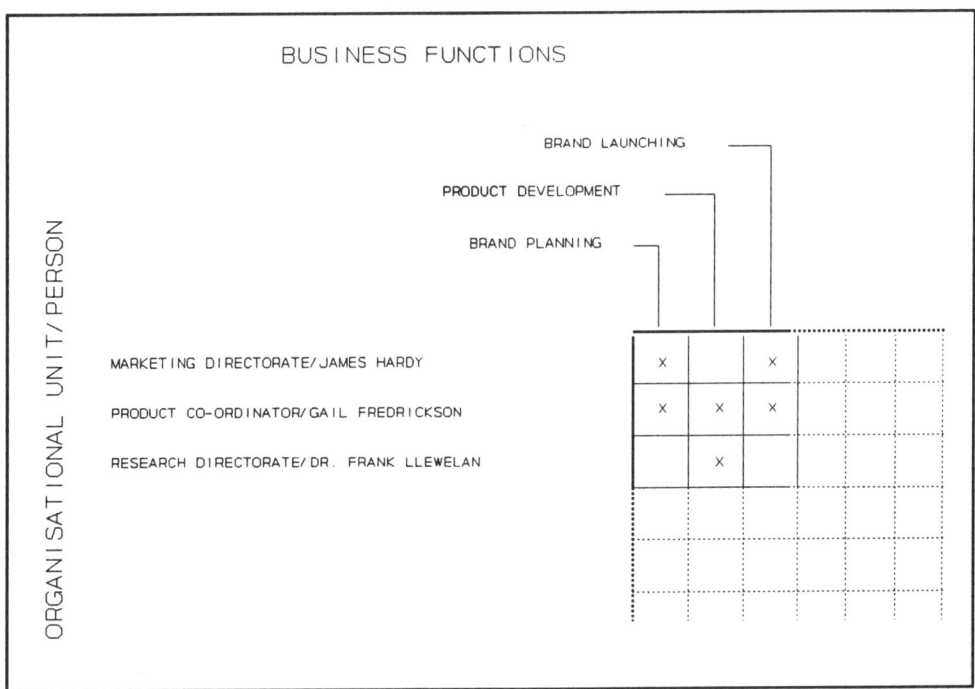

Figure 4.4 Function/Organisational Unit Matrix

may later provide valuable input to future Business Area Analysis projects.

4.2.4   Understanding the Current Technical Environment

At the same time as information is gathered about the business functionality of existing systems, it is necessary to collate information about the technical environment that they operate in. The questionnaires about current systems should also include sections on the hardware and software platforms that the systems run on. This information is collated and used as the basic starting point for the development of a Technical Architecture for the corporation, a topic further discussed in section 4.3.3. It allows an organisation to highlight potential technical problem areas: for example, one organisation was shocked to discover that almost forty different programming languages and development environments were in current use.

4.3   The Corporate Information Architectures

The Corporate Information Architectures lie at the core of the IE approach to the development of information systems to support business needs. The three architectures that are developed as part of the ISP phase together constitute a blueprint and frame of reference for the whole organisation's approach to information systems. The raw information about the business and its information requirements discussed in sections

4.1 and 4.2 is further analyzed and combined in order to construct these architectures. Section 4.3.1 describes how the interaction between the high-level information needs that have been identified and modelled is analyzed against the business functions so that an Information Architecture for the business based on common information usage is defined. This is then used as a framework for the identification of the conceptual systems and databases that will be required to support the business. The conceptual systems and databases, placed within the context of the Information Architecture, constitute the Business Systems Architecture, which is discussed in section 4.3.2, and against which existing systems are mapped. Lastly, the business requirements for systems, as reflected in the Business Systems Architecture, are used to create a potential Technical Architecture required by the overall business to support its operational needs for information systems. In drawing this up, consideration must be given to the current technical environment, as it represents the starting point for the growth of any future technical view of the organisation and strategy for it. The development of the Technical Architecture is explained in section 4.3.3.

4.3.1   The Business Information Architecture

The basic components of a Business Information Architecture are the data entities and business functions that have been identified and defined as part of the high-level analysis of the business. Now these are used to identify and understand the fundamental information structure that underpins the business. **This is achieved by analyzing the interaction between the two constituent parts of the developing high-level Business Model: its data elements, and its functional elements.** The key tool used for interaction analysis at this level of the business is a CRUD matrix: this is a matrix that maps each business function to the data entities that it interacts with. For each cell of the matrix in which interaction occurs the letters C, R, U and D indicate whether the function Creates, Reads, Updates, or Deletes the entity. The matrix can then be clustered[6] based on where the most common interactions occur so that functions with similar data interaction are grouped together as is shown in Figure 4.5.[7] Tight functional cohesion based on interaction with data allows business functions to be grouped together based on their logical cohesiveness rather than by how they are currently being performed within the organisational structure. The resultant clustered functional hierarchy identifies those **Business Areas** that are of relevance to the business as a whole, and that it makes business sense to view as a cohesive unit.

---

[6] Many CASE tools that allow for the construction of CRUD matrices also provide the facility for the running of clustering algorithms automatically. The person running the algorithm can usually set and adjust various parameters which will affect the results of each clustering.

[7] The results of an automatic clustering are never clear-cut. Each iteration through a clustering algorithm needs to be carefully studied and its business implications understood.

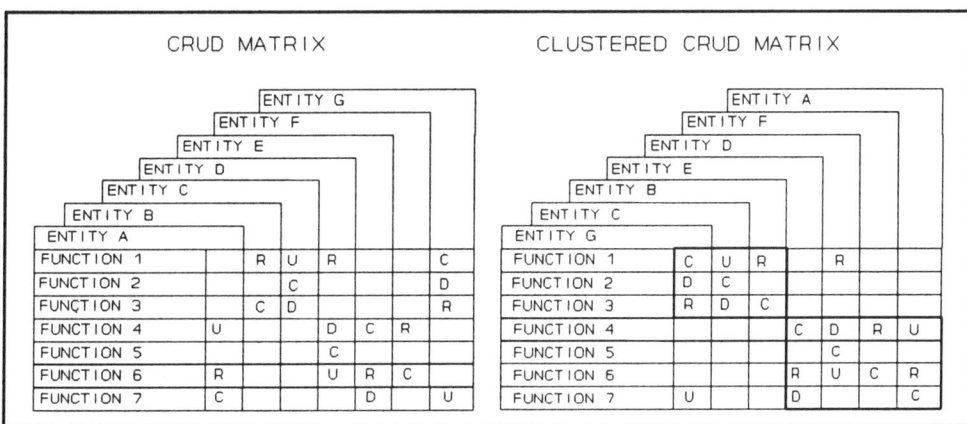

Figure 4.5 Clustered CRUD Matrix

Each Business Area so identified becomes a candidate for a Business Area Analysis project, but the determination of which BAA projects to tackle when is part of the subject of the Information Strategy Plan (section 4.4). The Business Information Architecture (shown in Figure 4.6) consists then of the overall business functional hierarchy based on the business's use of information. This is supported by the high-level data model, which in itself contains high-level data entities which can be conveniently grouped into Subject Areas based both on business perceptions of them, and on the common usage of information represented in the clustered CRUD matrix. Of course, the CRUD matrix itself is part of the Business Information Architecture in

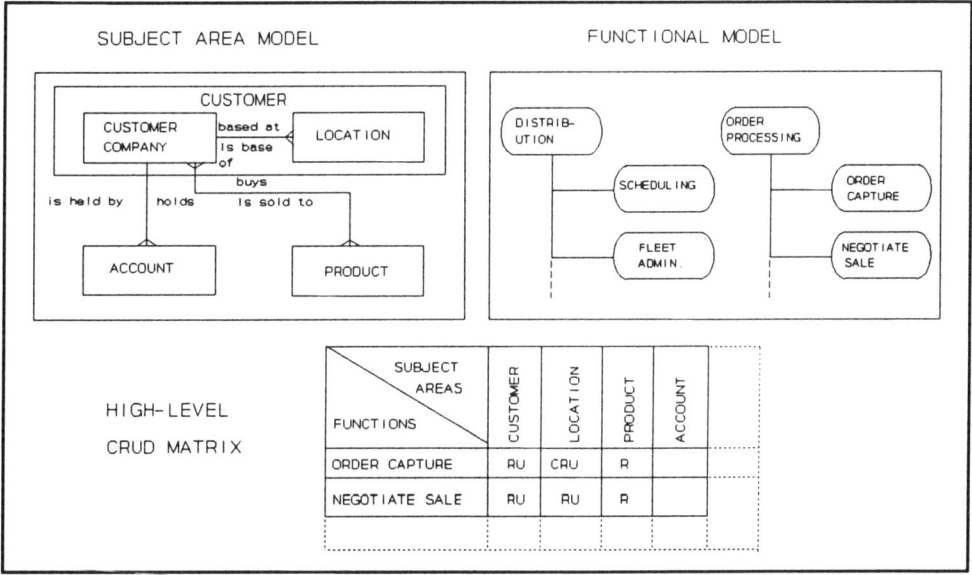

Figure 4.6 Business Information Architecture

that it provides the top-level cohesion between what the business does (its functions) and the things it needs to know about (the data entities).

The Business Information Architecture so defined becomes the framework for the definition of the Business System Architecture which is the topic of the next section. Each Business Area defined in the Business Information Architecture constitutes a subset of the architecture that provides the scope for a BAA project (see further section 7.2). The architecture itself provides the context within which new systems can be developed, and against which existing systems can be mapped.

4.3.2   The Business Systems Architecture

Once the Business Information Architecture has begun to emerge, it becomes possible to begin to identify all the potential systems[8] that may exist within each Business Area. It is often helpful to do this by designating those systems as being **Strategic**, with a time-frame that is long-term, year-by-year, month-by-month; **Support** with a time-frame that is medium-term, week-by-week, day-by-day; and **Operational** with a time-frame that is hour-by-hour, minute-by-minute. A subset of the Business System Architecture illustrating this concept is shown in Figure 4.7. Each system identified should contain a brief verbal description, and a definition of the system scope may also include a mapping of the system to the functions and entities that have been defined as part of the Business Information Architecture.

It now becomes possible, using the information gained in section 4.2.3, to map existing systems onto the Business System Architecture and to signify which conceptual systems exist, and, where they do exist, whether they are satisfactory in terms of business coverage and effectiveness or not. This final form of the Business System Architecture is shown in Figure 4.8.

It is also possible to use the Information Architecture CRUD matrix as the basis for determining what candidate databases may be required to support the envisioned conceptual systems. Depending on the information structure of the organisation and its specific information needs, such candidate databases may cut across a number of business areas or may be limited to one business area. For example, it is possible to imagine an organisation where a Sales database with information about Customers, their preferences, and actual sales is used by the Customer Services and Sales business areas, while summary data about trends in sales is consolidated with other strategic information in a Planning database that is used across the organisation (and across business areas) for all long-term planning functions.

---

[8] Sometimes known as "Conceptual Systems."

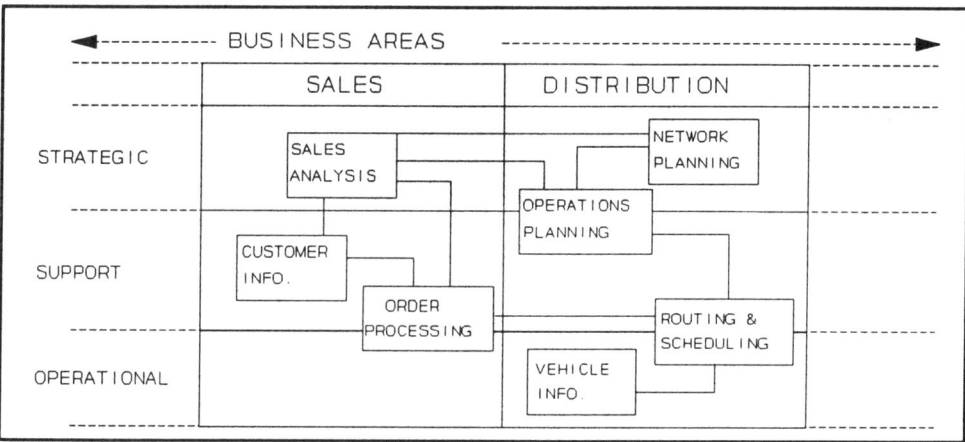

Figure 4.7 Subset of the Business System Architecture

4.3.3 The Technical Architecture

The starting point of the development of a Technical Architecture for the organisation is the understanding of the current technical environment that has been gained as a result of the effort outlined in section 4.2.4.

Business objectives need to be considered in defining the technical architecture that will be needed to support the conceptual systems and candidate databases identified as part of the Business Systems Architecture. For example, if sales representatives,

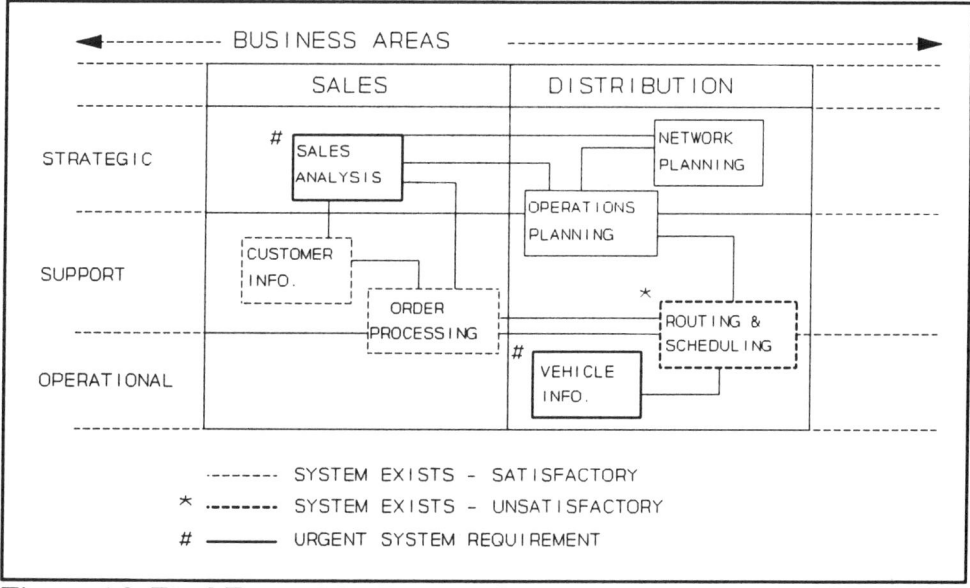

Figure 4.8 Final Form of the Business Systems Architecture

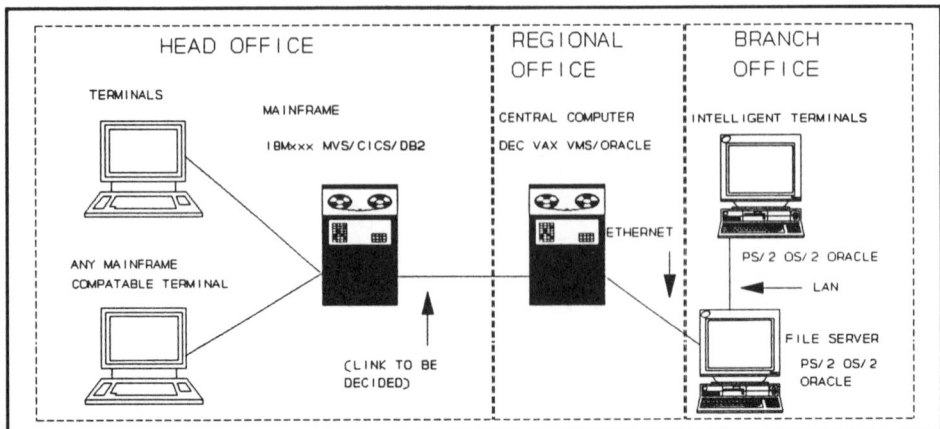

Figure 4.9 Technical Architecture

who spend most of their time on the road need to be able to have the latest product and pricing information for a very large product portfolio that changes on a regular basis, then the Technical Architecture will have to take into account their need for up-to-date information locally, and the means of distributing that information to them.

The Technical Architecture is the area of the Corporate Information Architectures that is most likely to require revision regularly over time as technological progress makes some specific aspects of it meaningless. Such an architecture developed five years ago would have recognised the sales representatives' business need and may have suggested home-based PCs with local printers and dial-up lines. The revised architecture today would have *looked similar*, but the requirement (if not yet addressed) may now be seen in terms of lap-top computers with no need for a printing facility.

An example of a fairly simple Technical Architecture is shown in Figure 4.9.

4.4   The Information Strategy Plan

The Information Strategy Plan grows out of a consolidation of the overall information issues faced by an organisation with the business issues that drive its need for information in the first place.

Initially the links between business and information issues are made by a series of matrices that map the business concerns such as key objectives and CSFs to the specific business functions and entities that will address them. As each business function and entity has also been related to conceptual systems and databases as part of the development of the overall Corporate Information Architectures, it now becomes possible to assess which potential systems are most likely to address the most pressing business needs. It is now possible to quantify these issues by comparing the potential benefits to the business that come from addressing particular business needs and opportunities, with the estimated cost of developing a candidate system or group of systems within the framework provided by the Technical Architecture. Optimisation of manpower can be achieved particularly where the paybacks lie in developing a series of systems within a particular area of the business that can be analyzed **once** as a cohesive unit. The resulting Business Area Analysis, which is the topic addressed comprehensively in Chapters 5 to 11, helps to ensure that synergy is achieved as the systems are designed based on a common, comprehensive view of the Business Area contained in a transformed and expanded business model. The systems that emerge from this process slot into a clearly understood place in the Corporate Information Architectures and help to meet the complete need for information within both an area of the business and the overall corporation.

The overall Information Strategy Plan then places the corporation's use of IT firmly within the context of its business needs. Senior executives can vote funds to development projects based on clear connections between the project and the overall corporate business needs and objectives. These are all seen within the context of the overall framework for the organic growth of corporate information systems that the architectures described in section 4.3 provide.

Chapter 5 The First Hurdle: Business Area Analysis (BAA)

One of the aspects of the IE approach that distinguishes it from other structured analysis and design methods is the way in which it analyses a cohesive area of the business as a whole. This synthetic way of viewing the business takes place in the phase known as Business Area Analysis or, simply, BAA. Because the shift in emphasis during this phase is so fundamentally different from that applied in traditional "systems analysis," BAA can prove to be a minefield for the unprepared and unwary. This problem is exacerbated by the fact that many of the techniques used in a BAA are familiar to analysts through their use in other structured approaches. As a result, some systems analysts are tempted to shrug off the challenges that Business Area modelling impose by assuming, "I have been here before," and getting on with specifying a system. But this is not the purpose behind Business Area Analysis. In order to understand the change of emphasis embodied in this approach, it is **essential** that the objectives behind the BAA are firmly rooted in the minds of all participants in the process. This is particularly true of the project manager, for the person who fills this role will have to determine **quickly** when things are going wrong and why, and take appropriate action.

I am aware of at least one BAA project that, after 18 months of elapsed time, and something like 12 to 15 person-years of effort, was still struggling to agree a first-cut data model. Among the problems experienced here was the "paralysis by analysis" syndrome that is particularly prevalent when BAA teams are attempting to achieve perfection in an imperfect world, are being steered by users whose expectations have been wrongly set in the first place, and are being managed by someone who has lost sight of the fundamental purpose behind Business Area Analysis. Preventing such disasters from occurring is the topic of section 7.4.

The key objective of a BAA project is to produce an integral model of the business area in terms of:
- **Data Entities;**
- **Business Processes; and**
- **the Interaction between Entities and Processes.**

Such a statement of objective, however, will not in itself tell us much. What we really have to keep in mind and in clear focus is the **purpose** behind producing a business model in the first place. There can be a number of reasons for doing so. More traditionally, IE has presented itself as a methodology for developing computer systems that better met and responded to business needs. In this context - the context of what is currently referred to as **forward engineering** - the Business Model plays a very clear role.

The business model is intended to be built in consultation with business users who understand the business area well. As such, the primary purpose is to develop and model a joint understanding of the area of the business **as an information system**. The business model plays two key roles:

- To develop an understanding of **what** the business does (in information usage terms), as opposed to **how** the business is currently doing it with the co-operation of the business users. Hence the business model illustrates **to the users** the analysts' understanding of the business.

- To serve as a structural basis for the building of systems that will provide support to the business. As such, it is directed **to the developers** as a starting point for their design of computerised systems. It represents an agreed user view of the business that can serve as the springboard for the design process.

Some key points arise from this recognition: a Business Model is **not** a functional specification: it is a working model of a part of the business at a point in time. Moreover, if correctly modelled, it is a relatively stable view of the business in that it is based on business data structures, and takes into account those aspects of the Business Area that are most stable. It is, moreover, a firm foundation upon which to base the specification of a system.

Taken from this perspective, the Business Area Model serves a number of additional objectives within the context of a Business Area Analysis:

- It provides an excellent basis for identifying potential business system solutions as well as a means of identifying potential system design projects.

- The enhanced understanding of the Business Area that the model represents can be related more succinctly to the organisation's goals, objectives, and critical success factors that were originally identified as part of the ISP. In so doing, it can provide the basis for the further refinement and steering of the organisation's investment in information systems.

Throughout a BAA project, an aspect of the evolving model that should be kept in mind is that it is merely a mechanism for representing the reality of the business, not that reality itself. As with any other project, an acceptable level of inaccuracy should be recognised: part of the BAA process itself is directed at minimising and, where possible, eliminating such inaccuracy where it is necessary to do so. But the purpose of building a Business Model in the first place is not to achieve the impossible - a one hundred percent accurate definition of the business. It is, rather, **to provide a firm basis for future systems development activity**. Building a Business Model is a case of applying the old eighty-twenty principle: a very acceptable and accurate Business

Model can be achieved by a pragmatic application of IE principles as long as the goal is kept in sight and the overall purpose of the exercise is recognised. Can anyone really distinguish between an eighty percent model and a ninety-five percent one? One suspects not - particularly when the areas of inaccuracy are most likely to be in those parts of the model that are of least current interest to the business: those where the payoffs are likely to be less. (There is no doubt that these areas *can* be addressed. The time and means for addressing them will arise as part of a normal business-driven demand. Until then, it makes sense to focus accuracy on those parts of the model where the business paybacks *are* perceived to lie.)

5.1   The Business Model in Package Selection

There is a further function that the Business Model can serve in the "forward engineering" process, and that has to do with the selection of packages. Encapsulated in the model is a clear view of what the business does in terms of elementary business processes, and the information the business requires to perform those processes in the form of entity types and relationships. It is possible very easily to construct two matrices that will allow sensible and accurate high-level assessments to be made about potential packages of interest to the package selectors. The first matrix, shown in Figure 5.1, maps the elementary business processes identified against the business procedures that the package supports. This allows the selectors to determine the appropriateness of the package's functional coverage to the business area in question, as well as to pinpoint any potential areas of functional deficiency. A second matrix can compare the entity types identified with those used in the package. Where no explicit data model exists for the package, it is possible to derive one from the given file layouts by the technique known as Canonical

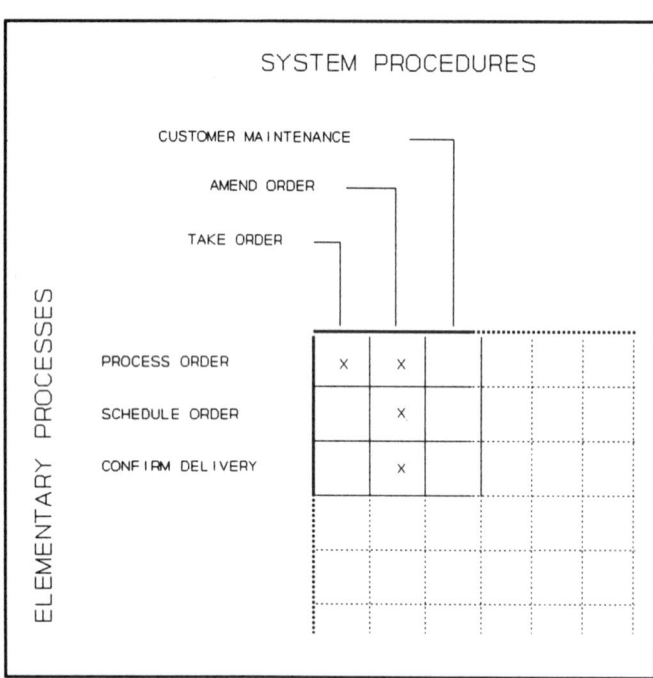

Figure 5.1 Elementary Processes/Package Procedures Matrix

Synthesis.[1] In all cases, once preliminary comparisons indicate that the package is a serious candidate, it is recommended that a more thorough comparison is made to the extent deemed necessary. This can involve the drawing up of a matrix that maps the entity/attributes of the Business Model with the file/fields of the given data model or derived one. This comparison serves two main purposes: it allows for a firm confirmation to be made that the two models do map closely to one another and, at the same time, problems with data coverage will be isolated at this early stage; secondly, the matrix will serve as a key source for determining any needed interfaces with existing systems, and will give some indication of the likely complexity of such interfaces. For this, the BAA data model serves as a constant point of reference both for the package(s), and for current systems: it acts as a base point for comparison.

This emphasis placed on the data issues in package selection is entirely in concert with the underlying data-driven approach behind IE. There is no real point in selecting a package that provides reasonable functional coverage if the effort saved by installing a package is going to be lost by the complexity of the interfaces to that package that are going to have to be built.

5.2   The Role of Current Systems Analysis

Where current systems exist that fall either partially or wholly within the Business Area being analyzed, the question must arise as to whether these should be analyzed at all, and if so, to what extent. It could be argued that these systems are going to be replaced anyway, or that the systems of the future have to transcend the current ones, so why bother? The analysis of current systems is seen to be part of the Business Area Analysis process. However, it would be foolish simply to go ahead and do it just because theory tells you to do so. We are aware of one company that decided that it needed to know something about a large and unwieldy existing system. Their project to document that system took 20 person-years using a team of 10 over a total of 2 elapsed years. Now they have two large shelves filled with "System Documentation." People point to it and say, "There's the system," but to the best of our knowledge, the volumes are barely used at all. Nobody bothered to ask the questions, "Why are we doing this? What is our **purpose?**"

Throughout this volume, stress will be laid on the question "Why?" If we can understand why we are undertaking any task or larger activity, we can understand to what extent we need to engage in it - fully, in some abridged form, or not at all - and, most importantly, **we can assess the risks of our approach.** While we shall cover some of the issues raised in undertaking current systems analysis (CSA) within the BAA context later (see section 5.2), it is necessary at this stage to appreciate the role that CSA **can** play in a BAA. This will allow us better to assess whether it is something we must do, can leave out with some risk, or need not undertake at all.

---

[1] This is discussed in detail in section 8.2.2.4.

In pure BAA theory, we build up a derived logical Business Model of the existing current system or systems in order to compare it with the Business Model we have built up top-down by examining the underlying structure of the Business Area. We do so in order to **verify and check** the BAA model. The comparison allows us to identify differences that inevitably will exist between the models, and **to account for them**.[2] In this way we can isolate areas of the model that are weak or deficient because of inadequate analysis, and that are incorrect through insufficient information or lack of understanding on the part of modellers. Corrective action can then be taken before errors become encapsulated in any system design models. So, in leaving out CSA, we are also depriving the BAA team of a powerful opportunity for checking its work.

There are instances where the risk of doing so is heightened by certain factors, or where doing CSA is a practical and pragmatic alternative given the absence of other essential resources. Some form of CSA should be undertaken in the circumstances outlined below, but the extent of that analysis will largely be dictated by additional specific circumstances: these are always a matter of informed judgement, which is, after all, the primary role of a good manager.

- Where there is an **absence of users** with the requisite business knowledge, existing systems may be a primary source for the construction of Business Models. This may prove to be the case where the people with key business experience and knowledge have retired. It may also be the case where individuals essential to the business are unavailable to the analysis team at the initial stages of the project. In such a case, it is better to have an initial, even if flawed, model to put on the table for discussion, rather than a blank sheet of paper.

- Where an existing system within the Business Area is **mission-critical**, the analysis team ignore it at their peril.

- Where an existing system represents **considerable investment in terms of business knowledge and experience**, common sense dictates that it should be treated with respect. Although it may not be appropriate to undertake a full-scale CSA of this system, those familiar with it, and its documentation (if current), should be incorporated into the analysis process.

- Where there is a **close match** between an existing system and the Business Area under analysis, CSA may be an appropriate route.

---

[2] See section 10.2.

5.3   Using the Business Model to Facilitate the Design Process

We have discussed the primary purpose behind building a Business Model, and the role that current systems analysis can play in that process. In order to understand the role played by a Business Model more fully, we need to have a clear view of its **uses in the process of developing computerised systems**. We have discussed its use in the evaluation of application packages, and now need to turn our attention to the more specific activity of designing and constructing systems.

5.3.1   Identify Potential Design Areas

The Business Model represents an understanding of the usage made of data within a particular Business Area. This understanding is used to determine the most effective groupings of elementary business functions against data entities so that separate design areas can be isolated that represent **sound structural bases for integrated systems**. This is done by clustering the CRUD matrix for entity types and elementary processes and analyzing the affinity data elements have for one another via the processes, as well as the implied coupling and cohesion that the processes have for one another via the data elements. While computerised algorithms are available to perform such analysis, the results of each execution of the algorithm require the informed manager to exercise analytic skills and judgement in understanding the implications of each clustering.

5.3.2   Determine Where the Payback Lies

At the end of the BAA process it is possible to map elementary processes against the goals, objectives, and critical success factors that were originally identified in the ISP. Effectively this involves an expansion of the original ISP matrix that mapped high-level business function to goals, objectives, and critical success factors. The new matrix can be reviewed afresh with management to confirm the currency of the issues it addresses, and then can be used to steer decisions about the scope of design areas, and the possible sequences in which they may be tackled. The matrix, and the issues it encapsulates, help to focus the scope of any cost/benefit analysis undertaken.

5.3.3   Scope Design Projects

Whatever extraneous influences come into play in the process of deciding the scope of future design projects (see section 11.1), the chosen scope can be established unambiguously in terms of the Business Model. The scope can be clearly expressed in terms of the elementary processes defined by the BAA, and these are supplemented by the requisite data entities to support the process in its execution.

5.3.4   Determine Potential Effects on Other Systems

As the scope of the data interaction within the design area can be tightly defined, it allows for the determining of the effects such a scope may have on other, already existing systems. Clear answers to questions like, "Where do data items come from?" (at an attribute level, if necessary) can be provided. Where this indicates the need for interfaces and/or bridging procedures to and from other systems, the nature and complexity of such additional computerised systems is determined at an early enough stage for the cost implications to be taken into account. Moreover, where it is clear that the "input data" does not lie within an already computerised system, the need for the construction of data capture and loading subsystems, particularly where they are "one off", is highlighted.

5.3.5   Determine the Phasing and Implementation Sequence of Design Projects

As it is clear from the model what data elements are needed in which processes, it becomes a relatively easy task to determine which defined design areas should be logically tackled in which sequence. This includes the assessment of interfacing and bridging issues discussed in the previous subsection. Problems that will then arise from varying this sequence due to other extraneous influences can be identified, and their cost implications can be assessed.

5.4   Other Uses for a Business Model

In the discussion above, the clear implication is that the Business Model will serve as a "bridge" between the business, and computerised systems that will support the business in its endeavour. However, the Business Model can also be used in a number of intriguing ways to deal with existing issues that the business may be tackling.

5.4.1   Documentation of Business Understanding

The Business Model can also be viewed as a formal representation and documentation of business understanding of a particular Business Area **in a standardised format**. This means that not only can it be constantly referred to by a range of different people, once they are conversant with the conventions used in it, it can also be used as a "baseline" view of the business. In this role, it becomes a growing point of reference: as aspects of business change, the model can (and should) be updated to reflect those changes. When a sub-area of a larger Business Area is better understood (perhaps because of some study or analysis project), the model can be expanded and enhanced accordingly. This concept is entirely in line with the role played by a repository or corporate encyclopedia in an organisation. As such, any model developed **and managed** within the IE context can be seen in terms of an ongoing investment in information by the organisation owning the model.

5.4.2   User "Specification" of the Business as an Information System

The model can also be seen as a business person's specification of their business as an information processing system. It clearly translates the business into a model that views that business in terms of its information processing and information requirements. As the model is constructed by users, and with their constant involvement in the building process, it can become **their view** of the business in information terms. The challenge for IT managers is to ensure that such a transfer of ownership and responsibility takes place in those (currently usual) cases where a BAA project is initiated by the IT function. Ways of rising to such a challenge are suggested in Chapter 6.

5.4.3   A Basis for Business Restructuring

Within a Business Area, the highest levels of the Business Model can be used (much as the ISP model can for the whole organisation) to serve as a basis for restructuring the business. The model itself can trigger off such a process by indicating where there is a loss of structural synergy in the current organisation. It may then also serve as a baseline against which to manage any planned changes. As the model changes over time to reflect business changes, the organisational structure itself can be assessed in clear and unambiguous fashion against the model.

5.4.4   A Basis for Re-engineering Business Procedures

Similar principles to those mentioned in section 5.4.3 can be applied to the current business procedures within a business area. They are often the product of a different and older style of management practice - one in which a significant role played by middle management was to authorise and control the activities of their subordinates. In a modern, information-driven business environment, such procedures may no longer be applicable or desirable. By viewing **what** the business does - a view encapsulated in the business model - and measuring it against current business practise, as entrenched in the business procedures, it is possible to determine the effectiveness of current operational practises and to decide how to re-engineer them to bring them into closer line with modern business needs. The BAA Business Model can play an important role in this process both in providing a fresh perspective on business practises, and in providing an indication of how those practises may be streamlined and amended to ensure greater overall synergy of effort.

5.4.5   A Basis for Systems Re-engineering

Lastly, the Business Model can also serve as a reference point for the re-engineering of existing systems. There are two main aspects to this: first, existing file structures can be mapped against the business data model. This can be used to identify redundant data elements as a means of reducing and even eliminating them in the process of normal maintenance and enhancement. Very often the additional effort required to engineer some of these fundamental structural changes is small when compared to the enhancement effort being undertaken. Secondly, the business process model can also serve as a point of reference for repackaging the existing functionality of a system: one system to which these principles were applied had been constructed around a menu structure that reflected a data processing view of the operations involved - there was a menu that led either to various "amend" functions, or to "insert" functions, or to "delete" functions. To perform a simple business procedure usually involved hopping up and down the menu tree a number of times. By recombining system modules in line with the business functional procedures, a significant productivity gain over the old system packaging was achieved, and the users found the changed system to be "more user friendly."

Of course the Business Model can also be used as a basis for more drastic reverse engineering of a system. In this case, either manually or via a suitable software tool, a derived logical model is constructed for the existing system. This can be compared with a top-down BAA model, where one exists; or it can itself form the logical model to which forward engineering principles are applied.

5.5   An Overview of the BAA Process

The distinct main steps of a BAA project are illustrated in Figure 5.2.

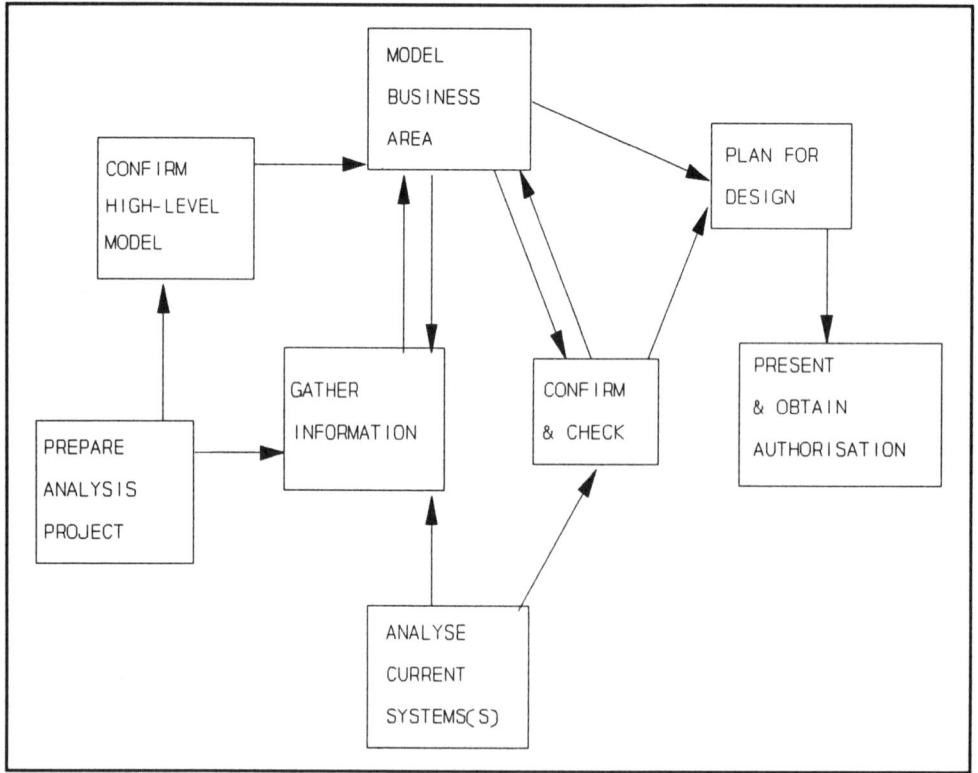

Figure 5.2 The Main Steps of a BAA Project

An illustration of these steps in relationship to the time taken to perform a BAA is given in Figure 5.3.

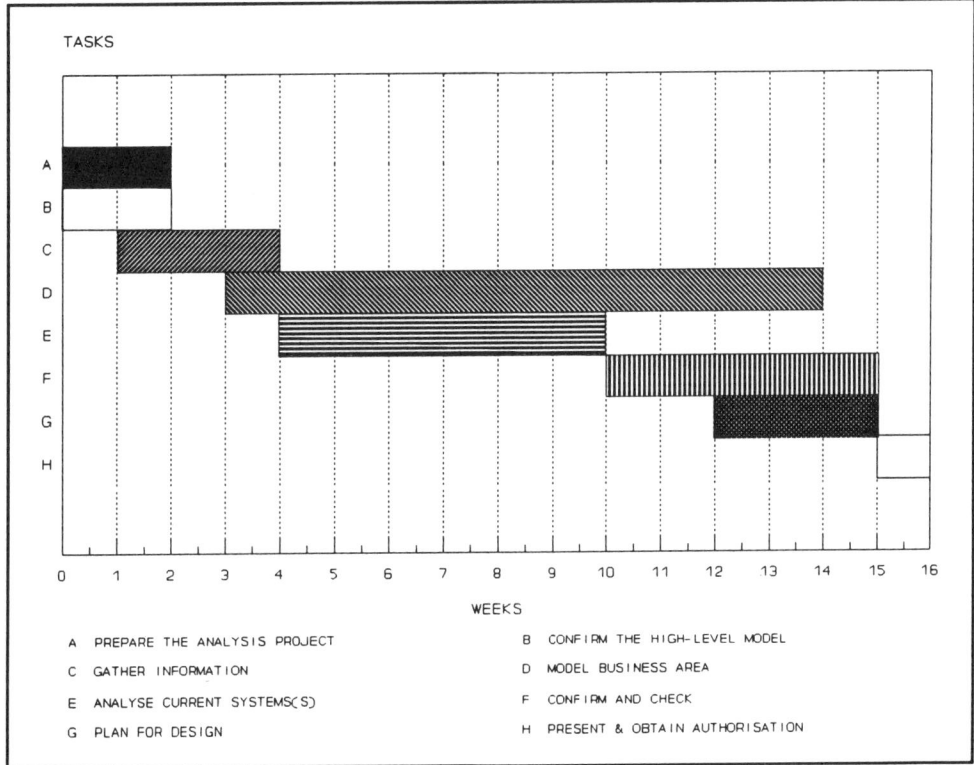

Figure 5.3 Time Taken to Complete a BAA Project

Each of the main steps of a BAA has a key set of objectives as well as clear deliverables. In this section we shall discuss these in overview before dealing with them in some detail in Chapters 6 to 11.

5.5.1   Planning and Preparing the BAA Project[3]

The main *objectives* of this step are:

●   To set up the necessary management structures to ensure that the project will be adequately controlled and supported.

---

[3] This topic is fully discussed in Chapter 6.

- To expand outline project plans in terms of tasks, deliverables, and time scales.

- To build a suitable project team structure to facilitate the success of the project. This includes the allocation of personnel to tasks.

- To ensure user commitment to, and involvement in, the BAA process.

- To devise a training plan that ensures that team members and users participating in the project will receive the appropriate training they require at the right time.

- To devise a quality plan that ensures that the assurance of quality is an intrinsic part of the BAA process.

The *deliverable* from this step is a detailed project plan that includes detailed training and quality assurance plans.

5.5.2   Scoping the BAA Project[4]

The main *objectives* of this step are:

- To confirm the scope of the analysis project in terms of both data subject areas/entities and business functions.

- To construct a preliminary entity model and functional hierarchy where none exists.

- To ensure that the project operates within the context of the corporate Information Strategy Plan by relating the project scope to the organisations's goals, critical success factors, and problems.

The *deliverable* from this step is an agreed project scope that is expressed in terms of a summary entity model and functional hierarchy.

5.5.3   Gathering Initial Information and Analyzing it[5]

The main *objectives* of this step are:

- To identify business and problems by means of structured interviews and/or intensive user analysis sessions.

---

[4] This topic is fully discussed in section 7.2.

[5] This topic is fully discussed in section 8.1.

- To analyze the interviews **and group** sessions with a view to building up initial business models for review.

- To confirm the analysis of interview and intensive user sessions with the participants.

The *deliverables* from this step are the signed-off interview analysis sheets and signed-off user intensive analysis sheets.

5.5.4   Modelling the Business Area[6]

The main *objectives* of this step are:

- To model the business in terms of its information usage and business activities.

- To achieve an understanding of **what** the business does regardless of **how** it currently operates.

- To illustrate the project team's understanding of the business to users in a form that they can comprehend.

The *deliverable* from this step is a fully reviewed business model of the business area under analysis.

5.5.5   Building Models of Current Systems[7]

The main *objective* of this step is:

- To model a current system (or current systems) in terms of its data and functionality.

The circumstances under which current systems analysis should be considered are fully discussed in section 5.2.

The *deliverables* from this step are models of existing systems in terms of data elements and relationships, and, optionally, business procedures.

---

[6] This topic is fully discussed in sections 8.2 to 10.1.

[7] This topic is fully discussed in sections 8.2.2.

5.5.6   Confirming and Checking the Business Area Model[8]

The main *objective* of this step is:

●   To check the business model in terms of its completeness, correctness, and stability.

The *deliverable* from this step is a business model of the business area under analysis that has been subjected to thorough internal and external quality and stability checking.

5.5.7   Planning for the Design Phase[9]

The main *objectives* of this step are:

●   To decide which parts of the Business Area are to be automated.

●   To determine how the parts to be automated are to be split into Business Design projects and to decide the order of priority of the Business Systems to be designed.

●   To examine the implications of time-scales and costs on potential Business System Design Projects.

The *deliverables* from this step are outline plans for the various design alternatives that have been accepted as viable.

5.5.8   Presenting the Business Area Analysis[10]

The main *objective* of this step is:

●   To present the results of the Business Area Analysis project to management in a form that will allow them to make informed decisions on how to proceed with the next phase.

The *deliverables* from this step are a Business Area Analysis report, an outline of which is given in section 7.1, and a formal management presentation of the project's conclusions.

---

[8]   This topic is fully discussed in section 10.2.

[9]   This topic is fully discussed in Chapter 11.

[10]   This topic is fully discussed in section 11.5.

As can be seen from Figure 5.3, **Modelling the Business Area** is by far the most complex and time-consuming of the BAA steps. It effectively consists of two main stages: in the first of these, data and process models are built in parallel, but more or less independently of one another; then, the two models are brought together in a systematic manner through the techniques of interaction analysis. Constantly, throughout these stages, quality checks are taking place so that the formal step of **Confirming and Checking the Business Area Model** is, in effect, a thorough Quality Assurance review of the quality checking matrices that have been produced, and the quality assurance reviews that have already taken place.

Table 5.1 summarises the main BAA steps in terms of their main tasks, and the deliverables that they produce.

BAA Step	Main Tasks	Deliverables
Plan and Prepare the Project	Define Project Tasks Assign Persons to Tasks Schedule Project	BAA Project Plan - Tasks, Assignments, Roles - Quality Plan - Training Plan
Scope the Project	Confirm BAA Model inherited from ISP or Build High-level BAA Model and confirm scope with sponsors	Scope Statement High-Level Entity Relationship Model High-Level Activity Hierarchy Diagram Activity/Entity CRUD Matrix Requirement/Problem vs Activity Matrix Requirement/Problem vs Entity Matrix

Gather Information	Identify sources of information Plan and schedule interviews Conduct interviews Analyze results of interviews	Agreed Interview Analysis Sheets and/or User Intensive Analysis Sheets
Model the Business Area	Build first-cut Data Model Build first-cut Process Model including: - Process Hierarchy Diagram - Process Dependency and/or Data Flow Diagrams Perform Interaction Analysis	Reviewed Business Model - Entities, Attributes and Relationships - Activities to Elementary Process Level - Entity/Element-ary Process CRUD Matrix Requirement/Problem vs Elementary Process Matrix Requirement/Problem vs Entity Matrix
Build Models of Current System(s)	Identify relevant current systems For each system identified, analyze to appropriate level of detail	Derived Data Model Entity/Attribute vs System File/Field Matrix Elementary Process/ System Procedure Matrix (optional)

Confirm and Check the Model	Confirm correctness of Model	Elementary Process/Entity CRUD Matrix
	Confirm completeness of Model	Stability Analysis Report
	Confirm stability of Model	QA Report
Plan for Design	Analyze design alternatives	Business System Design Plan
	Conduct cost/benefit analysis of viable options	
	Prepare BSD Plan	
Present the BAA	Compile BAA Report	BAA Report
	Present BAA Report to management	

Table 5.1 Main BAA Steps: Tasks and Deliverables

Chapter 6 Clearing the Hurdle

Many Business Area Analysis projects have been approached in an almost cavalier fashion, as though they were merely another Systems Analysis project without any of the broader repercussions that the IE approach implies (see Chapter 2). Were the project simply to exist in isolation, then it is arguable that such an approach would suffice. However, by its very nature, Business Area Analysis requires a broader context within which to be effective, and is likely to spawn a series of development projects, the co-ordination of which it will be vital to control. The brief history of IE in practice is already littered with the carcasses of BAA projects that have never seen their expected end point. The common factors that underlie the failures always relate very strongly to project management issues. Either there has been a lack of supporting structure and context within which the project can proceed, or the project manager responsible for the project has lacked an understanding (sometimes because of the initial learning curve) of the BAA process and so has failed to detect early warning signals and to respond effectively to them. The most disastrous failures have, of course, been the projects where both of these factors have been evident.

The most critical point to bear in mind throughout an IE project, and particularly in the BAA stage, is that **methodology and CASE tools are not a substitute for competent project management procedures and practices.** For a BAA to succeed, there **must** be an adequate supporting management structure for the project to operate within. Moreover, the project team itself needs to be structured in such a way that the roles played by individuals in it complement one another.

This chapter, while dealing with these issues, is not a short-cut course on the art of project management: it merely attempts to highlight the project management issues that will help or hinder the success of a BAA project. In applying some of the practices suggested, careful consideration needs to be given to the corporate cultural context within which the project is operating. There is no way in which a computer development project is going to impose new cultural norms on an organisation! There is a fundamental contradiction here though, because the IE approach is likely to "rock the boat" as it places areas of the business under the information microscope, so lesson number one is: keep the project close to the users - particularly to user management. The key to a successful BAA starts with the users: and the project requires both their active involvement and their commitment. Many of the practises outlined below are key to obtaining and maintaining such user commitment.

As outlined in Chapter 5, the first phase of a BAA project involves the planning of the project and the setting up of the right project management structures to ensure that the project will be adequately controlled and supported. It is to these issues that we shall initially turn.

6.1   Controlling the BAA Project

Business Area Analysis starts and ends with the business. The full commitment of the business users to the project is essential to its success. How the project is run and controlled plays a critical part in obtaining and maintaining such user commitment. Besides the obvious active user participation in the project team, which will be addressed more fully in section 6.8.2, the overall project should be financed, and hence, controlled by the users. This is best achieved through a Project Steering Committee which is chaired by the main user sponsor, and also comprises the senior managers from any part of the current business organisational structure that has anything to do with the Business Area under investigation. Also represented on the Project Steering Committee should be a senior manager from the IT department (preferably the Development Manager), and the senior manager from the Quality Assurance department. The BAA project manager should be directly accountable to the Project Steering Committee for both progress and costs, and regular (ideally monthly) progress meeting should be held. These should be supplemented with *ad hoc* meetings to review formally all interim deliverables and, where necessary, to deal with crisis issues should they arise.

There should be three additional bodies providing support to the project team, and specialised advice to the steering committee: the User Liaison Group, IT Support Group, and Quality Control Group.

The interrelationship between these groups and the steering committee in controlling the BAA project team is illustrated in Figure 6.1.

6.1.1   User Liaison Group

This group consists of members of the user community who know aspects of the Business Area well, have a particular area of expertise, or are well respected by their peers. Their role is twofold: they are required to supplement the business knowledge of the user representative who is an active member of the BAA team (see section 6.4.2 below), and they are required to communicate and even "sell" the work of the BAA team back into the user community. In playing these roles, the User Liaison Group members will constantly be asked to review parts of the emerging business model and to participate in its construction. They can communicate their confidence or concerns with the model back to their management who should be represented on the Project Steering Committee.

It is via this group that **business issues** relating to the project, and particularly to the business model being constructed, are addressed and brought to the attention of the Project Steering Committee. When the steering committee reviews interim and final deliverables, this should not be an arduous task, as these products of the project team should already have been reviewed and approved by the User Liaison Group, and the steering group should find it possible to follow their recommendations.

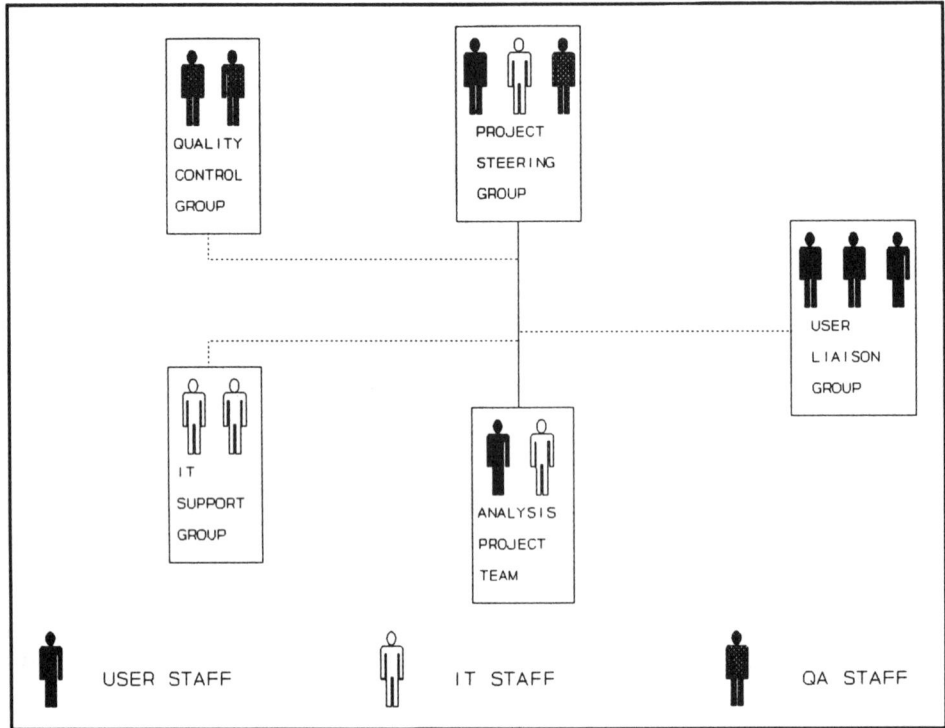

Figure 6.1 Controlling the BAA Project Team

The User Liaison Group provides the essential channels of communication from the project team back into the broader user community, and to user management.

6.1.2   IT Support Group

The primary purpose of the IT Support Group in the IE context is to provide technical help and support to the project team. Such help relates specifically to practical matters like the application of IE principles and techniques within the project context, and how best to use the chosen supporting CASE tool. Any technical problems experienced with the CASE tool are referred to the IT Support Group, and they liaise directly with the suppliers on behalf of the whole corporation. This allows them both to co-ordinate problems, experiences, and advice given, and to bring strong pressure to bear on particular suppliers by being a central focus for all problems.

The IT Support Group provides input to the steering committee on technical issues indirectly via the IT development manager, but may also be called upon to explain the significance of project deliverables or of techniques used in the analysis.

6.1.3 Quality Control Group

This group plays the role of external auditors to the project team and hence provides an independent means of quality control to the steering committee. Via the Quality Assurance manager, they should be communicating the results of their scheduled and *ad hoc* QA reviews to the group, and voicing any concerns they may have of the way in which the project team is applying corporate standards and the project quality plan.

6.2 Controlling a Multi-Project Environment

The controlling management structure described in section 6.1 needs to be set up **for every IE project undertaken**. This ensures that the interests of the business community - for whom the project has been undertaken and who are funding it - are fully addressed and supported. However, in a single organisation, it is probable that many IE projects will be running simultaneously, with each being at a different stage in the IE life cycle. Such a multi-project environment becomes increasingly difficult to manage, and it is essential that adequate project co-ordination structures are put in place **before** two or more projects are running simultaneously. There are three internal co-ordination functions that are essential to the successful management of a multi-project environment: without them in place and functioning, a great deal of time will be lost "re-inventing the wheel" and redoing work that has already been completed and signed off.

The interrelationship between these three support groups in a multi-project environment is illustrated in Figure 6.2.

6.2.1 Standards Steering Group

This group should consist of representatives from the IT department (whose job it will be to apply and use the standards), the QA department (whose job it will be to enforce the standards), and the user community (who will have to use the results of such standards in the form of names, standard screen layouts, etc.). The work of the group will be to approve standards to be used on a corporate-wide basis for the whole of the IE initiative. Project teams will either request that specific standards be put in place, or request changes to already existing ones. It will be this group's task to make sure that adequate standards are issued and/or revised efficiently and effectively.

6.2.2 Corporate Model/Data Co-ordination Group

This group is likely to be entirely IT staffed, and will very often grow out of existing data management structures. Its task will initially be to co-ordinate the overall corporate data model. Its scope, however, expands as BAA projects reach their conclusion. At a later stage, this group will also find itself becoming the custodian of common blocks of business logic and business algorithms that are used in many areas of the business (e.g. stock allocation rules) and that cannot be tampered with by one

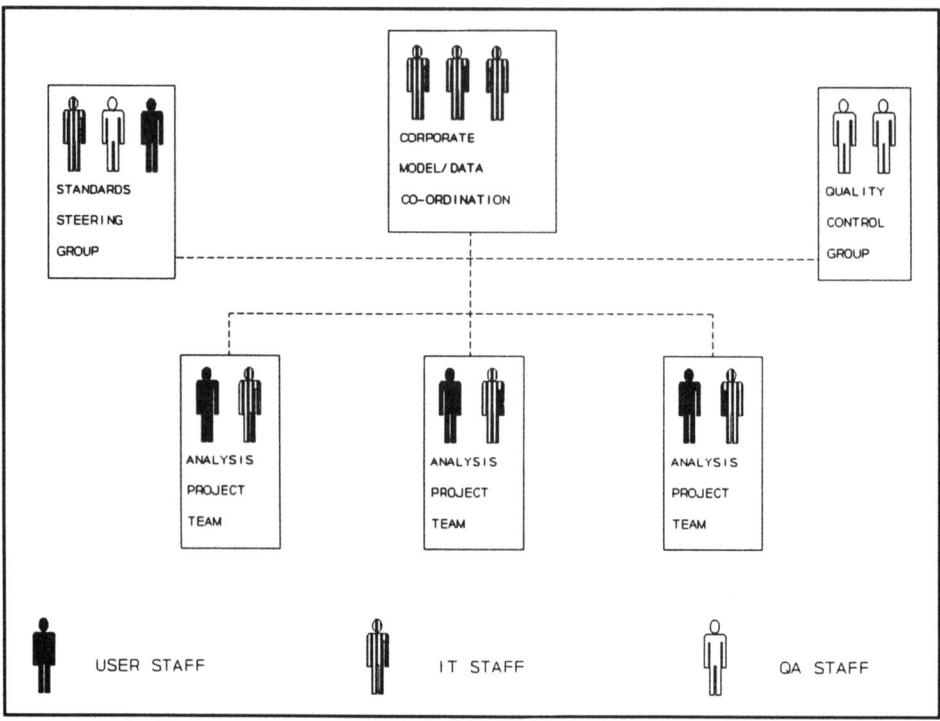

Figure 6.2 Supporting the Multi-Project Environment

team without jeopardising the integrity of the business models of other teams.

The Corporate Model/Data Co-ordination Group will function at two levels of detail: on the more conceptual one, it will need to take a **corporate view of data** which will involve it in acting as a "referee" between project teams who share the ownership of data entity types. They will also have to be instrumental in determining (in conjunction with representatives of the user community) when and whether a project team has sole ownership of an entity type. For example, it is clear that the entity types PRODUCT or CUSTOMER will be shared by many Business Areas. However, it is possible that a Business Area like Product Development could fundamentally own PRODUCT, in which case any changes proposed to the entity type (including its attributes and relationships) would have to be approved by the Product Development BAA team. Where, however, an entity type is shared by many Business Areas, the Corporate Model/Data Co-ordination Group would have to approve suggested changes to its structure, and consolidate each BAA team's business view of the entity type into a corporate one.

Although the group is likely to consist of IT personnel, it is clear that it cannot function effectively without the close co-operation of the various project teams, and of the business community via its various team representatives.

6.2.3 Quality Control Group

As mentioned in section 6.1.3, this group plays the role of external auditors to the various project teams. It ensures that the standards that have been agreed and issued by the Standards Steering Group (section 6.2.1) are followed to an equal and adequate extent across the whole corporation. The group's role is to see that deliverables are produced to a consistent standard, and that procedures and techniques are applied in a common way.

6.3 The BAA Process and the Role of a Project Plan

A way in which a Project Steering Committee can maintain overall involvement with a project and ensure that it is in control is by monitoring the progress of the project against a project plan. This statement, though apparently obvious to many, is one that seems often to have been ignored in the IE context. Part of the reason for this is that traditional IT development plans have been task-oriented, each task producing a deliverable that feeds into the next stage of the development process. With an IE project, the interrelationship between deliverables is extremely complex - so much so that a major justification behind the use of CASE tools is to ensure consistency of the models produced, and to provide an automated means of checking deliverables and

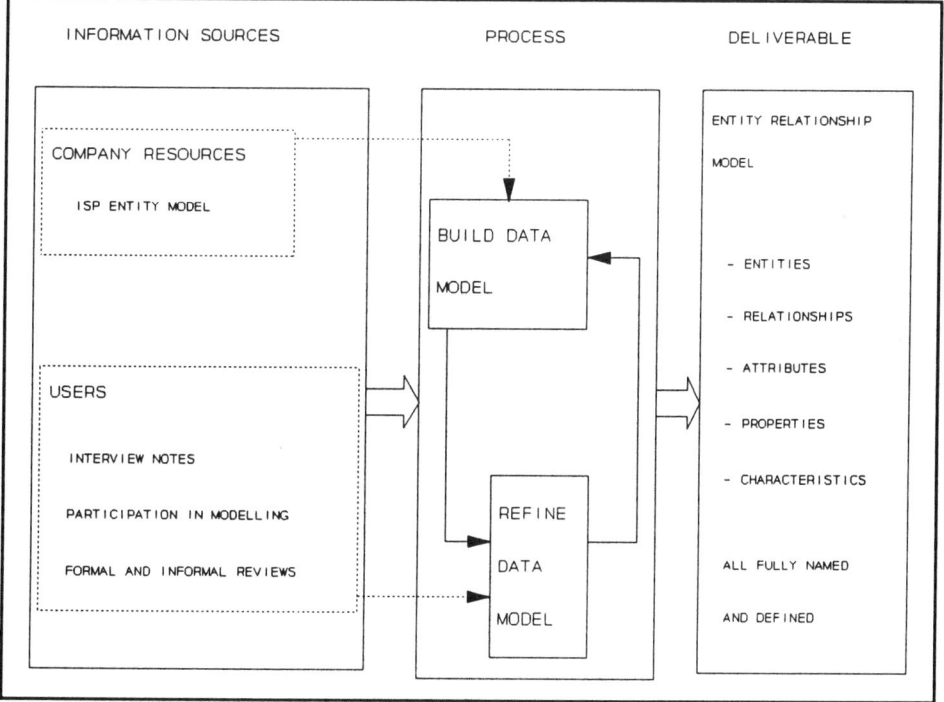

Figure 6.3 Building a Data Model

models for completeness and correctness. This complexity is further increased by the iterative nature of the model-building process itself: as Figure 6.3 illustrates, in the BAA phase, a data model is drawn up by an iterative process of gathering information from users, applying that knowledge to the construction of the data model, and then reviewing the results with users again.

This (and each subsequent) review is in effect a further gathering of information that is very often applied immediately to the model under review. At times the review also results in the gathering of further information outside of the review session and then applying it to the model, for a further review, and so on.... At what point is there a deliverable? When can one safely say that there is a first-cut data model in place, or for that matter a complete one? Another way of asking this question is perhaps, when can one safely get out of the loop?

At the risk of further complicating the issue, once the data model is reasonably complete, it is then subjected to a thorough review via the application to it of the techniques of interaction analysis, when the data model and the process model are brought together. As Figure 6.4 shows, this process too is an iterative one, subject to the constant review of users and the resulting constant change and refinement of

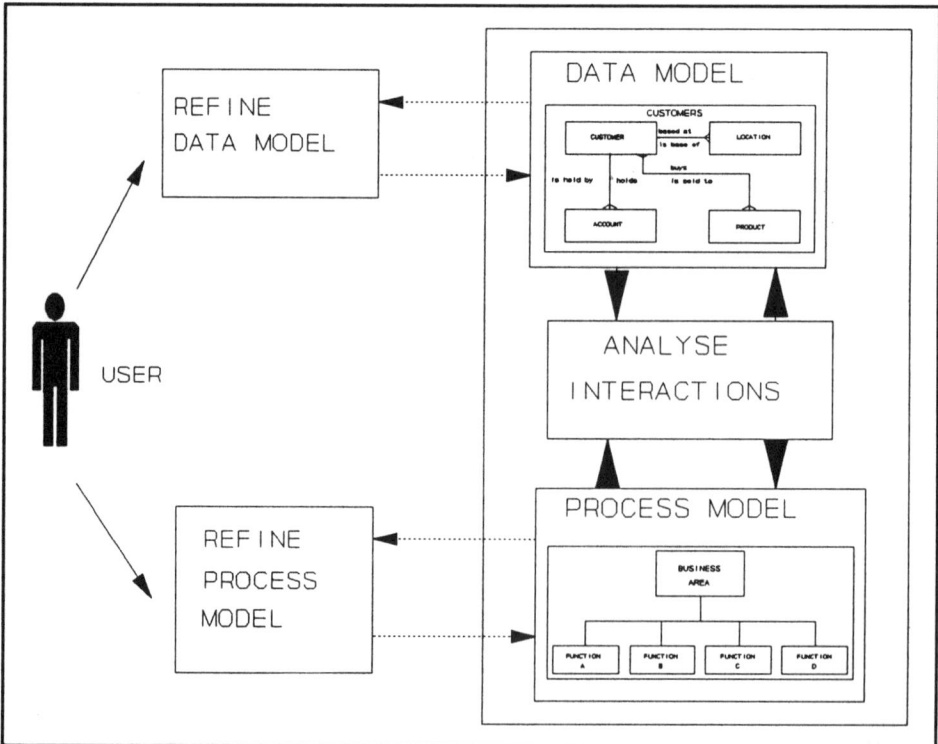

Figure 6.4 Interaction Analysis

deliverables.

The problem is that deliverables previously regarded as "stable" or "reviewed" are changed and affected by the process of interaction analysis. In a sense, deliverables are never complete, for the business itself (which the model is attempting to reflect in information terms) is a living and changing entity in its own right. How then do we know when to stop or when deliverables are "good enough" to proceed with?

A plan for a BAA project will have to take into account the iterative nature of the BAA process itself, while simultaneously recognising the need on the part of a steering group - and, for that matter, a project team - to have clear milestones and deliverables associated with each milestone. An effective approach to this problem is for a project manager, who is charged with developing the detailed project plan, to understand the tasks and deliverables involved in a BAA, and to understand **why** each task is being undertaken. Most importantly the project manager needs to determine **what the risks are of the task (and its associated deliverable) being either left out entirely, or only partially completed.** In order to do so, a project manager needs to have a rough feel for the major activities involved in a BAA (such as have been outlined in section 5.5), **and for the likely duration of each activity.** A typical BAA project that takes no account of a team's learning curve will take around four to six months to complete. If it is going to take much longer than that, then the scope of the project is probably too wide. If there is a significant learning curve for the team to overcome, then as much as two elapsed months can be added to the duration of the project. Figure 6.5 shows the typical spread of activities against time of a BAA project lasting around four months.

Two points become immediately clear from this figure:

● The major activity of Business Area Analysis is **Model the Business Area**. It is the most time-consuming process, taking at least 75% of the elapsed time of a project. When we view the activity in detail (sections 8.2 to 10.1) it will become apparent that there are two distinct phases to this activity, with some options that can be exercised to make the task less time intensive; but the risks of leaving flaws in the model are thereby increased.

● The other two activities that also take up a large part of the project's time and effort are **Analyze Current System(s)** and **Confirm and Check the Model**. The extent to which a project team engages in the former is determined by a number of factors that are discussed more fully in section 6.7, so there is some scope for leeway. However, the formal checking and confirming of the model is a compulsory and ongoing activity that needs to be undertaken in a formal manner once interaction analysis begins. Constant monitoring of quality is an intrinsic part of the project and should be fully documented in the project quality plan; the formal **Confirm and Check the Model** activity is an essential component not only of the quality issue, but also in the way it

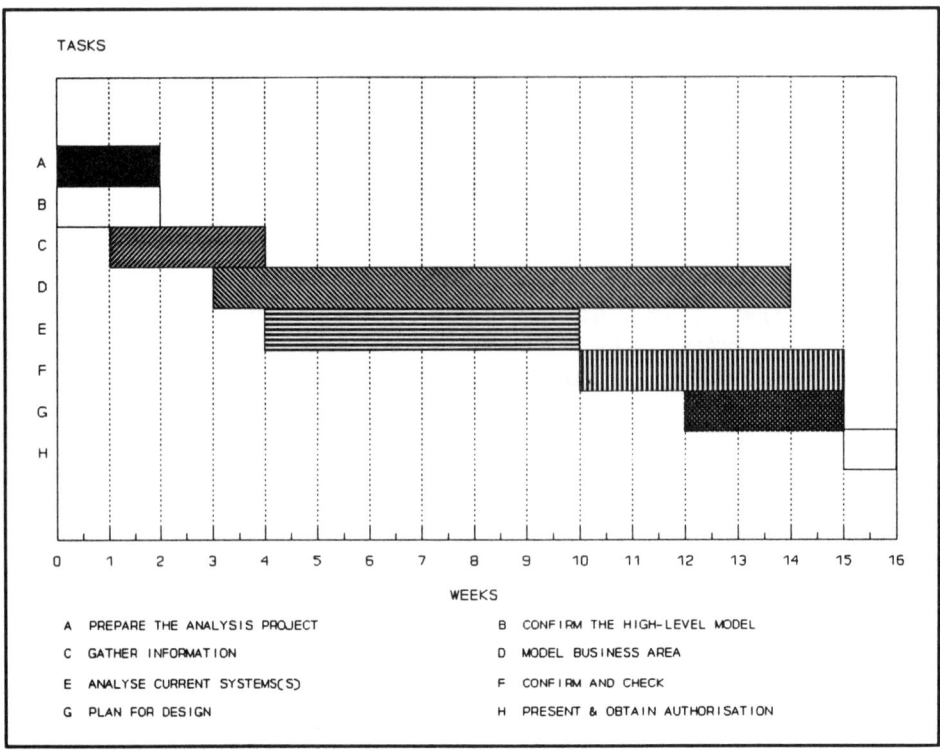

Figure 6.5 Typical Timing of a BAA Project

produces deliverables which help to guide decisions relating to how to progress beyond the BAA stage.[1]

It is worth considering each of the smaller activities in order to understand what they do, and what options there may be with regard to their timing and duration.

The two overlapping activities that occur at the project's inception - **Prepare the Analysis Project** and **Confirm the High Level Model** - involve both the planning of the project and the settling of its scope. They are interrelated activities in that they result in the setting up of the full project framework in terms of its supporting structures - both internal and managerial - and in terms of the area to be covered by the project's investigation. Too often these vital activities are either ignored or brushed over, and the inevitable consequences of this include projects raging out of control, arguments about the project's (shifting) scope, and disappointed users. Much of this chapter deals explicitly with the planning activity. The setting of the project scope is addressed fully in section 7.2.

---

[1]   See section 10.2.

The activity, **Gather Information**, results in the basic referential points for the project being gathered and formulated. Key players in the user community are interviewed, and the results of the interviews are analyzed, documented in a structured fashion, agreed with the interviewees, and then form the source and basis for all future analytic work and model building. The amount of time and effort spent on this activity will, of course, depend on the number of people being interviewed. If each is going to be interviewed individually, this will take at least one elapsed day (and two person-days) of effort: two team members prepare for, conduct, and analyze each interview, which generally will be around two hours in duration. It is possible to compress some of the time involved in this activity by conducting User Intensive Analysis sessions which involve a number of users, last anything from a day to a week, and which produce first-cut models. The **Gather Information** activity is discussed more fully in section 8.1.

Plan for Design is shown as lasting for some three elapsed weeks. It is an activity that can only be performed with confidence once the overall Business Model has reached some state of final stability. However, it is not uncommon for user management to begin asking a number of questions about "future systems" (generally related to cost and broad options) earlier in the analysis process. The activity itself is dependent on a number of factors which are more fully dealt with in Chapter 11. Early estimations will contain greater uncertainty, and it is the project manager's task to bring this fact clearly to the attention of the steering committee. Too much early attention on these issues is wasteful of time, but a project manager can make virtue of necessity by using any time spent on this issue to construct the basic matrices that will be required for this activity. Factors that will affect the amount of time finally spent on this activity include: whether or not package implementation is a viable option, and whether potential packages have already been identified; the design approach to be adopted - will a 4GL and prototyping be used, and will this be done in an environment outside of the I-CASE tool chosen for the analysis itself; what is the political sensitivity of the project and does it have high visibility in the organisation. The overall activity cannot be left out, as it is a prerequisite to the successful transformation of the analysis phase into those of design and construction.

The final activity, **Present and Obtain Authorization**, consists of the formal packaging of the results of the analysis phases, usually in the form of a report supported by its formal presentation to the steering committee. The content of the report (see section 7.1) and the presentation can basically be produced from the contents of the I-CASE encyclopedia, but it does require some time to be packaged together and printed in bulk. The report may have special requirements such as colour copying, and these add to the elapsed time to produce it. Lastly, it is worth bearing in mind that the time to gain formal approval to proceed into design and construction can vary widely, dependent on the organisation's own internal procedures. In planning the duration of an analysis project and the likely start date of subsequent design projects, it goes without saying that these factors need to be taken into account.

6.4   Structuring the Project Team

Having taken a brief overview of the overall likely duration of a BAA project and the broad factors that come into play in estimating time and effort, it is necessary to consider the roles to be played by individuals who are likely to be actively involved in the BAA as part of the project team. While it is recommended that the overall team size is kept to about 4 to 6 people, in projects where the scope is small and containable a team of only 2 or 3 is possible. A team much larger than 6 becomes extremely difficult to organise and especially to co-ordinate in a project where internal communication will prove to be a crucial success factor. If it seems that the project warrants such a large project team, the project manager should seriously question the size of the overall project scope, and where this cannot be changed, should then consider whether it is possible to divide the scope among sub-teams, recognising that additional time and effort will have to be taken to co-ordinate the various sub-teams.

The following are the roles that are required to be played by project team members at various times during the duration of a BAA project. It is clear that one team member may be called upon to play more than one role at a particular point in the project. Some of these roles require responsibility to be assigned to them for aspects of the

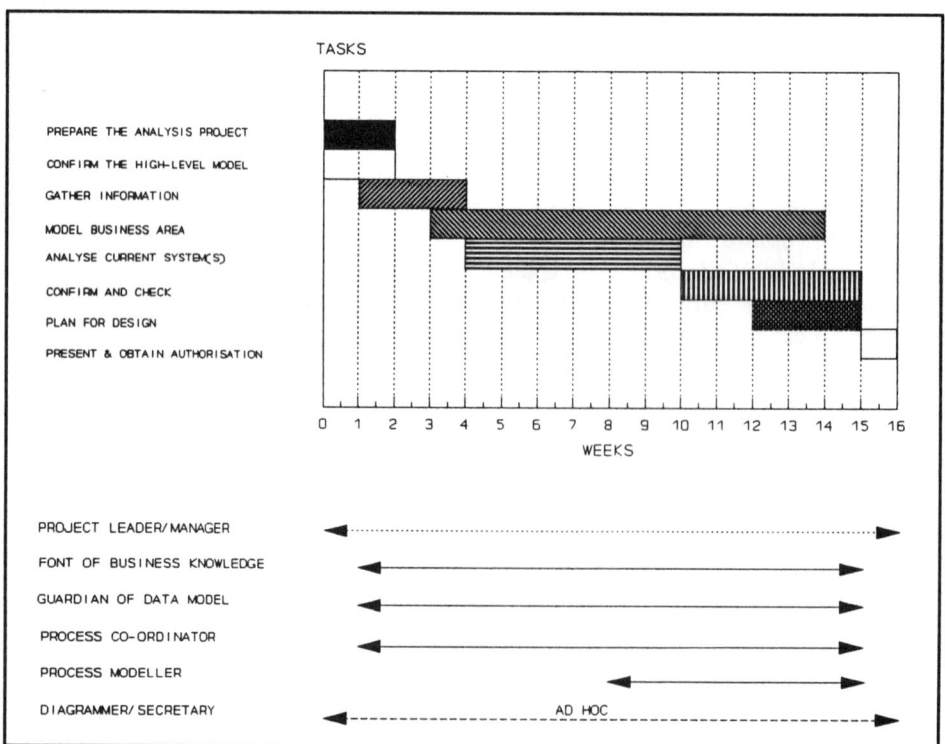

Figure 6.6 Involvement of Team Roles in a Typical BAA Project

developing model: these roles facilitate the communication between team members while at the same time making it quite clear to all where final accountability for an aspect of the model (and hence, of the project) lies. The likely involvement of each team role during the project duration is shown in Figure 6.6.

6.4.1 Project Leader/Manager

This role should be played by a user so as to ensure user commitment and accountability for the project. The Project Manager should understand the IT issues involved in the project, and is ultimately responsible for all aspects of the project, and is directly accountable to the steering committee for the project's progress against plan, the quality of the deliverables, and the controlling of costs. The activities that the manager will be directly responsible for and will usually perform include all the up-front planning, the definition and agreement of the project scope, the monitoring of team progress, internal quality control, planning for design, and the final presentation of the BAA deliverables to the steering committee. Generally this person should be well versed with project management issues, understand IE in theory and in practice, and preferably have a broad understanding of the Business Area being analyzed or credibility with the business users. The Project Manager is involved with the project from its inception right through to its completion.

6.4.2 Font of Business Knowledge

This person must be a user, as this role is the primary source of all detailed business knowledge to the team. Any query related to business procedures, practice, and policy by any team member should be directed primarily to this person. The individual who plays this role will usually not know all there is to know about the Business Area being analyzed, unless the Business Area is a fairly small one. However, it requires knowledge of where to find the answers to business questions being sought by team members: who to speak to, and which department or group deals with the issue. More formally, the Font of Business Knowledge should bear accountability to the business community for the accuracy and correctness of the model being developed by the BAA team. The formal channel for ensuring this is via the User Liaison Group (see section 6.1.1), which will provide views and decisions on issues that embrace the user community as a whole or that cut across current organisational structures. It is this role which reviews, from a business perspective, the accuracy of all deliverables produced, to ensure that they are formally reviewed and approved by the User Liaison Group, and to make sure that any new ideas, concepts or terms arising from the project's work are introduced into and accepted by the user community.

This person needs to be involved in the project from its earliest days - certainly by the time that any gathering of information has begun - and should be involved in the project until all formal checking of the model is complete.

6.4.3   Guardian of the Data Model

In a methodology that is posited on a data-driven approach to analysis and design, it is essential that throughout the lifetime of the project, a formal, single view of the data model is in place. This is particularly needed during the early stages of BAA, when the data model is in constant flux as it evolves, and again during the early stages of interaction analysis when the data model is being exercised and proven, and is again, in effect, subject to a great deal of change. The Guardian of the Data Model is responsible at all times for the completeness and accuracy of the data model, and is the one source of information for the definitive state of the model at any given point in time, whether that be the current definition for an Entity Type, or the current length of an Attribute.

As the project proceeds. better knowledge of an aspect of the business may generate a potential need for an aspect of the data model to change. Such change can only take place with the approval and participation of the individual filling this role. The Guardian views the Data Model of a BAA from a project perspective, and ensures that the model reflects the overall information needs of the Business Area. All changes to the Data Model are communicated to the rest of the BAA team by the Guardian.

In an environment where many IE projects are being undertaken simultaneously, the specific data interests of each project team are represented to the Corporate Model/Data Co-ordination Group (see section 6.2.2) by its Data Model Guardian.

This person needs to be involved in the project from the time when the exercise of gathering information begins. The role is to transform the information gathered into a first-cut detailed Entity Relationship Model for review by the user community. The Data Model Guardian needs to remain involved in the project until all formal checking of the model is complete.

6.4.4   Process Model Co-ordinator

Throughout the BAA process, but especially once interaction analysis begins, there is a need for a single person to maintain a formal view of the business process model as it evolves and becomes more refined. It is possible that in the early stages of the BAA this role can be adequately filled by either the Project Manager or the Font of Business Knowledge. However, once interaction analysis begins, a number of issues arise that are best coordinated and resolved by a single person who has detailed understanding of the way in which process logic is formally being recorded particularly by means of Process Action Diagrams (PADs). The first factor that must be ensured is that there is a consistency in style and layout of the PADs. Secondly, in the act of formally constructing PADs, the scope of each Elementary Process is being unequivocally defined. One person needs to understand where each part of the Business Area fits into the overall Process Model at any given time. Lastly, within various Elementary Processes, it is possible that the same business rule or algorithm is applied (for example a rule for allocating stock balances following an internal transfer of stock). The formal recording of the rule (as a reusable Process Action Block (PAB) or Algorithm) needs to be controlled, because its use within the Business Area needs to be consistent. The problem becomes more complex when such a PAB or Algorithm applies within Elementary Processes that occur across **different** Business Areas. The role of process co-ordination then falls within the ambit of the Corporate Model/Data Co-ordination Group, and the Process Model Co-ordinator from each project team will represent the team's view and interests to this group.

The Process Model Co-ordinator needs to be active in the project from the time the exercise of gathering information begins until all formal checking of the model is complete. It is a role that gains in importance once the interaction analysis aspect of the project begins. At this crucial later stage of the project, the person playing this role needs to understand how PADs work in detail. This requires an understanding of formal computing logic constructs, and so it is likely that the Co-ordinator will come from a computing background.

6.4.5   Process Modeller

This role only comes into play once interaction analysis begins. The various Process Modellers on the team are employed to capture the formal business logic that underlies each Elementary Process particularly in the form of Process Action Diagrams. To do so, a detailed understanding of formal computing logic constructs is required, and so it is essential that they come from a computing background. It is likely that they will have had some previous experience both with programming, and with the specification of programs and/or systems.

During interaction analysis, it is likely that more than one person will play the role of Process Modeller, as the activity of formally capturing what the business does is very labour-intensive: in fact, the task of formally recording the rules of business logic, together with the checking of the model, are likely to take up around half of the elapsed time of the business modelling task.[2] The various Process Modellers are co-ordinated, of course, by the Process Model Co-ordinator. They are also required to be actively involved in the formal job of checking the correctness and completeness of the model (see section 10.2).

6.4.6   Diagrammer/Secretary

At various points in the project, there will be a need for information to be recorded either in diagrammatic or in textual format. Depending on which I-CASE tool is being used by the project team, and the stage the project has reached, the most time-effective

---

[2] This time will depend on the level of detail that is captured in the PADs. This issue is discussed further in section 10.1.3.

way of recording information may be for the team to draw it up for subsequent capture in the project encyclopedia or repository. The task of entering the analyzed material can then be done by someone who is able to use the software, but does not necessarily possess the scarcer analytic skills required to develop and fine-tune the models.

At other times, there may be a need for material to be collated purely for presentation purposes. If a reasonable I-CASE tool is being used for recording project data, then the information will be available, but its suitability for formal presentations may not always be appropriate. The task of extracting and reformatting the material is best delegated to the person playing the role of Diagrammer/Secretary.

The requirement for such a role through the project's duration is usually *ad hoc*, though it can be predicted from the project plan when major walk-throughs of deliverables are scheduled with users, and when the final BAA project report is to be presented to the steering committee.

6.5   Planning the Project

The first major task to be performed by the Project Manager will be to expand any outline project plan (that should have been a deliverable from the ISP) in terms of tasks, deliverables, and time scales. This is essential if full visibility of the project is to be ensured. Visibility is desirable so that progress can be seen to be occurring, and so that problems can be foreseen and highlighted. The plan, and any subsequent agreed changes to it, will become the means of project co-ordination not just among the team members, but also between the team and the various support structures that will have to interface with it.

It is, of course, impossible to draw up a detailed project plan until and unless the project scope is agreed. This aspect of the project is fully discussed in section 7.2.

Once the overall project tasks and deliverables are agreed in concept, the project manager will have to allocate personnel to the tasks identified, and determine accountability of these people against the specific roles they will be playing through the project life-span.

6.5.1   The Training Plan

Having identified the specific team members as well as the key users to be involved in the project, the project manager should map each individual's skills and exposure to IE against the skills that will be required by that person through the project. A Person/Skills-Required matrix such as the one illustrated in Figure 6.7 is a useful means of doing this.

The purpose of such an exercise is to identify skill deficiencies in order to devise a training plan that ensures that team members and users participating in the project will receive the appropriate training they require at the right time. The training plan should be an integral part of the project plan, and should be kept in line with any changes made to project priorities and timings. It should include both specific skills training for project team members, and awareness training, particularly for the steering committee members and for members of the user community who will have to interact with the project team.

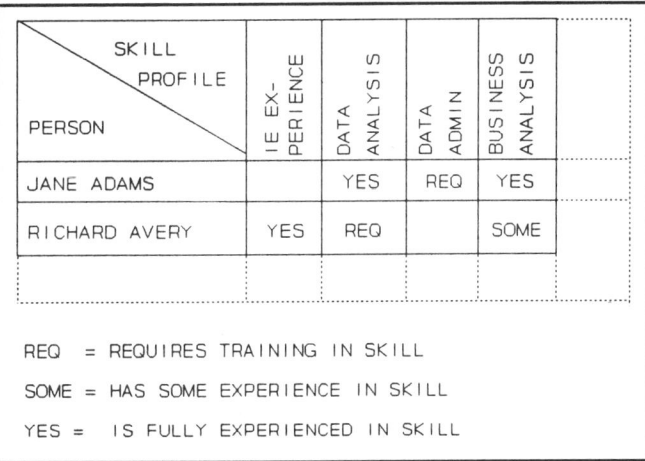

Figure 6.7 Person/Skills Requirement Matrix

6.5.2   The Quality Plan

The project plan should address the issue of quality explicitly in the form of a quality plan. This is a formal document that describes how the quality of the project (both its process and deliverables) will be controlled.

Whilst a full treatment of quality management is outside the scope of this book, it is an issue that should be seen as an intrinsic part of any IE project. **It should not be addressed outside of the project, nor should it be something that is tacked on later.** A further and more detailed treatment of quality issues is given when the checking of the model is discussed in section 10.2, but it must be stressed that the process of quality control and monitoring must be made an integral part of the project from its outset. It is impossible to address quality adequately as a single task tacked onto the end of a BAA project.

6.6   User Expectations

It is critical for the success of any project that the users' expectations from the project are met. This can be particularly difficult to do in a BAA project if the users have not been properly informed about the purposes of the project, and of the overall IE process. The project is guaranteed to fail if the users are expecting to receive a working system, and all they get is a Business Model!

As described in section 6.5.1, awareness training for users should form part of any BAA project plan. Such awareness must include an understanding of the deliverables produced in the BAA **and their purpose.** This necessarily involves some understanding of the BAA process itself, and how it fits in with the IE approach. Unless the overall implications of the IE approach (more fully discussed in Chapter 2) are taken on board by senior user management, no amount of enthusiasm by those reporting to them will suffice in convincing them that their money has been well spent, despite that fact that no system is yet on the horizon. The shift from viewing information and the provision of it as nothing more than an expense, to seeing and treating information as a corporate asset, needs to permeate the organisation at all levels, and preferably should be led from the very top. Even if it is, it will be essential to remind senior user managers periodically of the overall IE context of their project, and to sketch progress against the complete corporate IT plan.

One must not forget that the early days of the introduction of IE to an organisation can be a very difficult and frustrating time for senior managers: they see a lot of money being spent, but no systems are being delivered. Traditionally, this has been a signal to them that the IT department is not performing adequately. They may have participated enthusiastically in the ISP exercise, which should have taken around six months to complete; now there is a BAA which in itself could take a further four to six months: already a year has passed, and no systems have been delivered! And then someone is going to tell them that the design phase has not yet even begun!

Unless senior management are well aware of what is being attempted, there is every likelihood that they will lose patience at this stage and pull the financial plug on the project(s) just a few months before the first systems are due to be delivered.[3] The result of such a decision would not only end the current IE initiative; it is likely to discredit the approach within the organisation for some time to come, and could, ultimately, place the organisation at a disadvantage when compared with its competitors who do manage to capitalise on their IE investment.

It is very important, therefore, not only to have senior managers behind the IE initiative, but also to make sure that they are kept well informed both about the project's progress, **and its objectives**. The expectations of senior managers, like those of all users involved in the project, need to be carefully managed.

6.6.1   The Business Model as a Basis for Constructing Computerised Systems

The primary purpose of the BAA project should not be lost sight of: the construction

---

[3] It is realistic to expect that in a "pure" IE context, this will occur, at the earliest, eighteen months into the IE process if a quick-path quick-win project has been carefully managed through. As users need to see results, the IE group should be pragmatic in its approach: a key objective of the IE implementation plan should be the production of a real, necessary, albeit modest system within the first twelve months, **even if the system represents a compromise on the corporate architectures, and on the "pure" application of IE principles.**

of a Business Model that reflects clearly and unambiguously the business itself in terms of its usage of and requirements for information. By its nature, such a model is likely to reflect the complexity of the business it is modelling. Nor should sight be lost as to the purposes of such a model - why the BAA is being undertaken in the first place.

It is worth highlighting clearly the main objectives that are intended to be achieved by creating a Business Model. These are:

●   To build a model of the Business Area in terms of its:

      -     Information requirements (what information it needs to operate);

      -     Information usage (what it does with that information).

●   To achieve an understanding of **what** the business does regardless of **how** it currently operates.

●   To illustrate the BAA team's understanding of the business as an information processing system to the users in a form that they can comprehend.

We should not forget that the starting point for the BAA model is the high-level Information Architecture that is the result of the ISP process (see section 4.3.1). The Business Model thus exists within the context of, and is determined by, the high-level Information Architecture. Its primary function is to act as a bridge between the complexity of the corporate enterprise itself and the computerised systems that will be required to support that enterprise. This point is illustrated in Figure 6.8.

In a sense, the BAA model can be seen as a description, or even specification, **from a user's (business) perspective** of an area of the business viewed **as a system that requires information to function effectively**. The model is then a description both of the information that the business area requires **and** of the ways in which it uses that information.

It is a representation of **what** the business does (or wishes to do were it not constrained by existing systems and ways of operating) as opposed to a temporal view of **how** the business goes about its activities. It is worth noting in passing that very often process-based ways of analyzing and/or recording user requirements have, when poorly applied, done little more than record the "how": very little analysis was applied to the observations being recorded, and so poor business practice was simply replicated (and ossified) in the systems that were produced. As discussed in Chapter 2, such systems are clearly incapable of responding to the changing needs of a dynamic business, for they encapsulate a static, time-based view of business practice in their very conception and design.

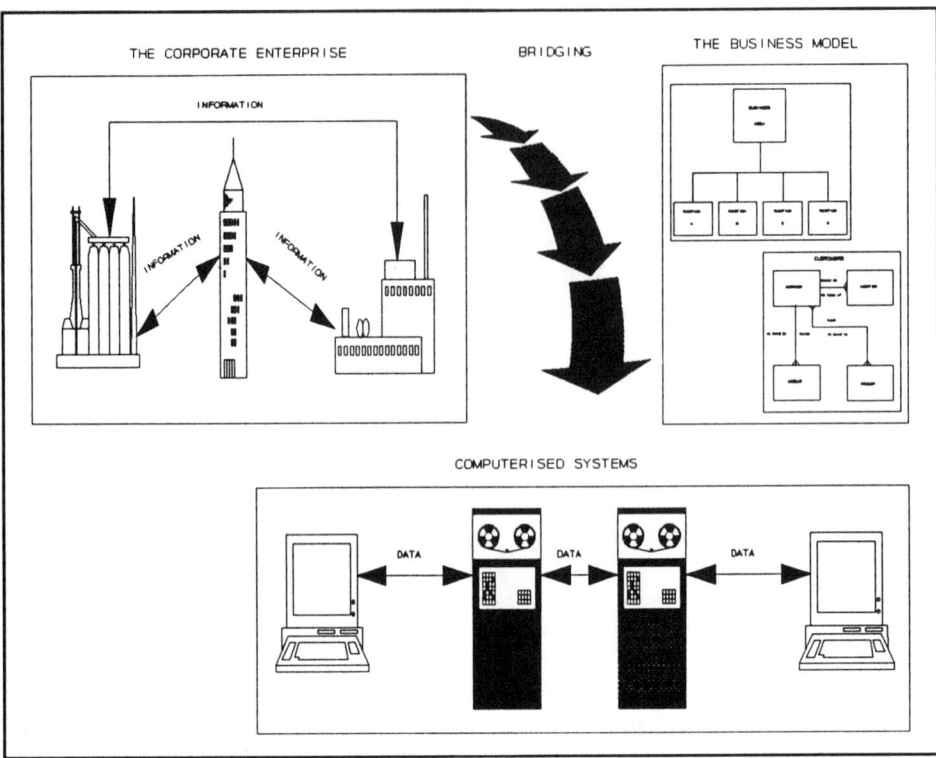

Figure 6.8 The Model as a Bridge between the Business and Systems

Users need to be made aware of these issues in order to appreciate the function that the Business Model serves. It may also be helpful to make them aware of where the model leads to, and how it can be used to drive the process that ultimately produces the systems that will help to drive and run the business of the future.

Within a Business Area, the model can help the analysts to determine how best to divide the area up into systems based on common information usage within the area (see section 11.1). A mapping of aspects of the model to key determining issues such as Critical Success Factors, Goals, and Business Objectives can help in determining or confirming where the key paybacks for systems lie within a Business Area. The model can then be used to scope each design area unambiguously in terms of the data and processes to be covered by the design project. The most effective phasing of the design projects and of their implementation can be determined using the model, as can the potential effects on other systems and/or interfaces with them. Lastly, the model provides an effective means for evaluating application packages in terms both of their functional and data coverage. The latter is vital as a means of coordinating interfaces between different packages and with existing systems. (For further discussion of this topic see section 11.3.)

6.6.2 Other Uses of the Business Model

Another way of understanding the function of the Business Model is to see it as a user "specification" of their **business seen as an information system**. In this sense, the users are involved in constructing their own model of the Business Area in terms of its information usage and requirements. This approach has a number of additional benefits besides those implied by the main thrust that has so far been emphasised - the Business Model as a basis for the construction of new systems to support the business.

The Business Model also provides a documentation of business understanding in a standardised format. As such it can be an ongoing source of investment in providing a "base-line view" of the business. Any additional or subsequent analysis work undertaken within the Business Area has a solid, comprehensible starting point due to the standardised format and structures used within the model. Secondly, in providing a view of what the business does, the model can be used as a base-line in its own right in coping with and accommodating to changes that may be affecting the business. The clearest application of this idea comes in two areas: systems re-engineering, and business re-engineering.

Systems Re-engineering

As will be discussed in section 13.2, systems that are built based upon the Business Model are able to respond more swiftly to business changes. What, however, about already-existing systems?

The Business Model can provide a basic point of reference for these as well. By the techniques of Normalisation and Canonical Synthesis (see section 8.2.2) an existing system's underlying structures can be analyzed and modelled. The Business Model then provides a means of steering that system from where it currently is to a position where it is more closely based on the Business Model. This process does not only refer to the complete re-writing of the old system based on a derived understanding of its structures; the principles involved in re-engineering systems can be applied in a controlled manner to existing systems within the context of normal maintenance. In one project, a small, highly successful system could no longer be easily amended to reflect changing and more sophisticated business needs without endangering the stability of the system. By a stroke of luck, a good Business Model that included in its scope the system's area of coverage had recently been constructed in a different context. The team looking after the system was able to gain access to the Business Model, and mapped their system to it. In the process, they discovered that most of their difficulties lay in redundant data items that were named differently, and hence were very difficult to recognise as such. As a result, any subsequent maintenance and enhancement they have undertaken on the system has taken the Business Model into account. Wherever possible, changes made in routine maintenance now include correcting the redundancies as well. Not only has the system gained a new lease on life, but the Business Model is providing users of the system with the basis for discussion of a new generation of systems that will better meet their expanding business needs. When the new systems are built, the Business Model will also provide the base-line for controlling the transition from the old system to the new one.

Business Re-engineering

In the process of Business Modelling, users often achieve a better understanding of the underlying structures of their business when it is not being constrained by the present organisation. Very often, current business procedures and patterns are historically based, and reflect the flow of control in an organisation that originally monitored decision-making by means of a flow of paper up and down the hierarchy. The Business Model can form the basis for rebuilding business procedures to reflect both what the organisation is actually doing, and the flatter overall organisation structure that is common today where businesses are attempting to place decision-making activities with individuals who are at the levels most suited to make them. It is recognised that improved operational procedures can help with achieving that business-motivated goal; in this context, the Business Model may provide added insights into the sorts of business procedures that are most appropriate to the current business operation. The model can provide a base-line against which to assess and manage any changes in procedures that are considered operationally necessary.

Summary

A full understanding of the function of the BAA model will help business users to understand why such a model is necessary, why the up-front activities that precede system development are so extensive and are taking so long, and how business information is being treated as an asset. Such an understanding will be an essential means of gaining end user commitment to the analytic process and in managing user expectations.

6.7   The Role of Current Systems Analysis[4]

In analyzing a Business Area with a view to providing enhanced and robust computerised system support for it, a question must arise whether, and to what extent, existing systems should be analyzed and modelled. In referring to existing or current systems most people tend to mean computer systems, but the remarks that follow are not intended to exclude current operational procedures that support part of the business and are either manual or mechanised to some extent.

The most important consideration in approaching an existing system is that it may in fact be **constraining** the way in which a business operates. The system may be imposing obsolete and/or clumsy business practises upon staff charged with doing the

---

[4] See also section 5.2.

job. These false constraints may actually blur the picture of **what** it is the business does by presenting a strong entrenchment of **how** it does it. Current systems and current practise may fossilise company mind-sets that are part of company culture, and may prevent any creative approach to the business itself. The job of analysis is to dig below these surface representations in order to understand and depict the fundamental structures upon which they are actually based.

Although this line of argument seems to imply that one should ignore current systems entirely, this is not the case. If they have been successful in any way (and many have effectively been supporting business operations for a long time) they must in themselves contain a vast amount of relevant business knowledge. The question that arises is how to capitalise on such knowledge?

IE theory clearly recognises a place for "The Analysis of Current Systems." However, many project teams have got so bogged down in that analysis that it appears to become an end in itself; or alternatively, they have not known what the purpose of the exercise is, and so have not fully utilised its results.

The main theoretical reason for undertaking CSA within a BAA project is in order to derive a data model of the existing system in order to compare it with the top-down model that the team has built up as a normal product of its analysis. The top-down model is **checked and verified** against the model(s) derived from the existing system(s). It is also possible to compare the functional coverage of the existing system(s) with the BAA process model.[5]

There are a number of instances in which it seems either sensible or essential to engage in CSA. The most important of these are discussed below.

6.7.1 Absence of Users

There may be an absence of users with an in-depth knowledge of the Business Area or particular aspects of it. At the same time, the computerised system may contain all, or a substantial part of that knowledge. In such a case, the existing system should be carefully analyzed in order to extract a view both of what it does and of the data structures it requires in order to operate.

6.7.2 Mission-Critical Systems

An existing system may form a key part of a business and be mission-critical to the operation of the business. It is then important to confirm either that the system lies completely within the scope of the Business Area as defined in the project scope, or else to have a clear view of where its boundaries with the Business Area lie. In either case,

---

[5] Further detail about these activities are contained in section 10.2.1.

but particularly in the former, the system can be used effectively to verify and check the analysis work the team has undertaken.

6.7.3   Investment in Business Knowledge

Very often a long-running system in itself represents a considerable investment in terms of business knowledge and experience. This cannot be ignored, and often there are good political reasons for not doing so. Any knowledge gained from such a system can be utilised well, both in the verification exercise and in activities such as populating the top-down entity model with attributes, and attribute definitions.

6.7.4   Functional Coverage

Lastly, it would be essential to analyze an existing system where either there is a close match between the system and the Business Area, or the project was undertaken with a view to replacing the system. In these cases, much valuable information could be gleaned from the system, and in the latter, the problems currently being experienced with the system, if well analyzed, offer excellent clues as to where the system is constraining or adversely affecting current business practice.

6.8   Critical Success Factors for a Business Area Analysis Project

Before embarking on a BAA project one should be aware of the factors that will affect the success or otherwise of the project. Some of these have already been mentioned in the discussion of the structures and methods required to control and support the project team. Others relate more to the ongoing practices of the teams as the project progresses, and will be addressed more appropriately in future chapters. It does seem appropriate though to be aware of Critical Success Factors (CSFs) before the project *per se* commences. It is far better, if possible, to prevent potential problems than to have to solve them once user confidence has already been compromised.

It will be noticed that **users** are the subject of the first two CSFs. They are the key to the success of any BAA project for, after all, it is **their** business that the team is attempting to model. It is with the users that the success of a project will start and end.

6.8.1   User Commitment

As discussed earlier, the project stands a far better chance of success if it belongs to the business community. The most effective way to achieve their commitment to the project is by having them own it fully. This requires both funding and control of the project by user management. The funding assures the commitment; and the control via a steering committee is essential, otherwise the users may begin to feel as though they have simply signed a cheque for the delivery of something - and a blank one at that if things start to go wrong. Final overall accountability for the project rests with a project manager, and it is most desirable that this role, too, be played by a user.

6.8.2   User Involvement

The concept of user involvement in a BAA project exists at a number of levels, the most basic of which is the presence of one or more representatives of the user community to play an active role on the project team. Such a user team member is the minimum involvement that is required for a project to stand any chance of success, but such involvement does need to be supplemented by the user commitment, without which an "us and them" situation can too quickly arise, especially in the event of the project encountering unforeseen difficulties.

Further levels of user commitment may exist via a wide-ranging user management presence on the Project Steering Committee. This can serve as a means of top-down communication back to the wider user community, as well as a way in which broader user commitment to the project is developed and consolidated. Lastly, user participation in the project via the User Liaison Group can be a very effective way of spreading user involvement beyond the aegis of a small group of managers and team members; it becomes a means for communicating the team's work back to the user community in a way that allows those who run the business at all its levels to own the products of the team and become involved in the cycle of their production.

6.8.3   Suitable Training for All Persons Involved in the Project

It is essential for the success of the project for all persons both directly and indirectly involved in it to have or to acquire those skills that are necessary for them to perform their jobs properly. For the team members, a specific training plan should be linked to their particular skill needs at a particular point in the project. Such training will generally cover both an understanding of the IE approach to analysis, and specific training both in the use of techniques and of the chosen I-CASE product. For all those who are on the periphery of the project, specific awareness programmes need to be set in place and run: for management, these need to build up an appreciation of the IE approach being applied, as well as a high-level understanding of any of the deliverables that they may be called upon to review; for other users, particularly those involved in reviewing and approving deliverables, the training will focus on an understanding of those deliverables, as well as their purpose and function within the BAA approach to analysis.

6.8.4   Clearly Defined Project Scope

The scope of the project must be clearly and unambiguously defined in terms that are understandable both to the team and to the project steering committee. If this is not done, then there is a great danger of a creep in project scope that could occur in an insidious manner. This will severely jeopardise the team's ability to meet the set targets, and is likely to be one of the primary contributory factors that will lead to the "paralysis through analysis" syndrome.

The topic of describing the scope of a BAA project unambiguously is dealt with comprehensively in section 7.2.

6.8.5   Realistic Expectations

It is impossible to meet user expectations if they have initially been wrongly set: the user expecting a system out of the BAA process will not be impressed when, at the end of the BAA phase, a series of Business Models are presented. Even if, somehow, a project manager succeeds in redeeming the situation at this stage, when the user is *then* told that there is still a BSD or Logical Design to be done, *and then* a Physical Design before "coding can start," it is doubtful whether the project stands any chance of survival.

The setting and managing of user expectations in terms of what they will receive, and when, is very closely linked to the users' understanding of the development approach the team will be adopting. The awareness training described in section 6.5.1 will play a vital role in ensuring that users will know **and understand** what the deliverables of each phase of the project will be. Continual involvement in and monitoring of the project by the steering committee will reinforce this perception, especially if the project team manages to produce a constant set of predefined deliverables regularly as scheduled in the project plan. Lastly, if in conjunction with a good understanding of the function of the deliverables, there is a clear and unambiguous shared understanding of the project's scope in terms of business coverage, chances are that user expectations and produced deliverables will match up.

It is important to recognise that user expectations have to be managed in a sensitive fashion throughout the project life-cycle. It is not enough for a project manager to wait for the end and then to say, "But we **told** you four months ago what we would deliver." By that stage it could be too late. User expectations, like the project itself, need to be constantly monitored, and where needed, appropriate action in the form of education and/or the review and explanation of deliverables produced must be taken to prevent them from slipping.

6.8.6   A Functional Team Structure that Facilitates the BAA Process

As has been more fully discussed in section 6.4, it is essential that an internal team structure is put into place that maximises each individual's strengths, and allows the team to operate effectively as a unit. This means that communications among team members, and between the team and the outside world, must be facilitated, not hindered, by the structure, and that roles to be played, and the associated responsibilities they carry, must be clearly defined.

6.8.7   Clear Goals and Objectives

The question of project scope is addressed fully in section 7.2. Supplementing the question of the overall aims and scope of the project, the team leader and team members must have a clear view of the goals and objectives of each of the tasks they are undertaking. For a team member, there is nothing more demoralising than being asked to perform an exercise that seems both pointless and meaningless just because "the book says it must be done." By the same token, the project manager needs to have a clear overview of the goals and objectives of each task so that the team can be more effectively steered on a day-to-day and week-to-week basis, and so that individual team members can be well managed, motivated, and directed.

6.8.8   Pragmatic and Realistic Use of Both the Methodology and the Techniques

A project manager's understanding of the goals and objectives of each task must be supplemented by a strong appreciation of **how they fit and work together**. This enables the project manager to decide how to apply each technique within the overall context of the methodology. Every project is under pressures of both time and budget, and if the risks of eliminating or modifying a technique within the overall project context are understood, the project manager can decide on the best course of action given the current status of the project and the pressures on it. Because of the way in which IE spans the full development life cycle, it is likely that decisions taken at one phase will have an impact on the next one. That impact too needs to be understood, for some short-cuts will effectively transfer work from one phase to the next - the work will still have to be done. In other cases, a short-cut may heighten the risks involved with an aspect of the project. If, for example, they most probably affect an area of the business that is unlikely ever to be automated, then the risks may well be worth taking. At other times, the transfer of work to the next phase may in fact be a preferred course. For example, if a decision has been made to use the powerful prototyping features of a 4GL that is not an integrated part of the I-CASE tool chosen, outline business logic may rather be captured at the BAA phase than attempting to record detailed business logic. In BSD then, when prototyping is undertaken, full understanding of the logic of the business is achieved as the prototype is created. What is lost in such an approach is the creation of a "pure" and complete model of the business as a point for future reference - and if this is a significant aim of the BAA process, such a short-cut should **not** be taken. What is gained, however, is a great deal of time and possibly user confidence with a prototype and working system being delivered significantly sooner, while the BAA model can still be checked using the outline logic, albeit less rigorously.[6]

---

[6] Fuller details of this particular aspect of capturing business logic is discussed in section 10.1.3.

This sort of pragmatic application of the principles of IE requires a clear understanding of the ways in which techniques interrelate both within and across phases. Some of that understanding can only be honed though practice and application, but it needs to be underpinned with an assessment of the risks involved for the overall project, and the immediate phase being undertaken.

6.8.9   Suitable Cross-team Co-ordination, Standards, and Support

Whenever the IE approach is being introduced and applied seriously within an organisation, the implication must be that there will soon be many teams analyzing areas of the business and building systems simultaneously. For such a multi-team environment to operate effectively, co-ordination across the various teams is vital. A great deal of effort is wasted when teams re-invent the wheel. Common standards need to be used and applied, and there must be informed support both for the I-CASE tool being used, and for the methodology and its practical application. These issues have been more fully addressed earlier in this chapter in section 6.2.

6.8.10   A Proper I-CASE Tool to Facilitate the Process

The ideal CASE tool that is needed to support IE is one that completely covers the development life cycle from ISP through to Construction via code generation. There are a number of reasons why that ideal may not be attainable: most current I-CASE tools are targeted at a **specific** operational environment, and that may not suit a particular company in terms of its own hardware and software strategy. The interim solution may be a bridge of some sort from one CASE tool to another, and this will most probably occur at the end of BAA, just into BSD, or possibly after the logical design has been completed. The pragmatic solution for the moment is to attempt to minimise rather than eliminate the need to bridge across tools; such bridging does introduce problems into the process, particularly if the bridge is one way only. These problems have to be managed (probably via a change control **mechanism**) until complete life cycle support is achieved either in one tool, or via a two-way bridge.

What the base CASE tool should provide, however, is the application and, in some cases, on-line enforcement of consistency rules. Where such rules are not automatically enforced, consistency and completeness checking after the event must be possible, though the former approach is preferable.

It would prove impossible to practice IE manually: not only would the sheer volume of material be unmanageable and indigestible, it would be quite impossible to control consistency and to enforce rules of association between objects in the models that have been produced. The I-CASE tool is **both** a documenting tool, **and** a tool for enforcing and checking such consistency. The tool chosen for the task should support the basic concepts and techniques that IE promotes. A more generalised CASE tool often compromises on some of these, and the compromises may become future pitfalls. It is important to anticipate what these might be before the event. It is also important to use the strengths of the tool as much as possible, even if its application of IE is not "pure", or it does not follow the corporation's recommended practices. For example, in a BAA, process modelling may be performed via Process Dependency Diagrams (PDD) or using Data Flow Diagrams (DFD). An organisation may prefer PDDs, but the chosen CASE tool (e.g. IEW™/ADW™) may only implement DFDs. In such an instance, it would be foolish to compromise on the strength of the CASE tool's consistency checking mechanisms based on DFDs by using the tool to represent PDDs without any real supporting structure behind them. (Potential difficulties with using DFDs for analysis in an IE context are discussed in section 10.1.1.1.)

Just as it would be foolish to attempt IE without CASE tool support, it would also be foolish to use a powerful I-CASE tool without a framing methodology, for in doing so, the methodology provides a solid guiding framework for the use of CASE tools.

***

Having addressed many of the management and infrastructural issues that need to be considered before embarking on a BAA project, it is now time for us to turn towards the project itself. The first questions we need to understand relate to the target we are aiming at, and when we know that our work is complete. Chapter 7 addresses the question of deliverables and their phasing through a BAA project.

Chapter 7 Getting It Right

It is very difficult to complete a BAA without a clear view of what it is that is being aimed at. In this chapter, we will begin in section 7.1 by looking at the sort of document that could be produced at the end of a BAA project. Then, in section 7.2, we turn to understanding what our starting point for a BAA needs to be so as to be able to proceed with the project without getting lost along the way. To do this we will examine how to scope the BAA project whether or not the project is the result of an ISP. Finally, we will look at the main milestones that occur in a BAA project in section 7.3.1, and the deliverables associated with each of these in section 7.3.2.

Closely related both to issues of scope and to deliverables is the question of knowing when a task is complete and a milestone has been reached. This is a particular problem in an IE and CASE environment, where the process of producing deliverables is often an iterative one so that deliverables that were once considered complete are revisited and drastically reworked. Some of the common pitfalls that plague BAA projects will be examined, and guidelines will be suggested for avoiding them in section 7.4.

7.1   The Business Area Analysis Report

At the end of a BAA project, the Project Steering Committee will be asked for authorization to proceed with the next phase of the project. This will involve the design and, ultimately, construction of one or more computerised systems to cover user requirements for information services within their Business Area. The approach to systems development may vary widely in different organisations, and may depend on a number of factors that are extraneous to the project itself. So, the way ahead may involve using a more traditional approach with the system being coded manually, even though this would counter some of the advantages of using IE and CASE in the first place. Where an I-CASE tool is being used, design and construction are likely to involve the use of 4GLs, prototyping and code generators. Whatever the development environment that is chosen, the Project Steering Committee will have to base its commitment of resources to the completion of the project on information presented to them. Such information is most likely to appear in the form of a **Business Area Analysis Report**.

Most of the information appearing in the report will reside in the I-CASE encyclopedia, and the production of the report will typically involve the extraction of this information, its reformatting so that it is in a form that is comprehensible to the readers, and the addition to it of some minimal textual commentary that ties the information together.

The report is not only essential as the basis for the securement of management approval, it is also necessary as a formal documentation of the end point of a project. As such, it is also the audit trail through the project, and the point of reference for all future work that will be undertaken based on the BAA.

The report is likely to consist of two main sections: the **Main Body**, which is really a summary of the BAA project in a format that is meaningful and comprehensible to the members of the Project Steering Committee. This part of the report is likely to be around 20 to 50 pages in length - the shorter, the better. The Main Body of the BAA Report is supplemented by a series of **Appendices** that contain the fully detailed work that was undertaken and that underpins that summary in the Main Body. The Appendices will contain the full audit trail through the project. Should a Project Steering Committee member wish to understand any aspect of the project and/or the resulting model in detail, the requisite information should be contained in an Appendix. The Appendices will also contain the frozen project model upon which any future design work is based.

7.1.1 The Business Area Analysis Report - Main Body

The Main Body of the BAA Report will consist of a number of sections that are outlined below. Some of these sections will only be present if the nature of the business area analyzed requires them. Sections that are optional have been indicated.

7.1.1.1 Management Summary

This is a one page summary of the main issues covered by the BAA project, the recommendations of the project team, and the key reasons for those recommendations. It is intended to be read not only by the members of the Project Steering Committee, but also by any other senior managers and directors to whom the project's recommendations may have to be justified.

Any costs and benefits related to the recommendation should be included in this summary, as should any key issues that may have a broader organisational impact. If appropriate, there should be clear cross-referencing to the relevant sections of the BAA Report Main Body for further information.

7.1.1.2 Project Background

The business reasons for the project are given. This can be a brief summary of the business needs that are being addressed, and/or the problems that the project was focusing on. A summary of the project scope should be included.

Details of how the project team tackled the issues placed before them, the team's *modus operandi*, its composition, involvement of business users in the process, and any acknowledgements are found in this section.

7.1.1.3 Information Needs

This section contains a summary of main business information needs that the project has identified. These are presented in the form of a summary of the highlights of the Project Data Model in terms that are easily recognisable to the business. High-level subject area diagrams containing the main data entity types (as illustrated in Figure 4.4) are supplemented by a brief narrative explanation of them.

The information contained in this section is backed up by extracts from the project encyclopedia that are contained in the BAA Report Appendices. These will cover: full details of the Entity Relationship Diagram, Entity Definitions, Attribute Definitions, and Entity Life Cycles (see sections 7.1.2.1, 7.1.2.2, 7.1.2.3 and 7.1.2.4).

7.1.1.4 Processing Requirements

This section contains a summary of the main business processing requirements that the project has identified. These are presented in the form of a *Process Hierarchy Diagram* (PHD)[1] which is supplemented by the short Function and Process Definitions that are held for each PHD entry in the encyclopedia.

The information contained in this section is backed up by the following extracts from the project encyclopedia that are presented in the BAA Report Appendices: Process Dependency Diagrams and/or Data Flow Diagrams, Detailed Definitions for all Functions and Processes identified, and Process Action Diagrams for all Elementary Processes (see sections 7.1.2.5, 7.1.2.6, 7.1.2.7, and 7.1.2.8).

Where issues of security and/or auditability are critical to the business, the ways in which the Business Model has been constructed to reflect these business needs are highlighted here. Full details of the incorporation of security and audit requirements into the Business Model are the subject of a separate appendix (see section 7.1.2.14).

7.1.1.5 Analysis of Current Systems

This section is only present where the analysis of existing computerised systems has been undertaken, or where a conscious decision has been made **not** to undertake this

---

[1] The PHD can also be formatted as an indented list. For example:
```
Top_Level_Function
       Sub_Function_1
              Process_1_1
                     Sub_Process_1_1_1
                     Sub_Process_1_1_2
       Sub_Function_2
              Process_2_1...
```

activity, even though there are a number of extant systems that could have been subjected to detailed analysis. In the latter case, the reasons for not undertaking Current Systems Analysis (CSA) should be explained.

The section briefly explains the scope of the CSA exercise, its purpose, and what the exercise achieved. The details to support the conclusions reached are found in the BAA Report Appendices in the format of a detailed Canonical Data Model for each system analyzed, and a series of matrices used to examine the areas of shared functional and data coverage between the Business Area Model and the Current Systems examined (see sections 7.1.2.9, 7.1.2.10, and 7.1.2.11). Any major discrepancies discovered as a result of the CSA exercise should be highlighted and explained in this section.

7.1.1.6 Package Selection

This section is only present if the possibilities of using an application package to meet all or some of the computerised business needs within the Business Area are desirable and/or considered to be feasible. The section should briefly cover the main packages considered, and the business reasons for accepting or rejecting them.

The documentation produced in examining the various packages should be included in the Appendices (see section 7.1.2.12) and is likely to include the package selection matrices, and, where appropriate, Canonical Data Models for the packages examined.

7.1.1.7 Distribution of Processes

This section is only present where different groupings of Elementary Processes that have been identified are likely to be computerised in different ways or groupings at various locations. For example, local offices may have a need for certain functions to be available on local machines, and others that are performed less frequently, to be available via remote access on regional computers. The configuration of processes at the regional and head office level may also differ, perhaps on a region by region basis. In such cases, the main business reasons for the determination of these groupings are given, and the details of the supporting analysis are contained in an appendix (see section 7.1.2.13).

7.1.1.8 Stability Analysis

The Business Model that has been produced should have taken into consideration possible changes to the business - both known and probable - that may affect it in the future. This section should outline the changes that have been considered, and explain whether and how the Business Model has been adapted to cater for them. Full details of the ways in which the model has been changed, or could be changed to cope with a possible change to the business area are documented in a separate appendix (see section 7.1.2.15).

7.1.1.9 Quality Control

Quality should be an intrinsic part of any BAA project, and this section should detail how the project's quality plan was implemented. Included should be a description of how business users were involved in the production and review of deliverables, and the types of quality audits and inspections that were part of the project process. The detailed results of any quality audits, and the project quality control sheets are documented in a separate appendix (see section 7.1.2.16).

7.1.1.10 Business System Design Plan

This section contains the detailed recommendations of the BAA project as to how to proceed with the design, construction, and implementation of one or more Business Systems to support the business in its operation. A chosen approach could include the use of application packages to meet business needs. Where more that one possible approach is being presented to the steering committee for its decision, the strengths and weaknesses of each approach should be concisely given together with a summary cost/benefit analysis of each alternative. The discussion in this section should be fully supported by the documents and matrices that were used in reaching the conclusions presented, and readers should be referred to the separate appendix in which they are contained (see section 7.1.2.17).

7.1.2   The Business Area Analysis Report - Appendices

The various appendices of the BAA Report contain full documentation of the Business Model. This is usually in the form of a comprehensive printout of the Model, which is supplemented by the BAA encyclopedia in machine readable format. Generally, the I-CASE tool used for the analysis will allow the relevant information to be extracted easily from the encyclopedia in a format that is suitable for inclusion in a document. Where this is not possible, some diagrams may have to be specially constructed for the sake of presenting a complete picture of the project model.

The appendices also contain all supplementary documentation used for the analysis project. This may include matrices that are external to the I-CASE tool used, and company-specific documentation of relevance to the project (eg. Quality Control Sheets).

7.1.2.1 Entity Relationship Model

A full graphical representation of the project ERM such as is illustrated in Figure 7.1 is contained in this appendix.

The ERM may be supplemented by Entity Horizon Diagrams (EHD) for entities that are supertypes. The EHD shows the entity subtypes and relationships for the entity supertype concerned. An example of this is illustrated in Figure 7.2.

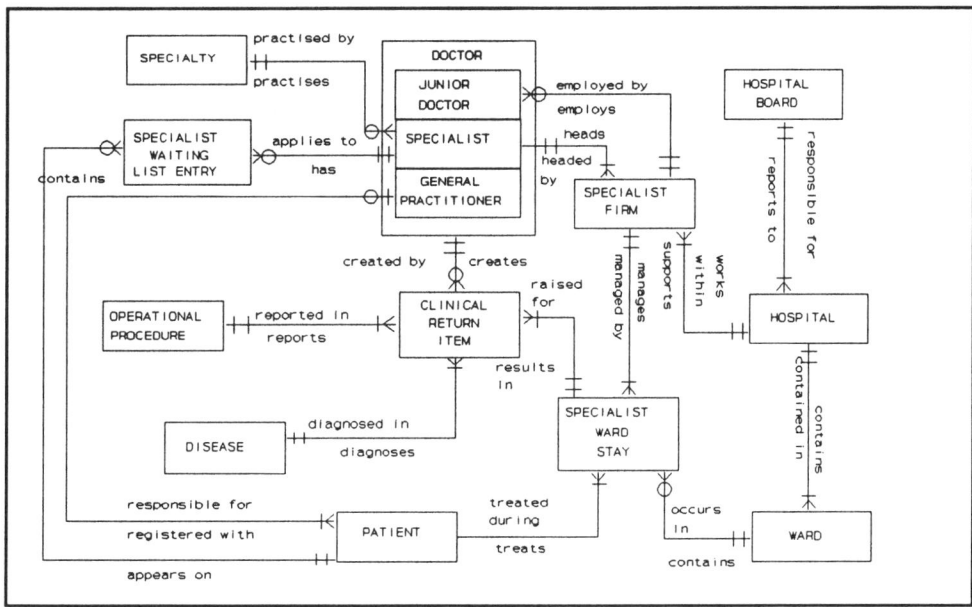

Figure 7.1 Entity Relationship Diagram

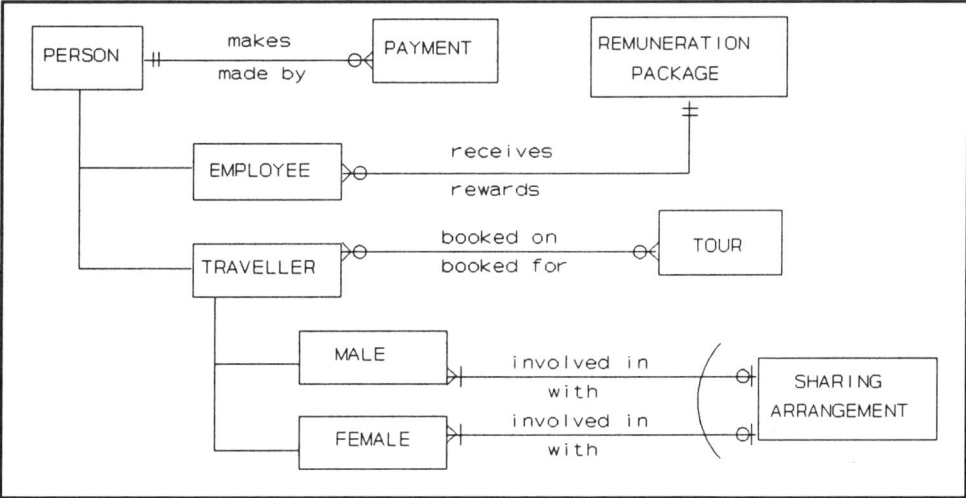

Figure 7.2 Entity Horizon Diagram

7.1.2.2 Entities and Subtypes

This section contains a complete listing of the Entity Types and their associated Subtypes, and contains the full encyclopedia definition for them. An example of such a printout from Texas Instrument's Information Engineering Facility (IEF™) is illustrated in Example 7.1 (1) - (3).

Model : PAYMENTS RECEIVED   19 Nov. 1991 08:28
Subset: (complete model)   page 7

                            Entity Definition

Entity: COMMUNICATION

Description: A record of a communication between the Owning
                     Company and an external Person or Organisation. This
                     can be incoming and outgoing, and includes any
                     medium eg. telephone, letter, fax etc.

Subject area: PAYMENTS_RECEIVED

Properties: Min Occ: 300000   Avg Occ: 10000000
            Max Occ: 15000000   Growth Rate: 3% per year

Attributes: MEDIUM
                     SYSTEM_REFERENCE
                     DIRECTION
Relationships:
Sometimes (0%) CONSISTS_OF many COMMUNICATION_DETAIL
     Cardinality Min: 1 (est) Max: 1 (est) Avg: 1
     cannot transfer.
Sometimes (0%) RESULTS many PAYMENT_FILE
     Cardinality Min: 1 (est) Max: 1 (est) Avg: 1
     cannot transfer.

Identifiers:
     1 SYSTEM_REFERENCE

Partitioned by: DIRECTION

Classifying Value	Subtype
O	LOGGED_OUTGOING_COMMUNICATION
I	INCOMING_COMMUNICATION

Example 7.1 (1) Entity Definitions

Model : PAYMENTS RECEIVED   19 Nov. 1991 08:28
Subset: (complete model)   page 7

Entity Definition

Entity: LOGGED_OUTGOING_COMMUNICATION

Description: A record of a COMMUNICATION from the Owning
                           Company directed to an external agency/organisation.
                           Actual content of a COMMUNICATION is referenced
                           within INFORMATION SERVICES. eg: Bill

Properties: Min Occ: 150000   Avg Occ: 6500000
                   Max Occ: 10000000   Growth Rate: 3% per year

Attributes: SENT_DATE
                          SENT_TIME
                          OUTGOING_REFERENCE
Subtype of: COMMUNICATION

Inherited Attributes:
       COMMUNICATION: MEDIUM
                                  SYSTEM_REFERENCE
                                  DIRECTION

Example 7.1 (2) Entity Definitions

```
┌─────────────────────────────────────────────────────────────────────┐
│                                                                       │
│  Model : PAYMENTS RECEIVED              19 Nov. 1991  08:28           │
│  Subset: (complete model)                  page 8                     │
│                                                                       │
│                      Entity Definition                                │
│  ───────────────────────────────────────────────────────────────     │
│                                                                       │
│     Entity:          INCOMING_COMMUNICATION                           │
│                                                                       │
│     Description:     A record of any incoming COMMUNICATION from an   │
│                      external contact/agency/Organisation of interest │
│                      to the Owning Company. eg. Request for work,     │
│                      customer enquiry.                                │
│                                                                       │
│     Properties: Min Occ:    150000      Avg Occ:      3500000         │
│                 Max Occ:    5000000     Growth Rate:  3% per year     │
│                                                                       │
│     Attributes:      RECEIVED_DATE                                    │
│                      LETTER_REFERENCE                                 │
│                      RECEIVED_TIME                                    │
│                      RESPONSE_REQUIRED_DATE                           │
│                      RESPONSE_REQUIRED_INDICATOR                      │
│     Subtype of:      COMMUNICATION                                    │
│                                                                       │
│     Inherited Attributes:                                            │
│     COMMUNICATION:   MEDIUM                                           │
│                      SYSTEM_REFERENCE                                 │
│                      DIRECTION                                        │
│                                                                       │
└─────────────────────────────────────────────────────────────────────┘
```

Example 7.1 (3) Entity Definitions

A similar printout from Knowledgeware Inc's IEW™/ADW™ is illustrated in Example 7.2.

Object Summary Report

Entity Type: Patient

Definition
A Person who is admitted to a HOSPITAL for treatment.

PROPERTY   VALUE

Purpose   FUNDAMENTAL
Last Update   1991/11/19 15:49 NEWUSER
Created   1991/05/10 09:55:32 NEWUSER

ASSOCIATION	TYPE	NAME
treated during	Entity Type	Specialist Ward Stay
appears on	Entity Type	Specialist Waiting List Entry
registered with	Entity Type	General Practitioner
Is Described by	Attribute Type	Patient Name
		Patient Number
		Date of Birth
Is Implemented by	Local Data Structure	Patient
		is for.Patient
		is made by.Patient
		is for.Patient

Object Summary Report

Relationship Type: Patient.appears on.Specialist Waiting List Entry

PROPERTY   VALUE

To From Name   contains
From To Minimum   0
From To Maximum   M
To From Minimum   1
To From Maximum   1
Last Update   1991/11/19 15:46 NEWUSER
Created   1991/05/10 09:59:34 NEWUSER

ASSOCIATION	TYPE	NAME

Example 7.2 Entity Definition

7.1.2.3 Attributes

This section contains a complete listing of the Attributes and their detailed definitions as contained in the project encyclopedia. An example of such a printout from the IEF™ is illustrated in Example 7.3.

Model : PAYMENTS RECEIVED   19 Nov. 1991 08:31
Subset: (complete model)   page 28

Attribute Definition

    Attribute: MEDIUM

    Subject Area: PAYMENTS_RECEIVED
    Entity Type: COMMUNICATION

    Description: This is the way in which a communication is transmitted. EG: Letter, phone call etc.

    Properties: Mandatory Basic Text
    Length: 10

    Default: none

       Permitted Values

          E MAIL

          TAPE

          FAX

          LETTER

          TELEPHONE

Example 7.3 Attribute Definition

A similar printout from Knowledgeware Inc's IEW™/ADW™ is illustrated in Example 7.4.

Object Summary Report

Attribute Type: Patient.Date of Birth

Definition
The Date of Birth of a PATIENT

     PROPERTY   VALUE

     Minimum per Subject 1
     Maximum per Subject 1
     Maximum per Value   M

     Last Update   1991/11/19 15:54 NEWUSER
     Created   1991/11/19 15:51:08 NEWUSER

     Type   ELEMENTARY
     Item Type   DATE
     Format   X(10)

     ASSOCIATION   TYPE   NAME

     Has   Data Type   date

Example 7.4 Attribute Definitions

7.1.2.4 Entity Life Cycles

Where Entity Life Cycle Diagrams have been constructed for the main entities in the Business Area, they are included in this section. An example of such a diagram is shown in Figure 7.3.

7.1.2.5 Process Dependency Diagrams

Where Process Dependency Diagrams have been constructed for the functions and processes in the Business Area, they are included in this section. An example of a PDD is shown in Figure 7.4.

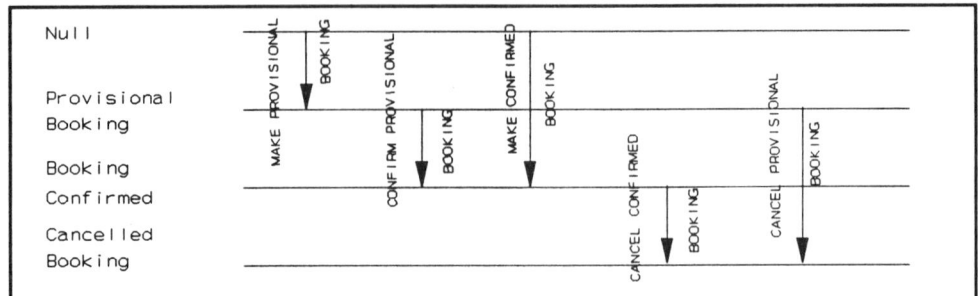

Figure 7.3 Entity Life Cycle Diagram

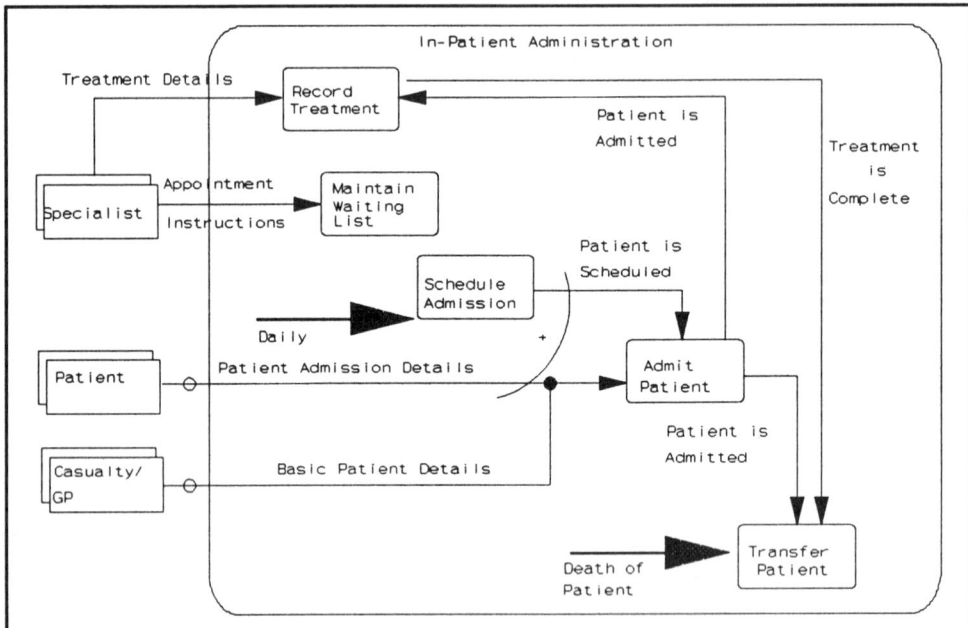

Figure 7.4 Process Dependency Diagram.

7.1.2.6 Data Flow Diagrams

Where Data Flow Diagrams have been constructed for the functions and processes in the Business Area, they are included in this section. An example of a DFD is shown in Figure 7.5.

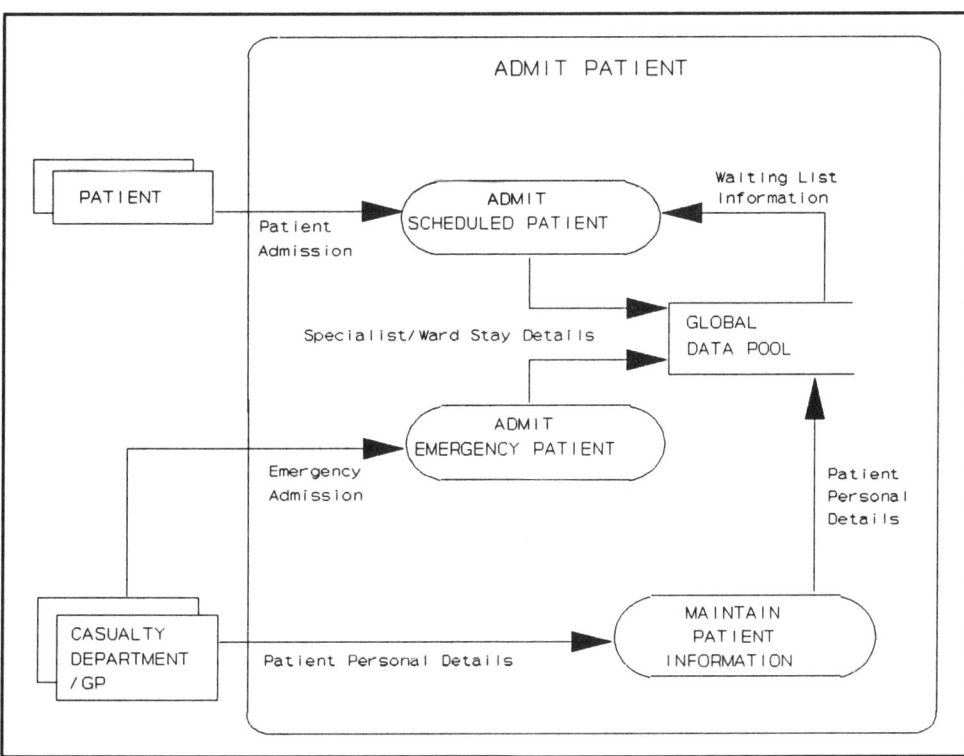

Figure 7.5 Data Flow Diagram

7.1.2.7 Detailed Process Definitions

For each Function and Process in the PHD, a full definition should exist which unambiguously defines the Activity and gives information about its business purpose. This appendix contains all such definitions, an example of which is shown in Example 7.5.

7.1.2.8 Process Action Diagrams

The detailed business logic for each elementary process that has been defined is contained in a PAD such as the one illustrated in Figure 7.6.

Model : PAYMENTS RECEIVED   23 Nov. 1991 08:35
Subset: (complete model)   page 33
                    Activity Definition

Name: MAINTAIN_CHEQUE_RETURN_REASON

Description: This process allows for the creation, amendment or deletion
                of the Reason for the Return of a Cheque.

                The screens for this process will not be generally available.

                All transactions will require authority and approval in
                accordance with company procedures.

                Amendments to the DESCRIPTION will only be allowed if
                they do not change the overall meaning of the description.
                Values of CODE will never be used twice. Deletions will
                only be allowed if there are no relationships to the DIRECT
                DEBIT RETURN REASON.

PRECONDITIONS: Details of Cheque Return Reason and requirements

POSTCONDITIONS: New, amended or deleted Cheque Return Reason

Type: Elementary process
                Not Repetitive
                Online implementation suggested

Subordinate of: REFERENCE_DATA_MAINTENANCE

Expected Effects:
        Entity Type   Expected Actions
        ----------   ----------------
        CHEQUE_RETURN_REASON   create
                                            update
                                            read
                                            delete
        PAYMENT_IN   read

Example 7.5 Process Definition

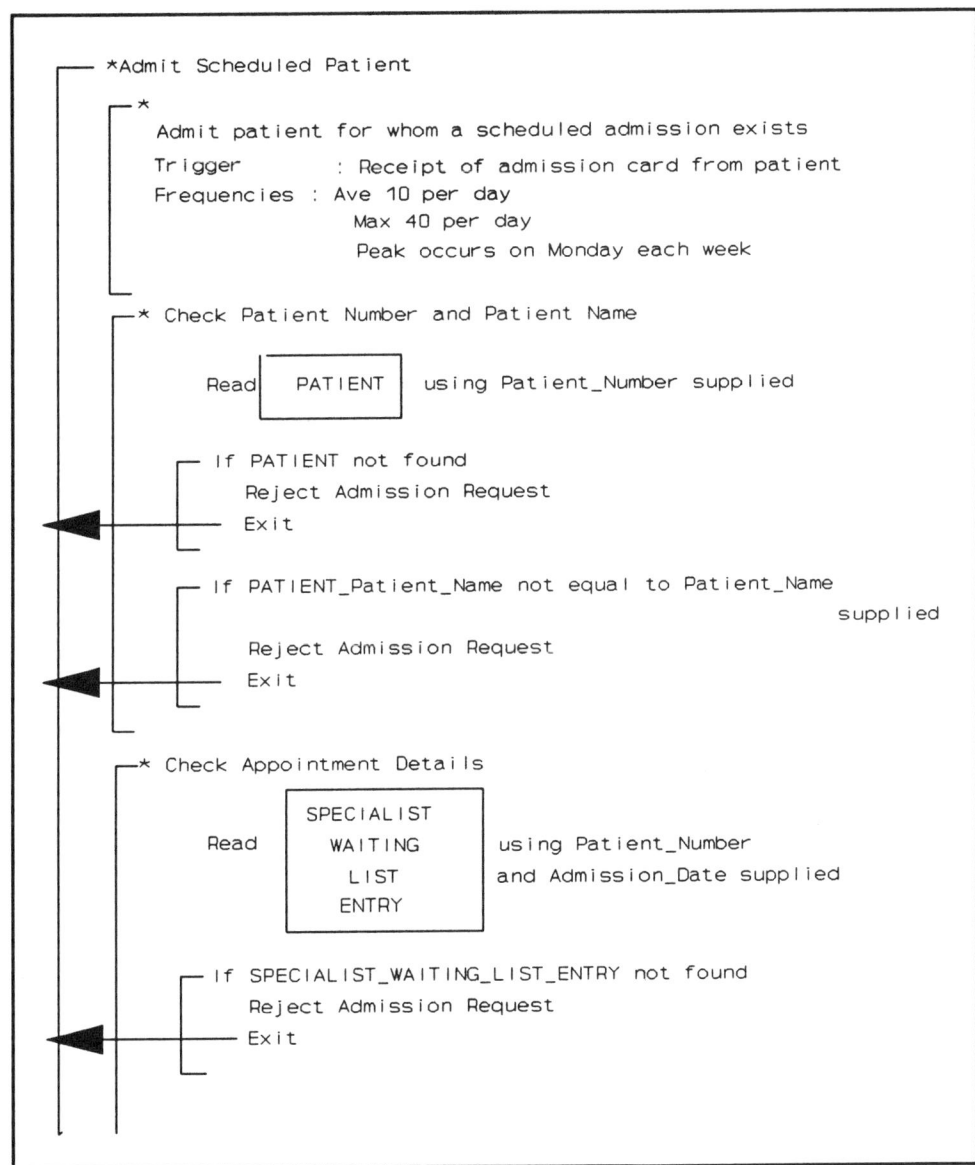

Figure 7.6 (1) Process Action Diagram

7.1.2.9 Current Systems: Canonical Model

This section will contain a derived logical data model for each of the current systems examined. Its format will be similar to the model illustrated in 7.1.2.1.

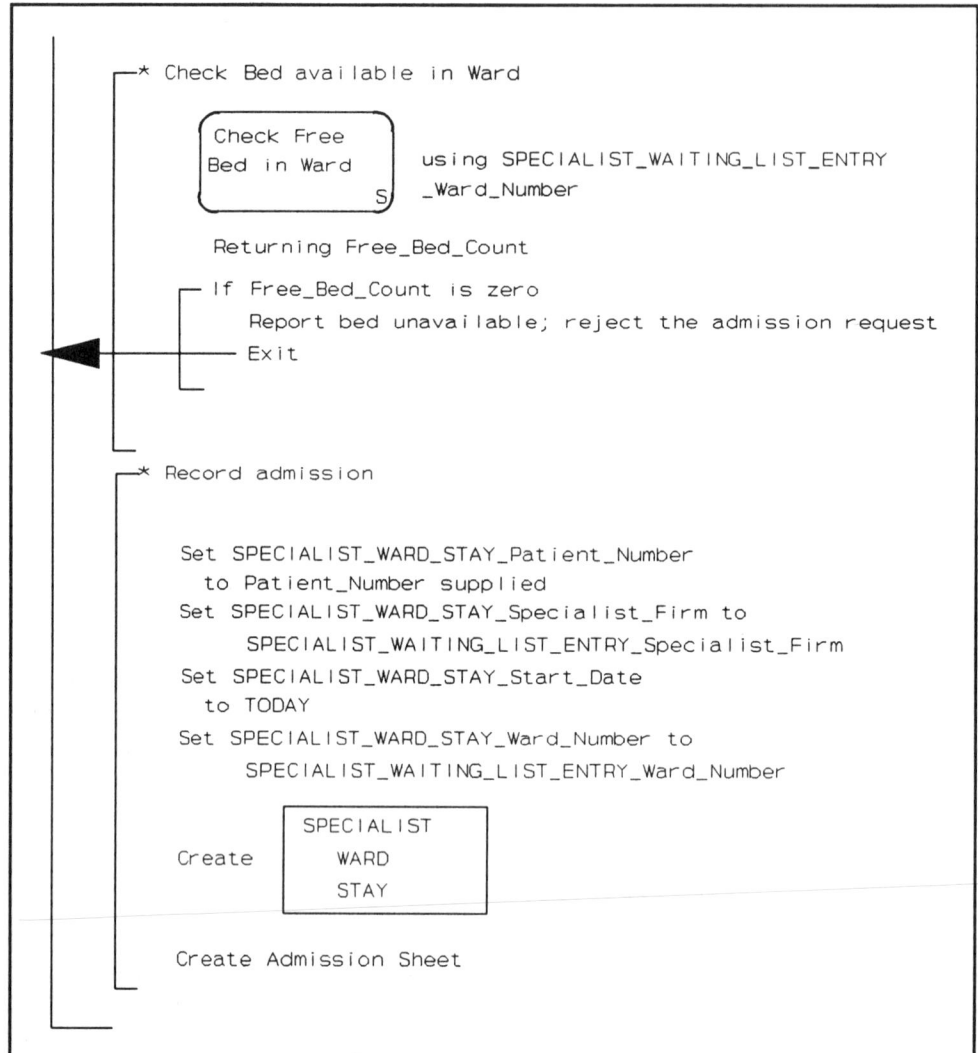

Figure 7.6 (2) Process Action Diagram

7.1.2.10 Current Systems: Comparison of Data Models

For each current system analyzed, this section will contain a matrix that compares the Business Area Entity/Attribute with the Current System's File/Field.

7.1.2.11 Current Systems: Comparison of Functional Coverage

For each current system analyzed, this section will contain a matrix that compares the Business Area Elementary Processes with the Current System's implemented

Procedures.

7.1.2.12 Package Selection Matrices and Models

For each package that has been analyzed, some or all of the following may be contained in this section: a derived logical data model for the system, a matrix that relates the Business Area Entity/Attributes to the Package File/Fields, and a matrix that shows the package coverage by comparing the Business Area Elementary Processes with the Procedures that are implemented in the package.

7.1.2.13 Distribution Matrices

Where Elementary Processes are to be implemented in more that one business location, this section will contain two matrices: one that maps each Elementary Process against Location, and a second that maps each Entity Type against Location. If required, the Entity Type/Location matrix can be constructed at an Entity Type/Attribute level which would then unambiguously illustrate where each Attribute is required to be present. These matrices will assist in the later design of distributed databases.

7.1.2.14 Security and Audit Considerations

This section documents the ways in which the Business Model incorporates the security and audit requirements of the business. It may contain narrative explaining how areas of the model work in the context of these requirements, and/or it might highlight aspects of the model (Attributes, Process Action Blocks) that have been expressly introduced to deal with these considerations.

7.1.2.15 Stability Considerations

This section documents the ways in which the Business Model incorporates issues that have been considered in the analysis of the model's stability and its ability to meet with known and foreseen changes to the business. It may contain narrative explaining how areas of the model work in the context of these changes, and/or it might highlight aspects of the model that have been expressly introduced to deal with its stability in the face of such changes.

7.1.2.16 Quality Control Sheets

This section contains any formal quality audit reports on the project, as well as the internal project Quality Control Sheets that have been used throughout the project to ensure completeness and consistency of the deliverables produced. An example of such a control sheet is shown in Example 7.6.

PROJECT XYZ BAA DELIVERABLES
ASSESSMENT OF COMPLETENESS AND CORRECTNESS

BAA:	Name of BAA Project
Functional Grouping:	Name of Functional Grouping **Page:** 1 of 1

Function Status: _____
(Actual Level of Completion in accordance with Standards)

Completeness and Correctness:

Correctness of Functional Grouping Deliverables (0_5) ____
Completeness of Functional Grouping Deliverables (0_5) ____
Completeness of Functional Grouping Underlying Data Model (0_5) ____

Review Status:

Reviewed by Project Manager (Y/N) ___
Reviewed with User Liaison Group (Y/N) ___
Reviewed with Process/Data Co_ordination (Y/N) ___
Reviewed with QA Group (Y/N) ___
Reviewed with Project Steering Group (Y/N) ___

Changes Incorporated (Y/N) ___

Signed off by User Liaison Group (Y/N) ___
Signed off by Process/Data Co_ordination (Y/N) ___
Signed off by QA Group (Y/N) ___
Signed off by Project Steering Group (Y/N) ___

Consistency:

PADs checked against Data Model (Y/N) ___
Inconsistencies Corrected (Y/N) ___

Comments:

Signed off by Project Manager: _____   Date: _____

Example 7.6 Quality Control Sheet

7.1.2.17 BSD Planning Matrices

As is discussed in Chapter 11, a series of matrices can be constructed at the end of a BAA project to assist in the planning of which way to go next. These BSD planning matrices should be included in this appendix.

7.2   Scoping the BAA Project

Where a BAA project is the result of an ISP exercise, its scope and the reasons for undertaking it will have been included in the Information Strategy Plan itself. This implies that a series of basic deliverables have already been produced that determine the project's scope. Those deliverables, which constitute the starting point for a BAA project, are discussed in section 7.2.1.

It is also realistic to assume that BAA projects are begun in a less structured and formalised fashion. In such a case, the scope of the project might be vague - no more than a statement or a wish list. Is it possible to perform Business Area Analysis in such a case, and what are the problems with doing so? How can one scope such a project in terms of recognisable IE deliverables? These issues are addressed in section 7.2.2.

7.2.1   Confirming the Scope of a BAA Project that is the Result of an ISP

As discussed in chapter 4, the ISP project should have identified a number of Business Areas for further analysis, and prioritised them based on the potential systems they encompass. In order to do this, a high level Business Information Architecture was constructed, and a portion of this provides the basis for scoping the BAA project.

It is important that the BAA project scope as defined in the ISP is confirmed in all cases. Clearly where an ISP was performed some time ago, its conclusions may no longer be valid. But, even with a more recent ISP, underlying business issues and priorities may have changed in the intervening period, and it is important that issues of scope and focus are sorted out in advance so as to maximise the control a project manager can assert over the project in ensuring that it meets its goals.

The high-level BAA model which is a subset of the ISP Business Information Architecture should contain three elements: a high-level entity relationship model, a functional hierarchy, and a data usage (CRUD) matrix that analyses the interactions between the functions/processes identified and the data model.

The high-level entity relationship model will function primarily at a Data Subject Area level. It is likely that the main subject areas have been expanded to include the important data entity types and relationships that they contain. For the BAA project, it is important that the main data entities and relationships relevant to the BAA project have been isolated, and that basic definitions for them are in place.

In parallel, a high-level activity hierarchy diagram depicts the functional scope of the Business Area. At its first level it consists of the Business Area itself fully defined. This is expanded into the main functions it contains, which are in turn further expanded until the first level of actual processes is identified. Each function and process is supported by a clear definition.

Lastly, the subset of the ISP data usage matrix that was clustered to define the Business Area is given. This is important as it shows the expected data interactions for each data entity and for each activity that has been defined.

While the deliverables described above are the **minimum** requisites for starting a BAA, they may be supported by the matrices that were used to determine the underlying business need for the particular BAA project being undertaken. These could include the following matrices (or at least some textual information from which they could be constructed): matrices that relate business objectives and critical success factors to the activities required to achieve them, and the data entities required to do so; matrices that relate business requirements and/or problems being experienced to activities and/or data entities. If these basic matrices are missing, it is recommended that they be constructed at this stage as an aid to confirming the scope of the BAA project. Their construction serves a number of purposes: it helps the project manager to understand the business reasons underlying the project and to confirm that understanding with the project steering group; the matrices serve as a basis, throughout the BAA, for steering the project efforts in the direction of the biggest business payoffs; and the matrices are used again at the end of the BAA stage as input to the planning of the BSD and in determining optimal system solutions to the business problems as they are better understood.

At this early stage of the BAA, it is necessary to ensure that the basic deliverables exist, that the assumptions underlying them have not changed (hence the need for the material mentioned in the previous paragraph), and that they contain no glaring errors or omissions.

These deliverables, which constitute a subset of the Business Information Architecture, need also to be viewed within the context of both the Business Systems Architecture, and the Technical Architecture that were also deliverables of the ISP study.

The relevant part of the Business Systems Architecture effectively shows the Business Area in question in terms of the conceptual systems that have been identified within it. It places these systems both into the context of existing actual computerised systems (and assesses whether they are effective or not in terms of supporting the business), thereby allowing the project manager to view the Business Area in terms of the **systems** that senior business managers envisage should be supporting their business.

Lastly, the BAA should be seen in the context of the Technical Architecture that forms part of the Information Strategy Plan. This architecture in effect places the potential systems within the Business Area in the context of an envisaged corporate technical environment. It allows the project manager to determine whether there are any pre-existing constraints on the types of systems the team might ultimately propose, and what future technical directions are planned for the organisation.

7.2.2 Scoping a BAA Project where No ISP has Taken Place

Where a BAA project has begun outside the context of an ISP exercise, there is a danger both that it will lack any firm context within the overall corporate IT strategy, and that its scope will be unclear. Even where there appears to be an unambiguous statement of scope, there still remains the danger that this scope has been based not on the underlying business information structures of a Business Area (or a cohesive part of one), but upon **a current view of the business**. It is necessary in such a case to use any scope statement as the basis for the construction of a preliminary Business Model that consists of a high-level ERM, high-level Activity Hierarchy Diagram (AHD), and a CRUD matrix that represents the interaction between them. In this way, a close approximation of the main scoping deliverables from an ISP as described in section 7.2.1 is achieved, but without the benefit of overall IT strategic architectures as an overall framework.

It is important that the three basic deliverables are carefully analyzed in their own right so as to determine how viable the project is as a cohesive unit. The main source of this information is the CRUD matrix. In its raw form, it will give a clear indication of whether there are entities and/or activities that are clearly absent from or extraneous to the project scope. Once it has been clustered, it is likely to indicate whether the chosen scope does in fact represent more than one cohesive project area, based on data usage. If this seems to be the case, then the project manager has two options: the steering committee can be alerted to the fact that the scope appears to cover more than one project, and a recommendation may be made to float two (or more) projects rather than just the one. Alternatively (and dependent on the political pressures surrounding the project) the project manager may chose to run the project as two discrete units, and in this way to control the inevitable ongoing expansion and contraction of scope that usually occurs as a symptom that more than one Business Area (or pieces of Business Areas) have been haphazardly included in a project scope.

In either of the cases where the scope encompasses more than one Business Area, it is important to have clearly designated each area's scope on the high-level ERM and AHD.

In all cases, it is also necessary to attempt to place the project(s) within an implicit IT strategy, and to confirm (or in effect, undertake) the initial cost/benefit analysis. The effect of this in reality will be an attempt to understand formally whether there are any real or implicit technical issues that constrain the project (in effect a *de facto* Technical Architecture). This will be supplemented by an initial formal linking of the project justification to corporate objectives, critical success factors, and problem areas in order to steer the project more visibly towards recognisable areas of business payback.

7.3   Milestones and Deliverables

The BAA process falls into a number of distinct stages, the major ones of which can be seen as milestones. Against each milestone, there should be a clear set of deliverables so that the progress of the project can be adequately measured.

7.3.1   BAA Milestones

The three main BAA milestones are illustrated in Figure 7.7. Each project milestone

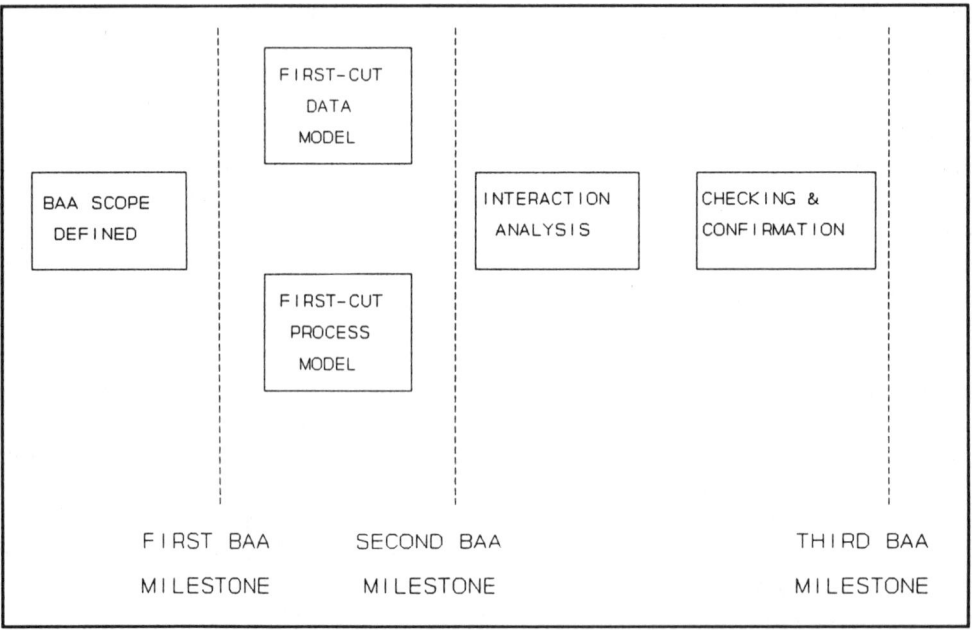

Figure 7.7 BAA Milestones

provides the Project Steering Group with an opportunity to review the team's progress so far against the project plan, and, where necessary, to take action to narrow or extend the project scope, to provide additional funding, or even to cancel the project in order to minimise the risks and costs that are associated with it. Each BAA milestone is briefly discussed below.

7.3.1.1 Milestone 1: Confirmation of Project Scope

Before a team launches out on a project that is likely to take them across unchartered and even perilous waters, it is absolutely necessary to have a clear view of where they are heading, and within what confines they are operating. These framing parameters are the Project Scope, and they need to be clearly stated and understood by all participants in the project, but especially by the Project Steering Group, and by the Team Leader/Manager. This point cannot be understated, because, while it is recognised that the **actual** scope of the project may well change over time, an unambiguous starting point will help to serve as a focal point of reference throughout the project duration. This will be especially the case when arguments occur about either extending or narrowing the scope of the project.

From a purely technical perspective, the basic deliverables required for this milestone are well described in section 7.2 above, and further emphasised in section 7.2.2. However, this milestone of the project has two additional major objectives: not only does it need to **establish and confirm the project scope**, it needs to ensure that the **project's objectives are clearly stated**. Where an ISP project has preceded the BAA, the justification for the BAA project should be clear through a number of base deliverables: the cost/benefit analysis should provide the key business justifications for the project. Underpinning it should be a series of matrices that link the project (either directly, or via its major Activities and Data Types) to Business Objectives, Critical Success Factors, and Business Problems. **It is essential that this first project milestone reconfirms the Business Reasons for undertaking the project.** If the ISP had been undertaken some time back, the business justifications for the project might have changed with a changing set of business priorities. There needs to be a clear, swift reappraisal of these by the Project Steering Group.

Even where no ISP has set the project scope, by the end of Milestone 1, the business case for the project, and hence the project's key objectives, must be formally acknowledged. Often an analysis project is the result of some preliminary Feasibility Study, and this should provide the basis for a business justification. In the absence of such a study, the team must pin down the project's business objectives. Here organisational internal politics may come into play and prevent a full cost/benefit analysis from being undertaken. The very least that is required is some linking (probably using matrices) of the project's scope (Activities and Entity Types) to Business Objectives and Critical Success Factors. These matrices provide both a point of reference should the sea become stormy with arguments about increasing or narrowing scope - they provide an unambiguous mapping of **business** goals and objectives to **project** scope - and a means for the project manager to steer the project team towards those parts of the Business Area that are most likely to provide a real payback to the business.

The activities required to complete this milestone are unlikely to take longer than two elapsed weeks (and one person-month) to complete. The main dependency will be on whether there is a clear project scope, and where the bases for a business case exist.

7.3.1.2 Milestone 2: Completion of First-Cut Data Model and First-Cut Process Model
(BAA Part 1)

Two activities now occur in parallel: the preliminary project Data Models and Activity
Hierarchy are developed more fully. These activities are dependent on the formal
gathering and documentation of information about the Business Area from key
business users. In the case of a BAA project, they are likely to be senior and middle
managers who have an overview either of the Business Area, or of one or more of the
key Functional areas contained within it. The project activity of gathering and
analyzing such information is described in section 8.1.

The objective of this milestone is to produce detailed models of the project's **Data and
Activities without** being confused by their interaction with one another. The main
reason for doing this is so as to gain a clear picture of **what it is that the Business
Area does, and of the information it requires to operate** without being drawn into
issues of **how it currently operates**. The two models developed more or less
independently of one another provide the best picture of the **informational structure**
that underpins the Business Area.

Wherever possible, the Guardian of the Data Model and the Process Coordinator are
the driving roles behind the development of these models. The techniques they will use
are: for developing a data model - Normalisation and Entity Relationship Modelling;
for process modelling - Process Decomposition and Process Dependency analysis (Data
Flow Analysis can also be used at this stage - some CASE tools permit its use only -
but it poses its own set of problems which are discussed in section 10.1.1.1).

The objective of this milestone is to achieve a thorough understanding of what the
Business Area does in information terms, **and to demonstrate that understanding
to users**. Their active participation in the activities that constitute this milestone is
essential.

7.3.1.3 Milestone 3: Completion of Interaction Analysis (BAA Part 2)

The primary purpose of interaction analysis is to ensure that the two aspects of the
Business Model that have been developed so far support one another. From a Data
perspective, this implies testing the data model to ensure that it can support what the
business does: are all the required Data Entities there, do they contain all the
Attributes that the business requires, and are the Relationships between them
sufficient to support the information requirements of the business? From the
perspective of the Business Activities, the questions to be answered are: do we
understand what it is that each Activity - especially each Elementary Process - is doing
in full detail, and particularly in relation to the data model, and have we identified all
the Business Activities that are undertaken within the Business Area?

Most of the team activity at this stage is likely to focus initially on the effects of their analysis on the data model. In every BAA project the author has been involved in, as Interaction Analysis begins, a wave of frustration hits the team as it watches its carefully constructed models becoming - in their eyes - destabilised. That the models change a lot initially is quite understandable: analyzing their interaction mercilessly exposes holes in the team's understanding of the business and of its information structures. You may well ask, if this is the case, why not do it all at once? Why the artificial separation of process and data in the first place? The question cannot easily be brushed off. Quite clearly this artificial separation between the data and what is done to it is becoming bridged by the theory and practices that are currently being developed and consolidated as "Object-Oriented Analysis." Over time, these techniques, and their accompanying tool sets will allow data details and business rules to be captured in the same way for such "Objects." Given that the distinction between data and process remains necessary for the moment, keeping them separate initially allows us to highlight clearly **the structural basis** of the Business Area as a "system" that processes information. Adding the issue of interaction too early in the process confuses the picture, and can bring the analysis dangerously close to **how** things are presently being done, thereby losing the Information Architecture component of the model.

Interaction analysis is a process of connection, amplification, and of checking. In more fully understanding what an Elementary Process does, the Data Structures supporting that process are also more fully and correctly understood. The issue that will always arise at this stage of the project is to what amount of detail does the team have to analyze things in order to complete its task? This, and other related pitfalls, are fully addressed in section 7.4. Depending on the answer to this question, rests the question, how long will the BAA take? If a full interaction analysis is completed with fully detailed Process Action Diagrams being drawn up for each Elementary Process, then the duration of the third milestone is likely to be as long as the project has taken to this point (around 2 months). There is clearly scope for some compromise here, but the full implications of any shortcuts need to be fully understood: sometimes they amount to no more than passing the problems on to the next BAA phase. These issues will also be discussed in section 7.4.

7.3.2 Deliverables at Each Milestone

Generally, project progress at a milestone will be judged by the deliverables that have been produced, and so it is necessary that there is a clear definition of expected project deliverables against each milestone identified. Table 7.1 matches the minimum set of deliverables described in section 7.1 against the major milestones described in section 7.3.1.

Major BAA Milestone	Deliverable
Milestone 1: Confirmation of Project Scope	Statement of Scope High-Level Entity Relationship Model High-Level Activity Hierarchy Diagram Activity/Entity CRUD Matrix Requirement/Problem vs Activity Matrix Requirement/Problem vs Entity Matrix
Milestone 2: Completion of First-Cut Data Model and First-Cut Process Model	Entity Relationship Model including: - Entities, - Entity Definitions - Relationships with cardinality and optionality - Sufficient Attributes, with definitions, to identify the entity unambiguously Process Model including: - Activity Hierarchy Diagram to Elementary Process Level - Activity Definitions including Expected Effects on the ERM - Process Dependency Diagrams - (Optional) Context Data Flow Diagram

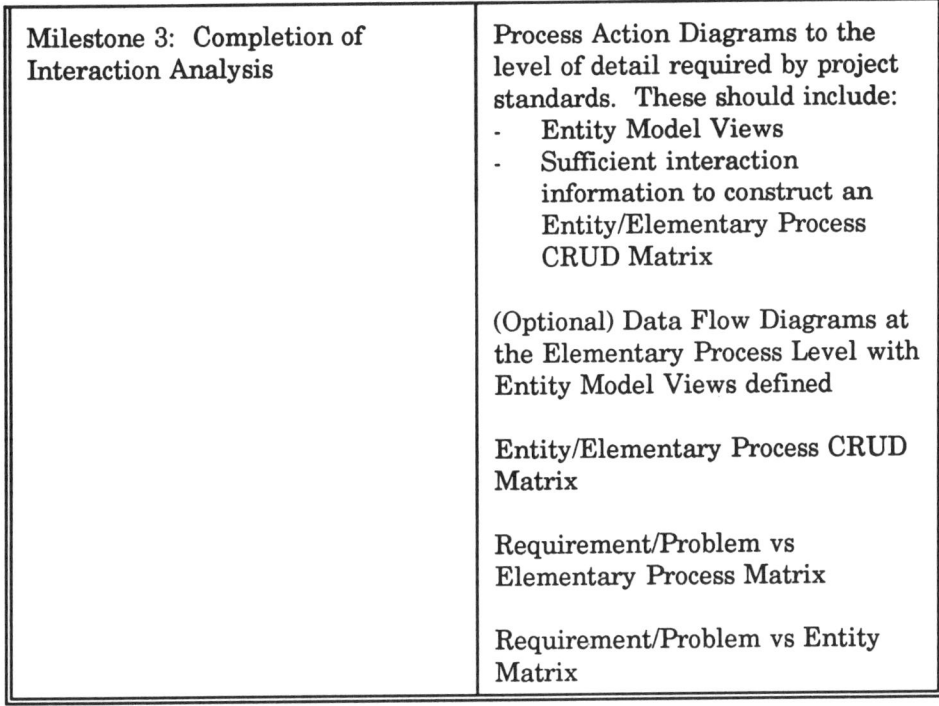

Milestone 3: Completion of Interaction Analysis	Process Action Diagrams to the level of detail required by project standards. These should include: - Entity Model Views - Sufficient interaction information to construct an Entity/Elementary Process CRUD Matrix (Optional) Data Flow Diagrams at the Elementary Process Level with Entity Model Views defined Entity/Elementary Process CRUD Matrix Requirement/Problem vs Elementary Process Matrix Requirement/Problem vs Entity Matrix

Table 7.1 Minimum Deliverables at Main Milestones

7.4   Common Pitfalls

Many BAA projects undertaken to date have experienced serious time and cost overruns. While it is possible to write some early instances of these off to a "learning curve," certain problems have recurred frequently. Detecting and recognising the symptoms of a problem early can allow a project manager to take action effectively to remedy it. The essential key to controlling an IE-based project remains sound, proven project management procedures and practices. This statement sounds so obvious that it ought not to be necessary. However, too often would-be IE practitioners have been told, "Do not worry, the CASE tool will ensure that standards are being met... the CASE tool will manage the project."

In the confusion with adopting both a new approach **and** new technology, this statement has too often become an excuse for sloppy project management. Seriously inaccurate estimates have, at worst, resulted in management by neglect, when the attitude becomes, "We cannot spend time managing the project because it was not in the original plan."

A detailed discussion of good project management practice is clearly outside of the scope of this book, but a common pitfall in overall IE projects is a lack of overall project control and steering. This has nothing to do with the nature of the project itself: using an IE approach to analyze and design a computer system. Lack of project control and steering remains an issue that has to be addressed by the senior project management with whom accountability for the project lies. It may also point to the problems that can result *if* a complex project is run by a person with sound and long-standing technical computing experience, but who does not understand the business focus underlying the IE approach, or who, as a technician, manages technology, not people.

Turning away from the "art" of project management *per se*, it is to some of the common technical pitfalls that we now direct our attention, so that non-technical project managers - often the users themselves - will not easily be baffled by jargon or the "technical mystification" of project issues by team members.

7.4.1   Drifting Project Scope

It is impossible to judge whether the scope of a project has changed, unless there is a baseline against which to measure this. In section 7.2, we have already examined the issue of setting and confirming the scope of the project **before** the project gets underway in some detail. It is essential to do so in order to avoid confusion later, and to circumvent the inevitable apportioning of blame if user expectations are not met by the project.

In order to remain in control of the project, and accountable for it, a project manager would prefer to pick up the warning signs that scope may be drifting before the event, rather than after ground has already been conceded. In order to do so, it is necessary to keep a constant watch on project scope as the early data and process models are being developed and expanded. Usually, the introduction of a number of major Entity Types previously considered outside of the project scope is an early signal. By asking what activities these are intended to support, the project manager can quickly determine whether the Entities are the product of an overzealous Data Model Guardian, the result of an analyst who, in trying to understand an unfamiliar Business Area, would rather get too much in than too little, or a genuine opening up or change in project focus. Because business users are often more activity- than data-oriented, changes of scope in the process model will be easier to spot and confirm; and so a suspected shift in scope in the data model can be quickly confirmed or denied by linking the data to business activities. Questions like, "What function does this entity serve?" and "What does this entity do in the data model?" will help to flush out scope drift.

In monitoring drift in scope, the project manager can also detect early symptoms of other potential problems with the project. A scope that appears to concertina - to expand and then contract, only to expand again - can indicate that the Business Area has been poorly defined in the first place, and that the project team may be facing more than one Business Area in the guise of a single project. This phenomenon is likely to occur where no ISP has been undertaken, and where the project scope contains, in effect, a temporal view of the business rather than a true Business Area based on the organisation's information structure. (It can also occur where a poor ISP has been done.) How the project manager chooses to deal with the situation may depend on the sensitivity of the project and/or the organisation: in some cases it may be best to raise the problem with the Project Steering Group in order to redefine the project's scope and objectives; in others, the project manager may well have to recognise the fact that the project covers say two Business Areas, and then chose to manage it as two mini-projects, invisible though to the Steering Group.

Constantly expanding project scope will inevitably lead to project overruns both in time and in cost, and the project manager needs to spell these out clearly as early as possible. In order to do so, it is necessary to have some view on the effect of adding a new Business Function, or a Data Entity. Some guidelines in this process are possible: in planning the project there must have been some assumptions made on the likely number of elementary processes the initial activity hierarchy was going to decompose into, and also on the number of data entities the final Business Model was likely to have. Cost estimates must have been made on these assumptions, and it is advisable to keep the original parameters used in estimating (usually this is most conveniently done in a spreadsheet). By applying the same parameters and adjusting the assumptions, the likely effects on cost and time can clearly be presented to the Project Steering Group, together with a request for some guidance on priorities based on what must surely be changed business objectives. Again, the Project Manager assumes control of the situation, rather than allowing the tail to wag the dog.

Drifting project scope can be detected if clear scope and objectives have been defined up front, **and** the Project Manager monitors the project through close involvement in it. Early evasive action can prevent a project from becoming a monster: often making the drift (and its likely cost effects) visible will be enough to ensure that the project does not run out of control.

7.4.2   The Never-Ending Data Model

The first major tasks of a BAA team are to come up with first-cut detailed process and data models that provide full cover for the Business Area's information processing requirements. Usually, decomposing the high level processes to elementary level and coming up with reasonable descriptions of them proves to be a finite task: users can quickly confirm that this is what they do, and that nothing of significance has been left out.

The first-cut data model has, however, proved to be more elusive. It is not constructing it that is difficult; it is knowing when to stop. This problem can be exacerbated by a number of contributing factors: the task of building a data model is often assigned to a data administrator. By nature, the person filling this role in an organisation has traditionally had to be a stickler for detail; database systems have failed or succeeded largely because a data administrator has kept a firm hand on the rein, and insisted that standards be followed to the letter. Such a person is unlikely to be content until the data model is perfect - small flaws will constantly be found, and these will be set right. (Often, too, the flaws that are being set right have to do with concern about how a database founded on this data model will perform, and so issues of physical constraint, totally inappropriate to the task at hand, are introduced when they are irrelevant.) A second contributing factor is that the very concept of data modelling may well be alien to users, and initially a little daunting to some. As a result, they are less able to relate to the process and its results than they are to process modelling. Furthermore, users are accustomed to having to get specifications **right** - any failure to do so has usually cost them dearly in the form of expensive system development overruns, and rewrites. The combination of an over-meticulous or pedantic data modeller, together with an uncertain user, can prove disastrous. They end up attempting to take an excellent first-cut data model that is perhaps 80% accurate, to a position where it is, if not perfect, pretty close to that. The problem here is that this final polishing is terribly time-intensive, and, worse, it is **totally unnecessary!** Once the first-cut data model contains all major business information requirements, and the users can give it a broad brush approval, **the process of Interaction Analysis will exercise the data model in such a way that its flaws and potential flaws will be mercilessly exposed.** In fact, the first few weeks of Interaction Analysis can be very disheartening for a BAA team: the data model becomes destabilised, and it would appear as if all their painstaking work in constructing it has been in vain.

Of course, the data model will settle down again, but this time it will have proved itself fully capable of supporting the business Elementary Processes that have been defined.

It is critical for the success of the project that the team manager prevents the data modelling team (or individual) from getting into an endless loop. It is to some extent a matter of judgement when the first-cut data model is good enough: when the users are beginning to make petty or pedantic criticisms of it the time has come to move on, and a competent project manager will recognise that, take the risk, and break the team out of its data modelling loop.

7.4.3   Reaching the Correct Level of Detail

Level of detail becomes an issue when the team is developing detailed analyses of the elementary processes that have been identified. In IE, this analysis is captured by means of a Process Action Diagram, a formal application in each of the I-CASE tools of the principles of Structured English that enforces rules of syntax and links them with the objects identified in the encyclopedia (see section 10.1.3). To many, the constructs of the PAD are reminiscent of procedural programming. While this is substantially true, PADs differ from programs in that they are not intended to support a physical implementation of the process directly; they are **formal and rigorous descriptions of Business Logic.** PADs describe unequivocally **what the business does.** They will form the basis for the construction (hopefully automatically) of program modules, but they are not the modules themselves. So, when one project manager proudly announced that his team's PAD could be converted directly into FORTRAN, this was a clear warning signal that the "wrong level of detail had been reached."[2] What the team had done in this case was not only capture business rules, they had strayed firmly into **how** those rules were to be (or, worse, currently being) implemented.

This problem does, however, raise an important question that is fully addressed in section 10.1.3.2: is it always necessary to construct PADs, and if so, are they required for all Elementary Processes? The simplified answer to both these questions is a qualified no. Certainly if the PAD (or its equivalent in a chosen I-CASE tool) is to be used as the driver for code generation **in that CASE tool**, then it is essential to do them, and to get them right. But, if not, then what is appropriate as a substitute, and to what level of detail should this "process logic specification" go?

Again, there are no glib answers. The least that is required is that the Interaction of the Elementary Process with the Data Model has been fully tested with two objectives in mind: the Data Model must be fully exercised so that all flaws in it are exposed and remedied; and the logic of the Elementary Process must be **unambiguously** understood. At that stage, sufficient detail has been reached to proceed: the formal process of confirming the model will identify any latent flaws. What is an essential element in deciding whether a sufficient level of detail has been reached for **this** project is the requirements of the CASE tool that will be used for design and construction. It is not uncommon for a team or organisation not to follow one I-CASE tool through from analysis to implementation of a system. At present this may be necessitated by the comparative immaturity of many I-CASE tools, but that situation will inevitably change over time, and the problem may diminish proportionately.

7.4.4   When is a BAA Complete?

The simplest answer to this question is that a BAA is complete when all the agreed deliverables have been produced to the standard outlined in the project Quality Plan, and the users are satisfied with them. This statement might sound like an oversimplification of the situation, but it is not. It again points towards the necessity for the project to have clear goals and objectives; and these include a clearly defined set of deliverables. Moreover, the implication is present that the users are also aware of those goals and objectives to the extent that they are able to judge the deliverables intelligently.

The Business Area Analysis project is, of necessity, **a joint venture between users**

---

[2] This is different from specifying a complex business rule or algorithm which, as a controllable Process Action Block (see section 10.1.3, page 167), might be kept as a "black box" of low-level code.

and IT professionals in the best interests of the business. For it to reach an agreed and successful conclusion, that partnership needs to function optimally; and that requires a constant openness between both parties which ensures that the joint goals are recognised from the beginning so that they can be defined when they are reached. It is those goals that should ultimately steer every technical decision faced by the project team, including those outlined in this section, that often lead projects into a mire. The needs of the business should drive the BAA process.

Technical issues will affect how goals are achieved, and it is essential that the Project Manager understands these too. What the key analytic techniques are, and how they fit together throughout the BAA process, is the focus of the next three chapters.

Chapter 8   The Main Techniques and How They Fit Together (1)

In chapters 8 to 10 the main techniques that can be used in a BAA project are discussed so that the reader can understand what the purpose of each is, when it can be most effectively used, its strengths and weaknesses, and the risks involved both with applying it, and, just as significant, with leaving it out or taking a short-cut through or around it.

Where applicable, the deliverables resulting from each of the following techniques are also illustrated, and their meaning and conventions are briefly discussed. For convenience, this chapter concentrates on Information Gathering and the building of the Data Model. The Process Model is covered in Chapter 9, while Interaction Analysis and the checking of the model are dealt with in Chapter 10. The topics covered are:

TOPIC	SECTION
Information Gathering and Documentation	8.1
Entity Modelling	8.2.1
Normalisation and Canonical Synthesis	8.2.2
Process Decomposition	9.1.1
Analyzing Process Dependencies	9.1.2
Analyzing Data Flows	10.1.1
The Analysis of Entity Model Views	10.1.2
Process Action Diagramming	10.1.3
Entity Life Cycle Analysis	10.1.4
Confirmation and Checking of the Business Model	10.2

8.1   Information Gathering and Documentation

The gathering together of information relevant to the project is the essential starting point from which the BAA model grows. The model itself is an attempt at representing the Business Area, and in order for that representation to bear a close relationship to the reality that it purports to reflect, it needs to be based on current and accurate information. It is not, however, enough for reams of information to be gathered. The information itself must be analyzed and made accessible and comprehensible primarily to the BAA team members who will use it throughout the project lifespan, but also to those who have been the main sources of that information. When information is analyzed and documented, there is the inevitable possibility that distortion of it can take place, and that the record of an interview is actually a distortion of the information that was conveyed. So, the recorded, analyzed interview needs to be reviewed and confirmed by the interviewee.

8.1.1   Objectives in Gathering Information and Documenting it Structurally

Essentially, the main purpose served by information gathering is the identification of business information requirements (both current and future ones) and problems experienced with meeting these requirements. The primary sources for such information are the users themselves, either in direct structured individual interviews, or via user intensive analysis sessions, which are also referred to as Joint Requirements Planning or Joint Application Development sessions.[1] A further indirect source of information is existing company documentation, often in the form of manuals of practices and procedures.

It is worth mentioning at this stage that, in most modern businesses, a vast wealth of business knowledge is contained in existing computerised systems. Preliminary analysis of this information can be made by a review of existing system documentation (where this exists), but if it is undertaken at this stage, it is recommended that the review is limited to gaining an overview of the business as it is represented in the system. Fuller analysis of existing computerised systems is presented in section 5.2 to which the reader should refer if this aspect of the Business Area to be analyzed is of particular importance.

In direct interviews with users, the discussions should be focused on the business - what is done and the information required to support its operations - but it is inevitable that, particularly where the interviewee discusses problems that are being experienced, a lot of information will also be gathered about current systems. This is understandable, because so many businesses operate via their computerised systems, and for many users, their view of the business is coloured by and even distorted through the ways in which a current computerised system constrains their business activities. All of this is good and valid information, but it should not simply be digested raw: this is where the task of analysis begins, and a skilful interviewer will probe behind the surface, and encourage the interviewee to explore business possibilities ("How would you like things to happen?") unconstrained by current

---

[1]   Joint Requirements Planning usually refers to the use of this technique in ISP and BAA; Joint Application Development, to its use in BSD, and sometimes, BAA.

problems. Moreover, the flip side of a problem is often a requirement, and the skilled interviewer will recognise and explore this fact.

8.1.2   Ways of Gathering Information

In BAA projects, the primary way in which information will be gathered is by direct structured interviews with the appropriate users. As the BAA effort is focused on a whole area of the business top-down, it is essential to interview senior and middle managers who can either give an overall view of the Business Area, or of a specific Functional Area or set of Functions within it. The initial objective on the part of the team will be to develop first-cut business models: as they begin to fill in more and more detail, they will become increasingly reliant for this information on the Font of Business Knowledge within the team, and via this resource, on the User Liaison Committee.

Structured interviews will involve a two-person team: one person conducts the interview, the other acts as a recorder. It is essential to plan the interview well in advance. Often the Project Steering Group will provide an initial list of potential interviewees (which should include all the user steering group members). The BAA team should in any case ascertain who in the business is responsible for each of the main business functions that lie within the scope of the BAA and make certain that all these functional areas are adequately covered. (The user team member is an excellent resource to determine this.) Interviews should be scheduled well in advance, and an interview brief should be submitted to each interviewee in order to ensure that they have adequate time to prepare. Often details that the team may require will not be at the interviewee's fingertips, and the brief will allow time for it to be located: this ensures that no-one's time is wasted unnecessarily. Furthermore, such an interview brief can provide a good structural basis for the interview itself. It will usually consist of a basic explanation of the BAA project and why it has been undertaken. This is then supplemented by a list of discussion topics and issues tailored for the specific user. It is a useful ploy to get the chairperson of the Project Steering Group to send out the initial brief: this serves the purpose of stamping a user authority on the activities of the BAA team, and serves as a powerful introduction of the non-user team members to the user community.

The interview itself should be limited to two hours, and the planned duration should be indicated in the interview briefing, and respected by the interviewing team. Generally, the majority of the information is likely to be gained in the first hour. If there is a genuine need to continue the interview beyond two hours, then a separate interview should be scheduled with a separate brief and focus. Such a course of action should, of course, be mutually agreed.

Wherever possible, follow the prepared structure: as the end of each topic is reached, the note taker should summarise what has been recorded, and ask for clarification of any issues that were either unclear, or skipped over in the course of the dialogue. It

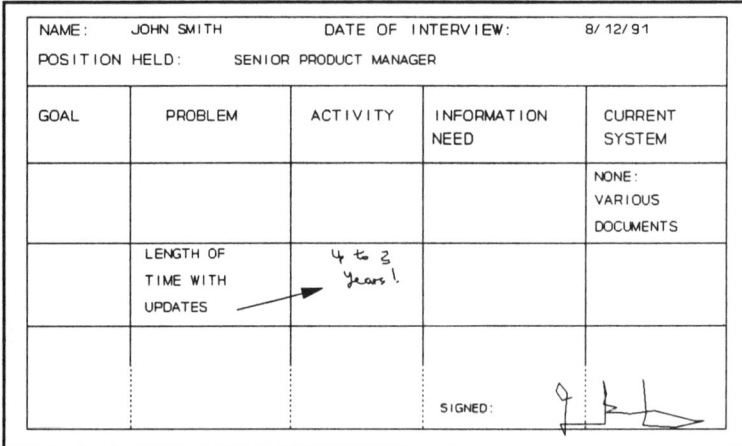

NAME: JOHN SMITH		DATE OF INTERVIEW:	8/ 12/ 91	
POSITION HELD: SENIOR PRODUCT MANAGER				
GOAL	PROBLEM	ACTIVITY	INFORMATION NEED	CURRENT SYSTEM
				NONE: VARIOUS DOCUMENTS
	LENGTH OF TIME WITH UPDATES	4 to 3 Years !.		
			SIGNED:	

Figure 8.1 Structured Interview Sheet

is clear from this that the recorder's role is not a passive one. Some recorders find it easy to analyze the discussion directly onto a structured interview sheet such as the one illustrated in Figure 8.1. Others prefer to take detailed notes and then to analyze the results onto the structured interview sheet. In either case, a manager planning the activity should recognise that the analysis of the interview can take as long as the interview itself! A general rule of thumb suggests that one should plan a full day (i.e. two person-days) for each interview: this allows for the time taken to schedule, prepare, conduct, and record the interview.

Throughout the interview, both questioner and recorder should be aware that the interviewee may wittingly or unwittingly be presenting any one of three views (or combination of views) to them: the **formal** view is a representation of what officially occurs, for example what the formal business procedures state should be done; in contrast to this an **assumed** view represents what the interviewee thinks is occurring or should occur; this in turn may differ from the **actual** view - the one being sought - which represents real business practice. Ferreting out the actual view may require some skill and experience from the interviewer.

The final aspect of an individual interview that should not be ignored is an agreement on the feedback and sign-off arrangements. The interviewee should be presented with an analyzed interview sheet as soon as possible after the interview has taken place, certainly within a week. The interviewing team should be cognisant of the fact that this is their first real opportunity to gain user confidence in the work that they are undertaking. For this reason alone, it is essential that the feedback should take place when it is promised, and that it is to a high quality. All information recorded by them should be verified by the user, and any differences or conflicts should be discussed, and **resolved** through mutual agreement.

There are occasions where it may be more appropriate to hold a User Intensive Analysis session. (This is also referred to in some contexts as a Joint Application Development (JAD) session, though the term is slightly misapplied in this context.) Such occasions are where **no viable first-cut model exists for the Business Area** (for example, where no ISP - or a poor one - has been undertaken). In this case, the primary purpose of the JAD session is to jointly develop such an initial view, and to achieve preliminary agreement.

The other instance in which such a technique is indicated is where **a number of key senior managers need to be consulted** and their agreement to a first-cut model achieved.

The User Intensive Analysis is a highly concentrated group analysis effort that can last from a single day up to a week, depending on the scope of the work to be covered and the objectives to be achieved. Where no ISP has been undertaken, the session is likely to last significantly longer than if agreement is being sought to a first-cut model.

The participants will usually include the key users, business analysts, and a moderator. The role of the analysts is to record the proceedings, and translate the conclusions into a first-cut model. Effective ways of doing this may include the use of a white board on which preliminary ideas are developed, models are sketched, and then recorded by the analysts for further development and capture in an I-CASE tool (a white board with an automatic print facility can help to ensure the accurate recording of agreed information). Some analysts prefer to capture the results of discussions directly into the CASE tool's encyclopedia, printing out aspects of the model periodically for further discussion.

The moderator's role calls for tact, and the ability to facilitate discussions. Whoever plays this role needs to ensure that the sessions keep to their chosen agenda, that rivalries between participants do not prevent a good outcome from being achieved, and, wherever possible, that differences of opinion or business practice are either resolved or recorded. It is sometimes a benefit for the moderator to have no in-depth business knowledge in order to remain neutral. There are cases, however, where business knowledge can be a great advantage in resolving complex issues.

The sorts of issues that can be discussed and recorded in these sessions include the business processes that are performed within the Business Area, main Entity Types and Relationships, and the dependencies that exist between business activities. In modelling these aspects, the project team will come away from the sessions with a good first-cut Business Model that has been agreed with and is subscribed to by the key users. Very often, the users themselves emerge from such sessions with a clearer, more structured view of the business they are so familiar with.

The final source of information that can be used in business modelling is various forms of company documentation. This may include technical literature covering existing systems, other business documentation such as standard procedures, forms, reports, and screens. Detailed analysis of some of these documents may not yet be appropriate, but identifying where they are obtainable, and that they exist, is of importance.

8.1.3   Effective Ways of Documenting and Analyzing Interviews

A long, verbatim record of an interview with a user is of little use, especially to someone who is either seeking information some time after the interview was recorded, or looking for a particular issue or answer. The time involved in reading through the interview notes is not cost effective, and different recorders' styles can be confusing, and open to ambiguous interpretation. A much more effective way of regrouping the information gathered in an interview is to analyze it into categories that are relevant to the process of Business Modelling. As is shown in Figure 8.1, grouping the content of the interview under headings such as Mission, Organisation, Goal/Objective, Problem/Inhibitor, Activity, Information Need, and Current System (this list is not intended to be comprehensive or mandatory: each team should chose from it and add to it as need dictates) allows a subsequent reader quickly to locate information that is relevant. Even some months after an interview took place, a team member who is querying an aspect of the data model can skim down the Information Need column, and, on locating the information required, determine if necessary which user was interviewed and who conducted the interview. This allows the team member easily to contact the relevant user, and pursue the problem further.

The analysis of an interview into the format shown in Figure 8.1 also creates a very positive initial impression on the person who has been interviewed. Instead of having to read verbatim text, the interviewee perceives that the interview was taken seriously enough for its content to be analyzed thoroughly and transformed into a format that will be useful. Moreover, the transformation from rough notes into structured analysis matrix exposes the interviewers' understanding of what has been imparted, and allows both parties to the interview to confirm their understanding of what was said.

The structured interview matrix is an important base document for the project, for all business modelling work is based upon the information that is contained in the collected interviews. At the end of a BAA, any feature of the model should be traceable back to these interview sheets: they mark the beginning of an important information audit trail through the project.

8.2   Techniques for Modelling Data

The final project Data Model will consist visually of a detailed Entity Relationship Model (ERM) that is supported by a further dimension of textual description and definition. The complete Data Model will contain information about the information that is required to support the operation of the Business Area, and in order to construct it or to understand and review it, it is necessary to be familiar with the conventions, rules, and practices that are intrinsic to data modelling. This section serves to explain them, but does not pretend to be a detailed overall guide to the subtle and at times intricate subject of data modelling itself.

First, in section 8.2.1, the ERM itself will be discussed; this will be followed in section

8.2.2 by an explanation of the basic rules of data normalisation, and the technique known as Canonical Synthesis, by which a derived logical data model can be built up by analyzing existing systems, whether they be computerised (including packages) or manual.

8.2.1 Building an Entity Relationship Model (ERM)

The ERM is a graphical representation of the Data Entity Types required to support a Business Area, and the Relationships that exist between the Entity Types. An example of an ERM can be seen in Figure 8.2.

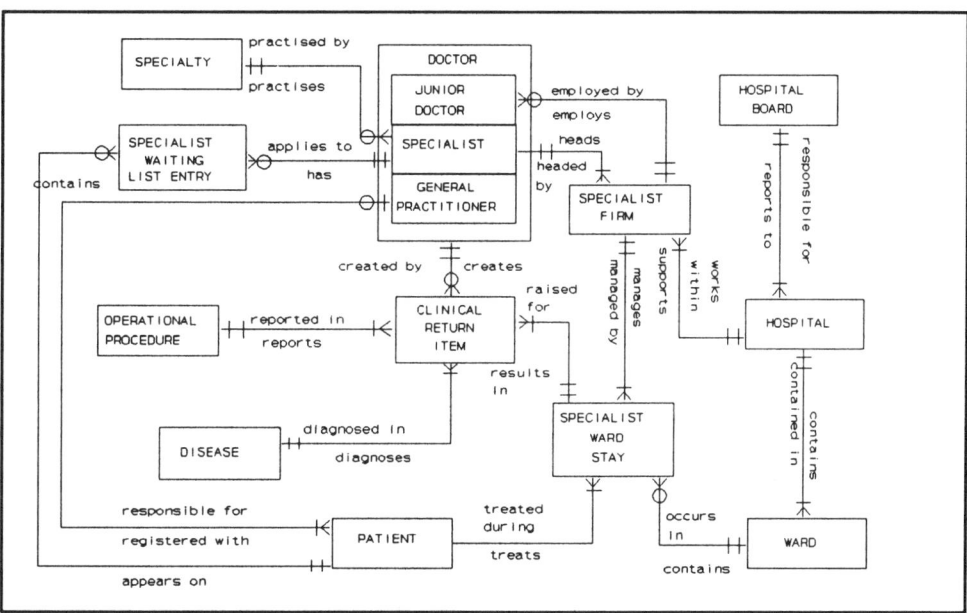

Figure 8.2 Entity Relationship Model

As discussed in section 7.2, the high-level ERM that provides a focus of scope for the BAA project derives directly from the ISP study, and is a sub-set of the overall corporate data model. The relationship between the high-level ERM and that produced during a BAA can be seen by comparing Figure 8.3 with Figure 8.2.

In the BAA project, the data subject areas and main data entities inherited from the ISP study are examined further: additional entity types are generally identified within subject areas, and ISP entity types are often found to contain additional levels of detail and complexity.

It is from the high-level ERM that the BAA begins working. This ERM is then

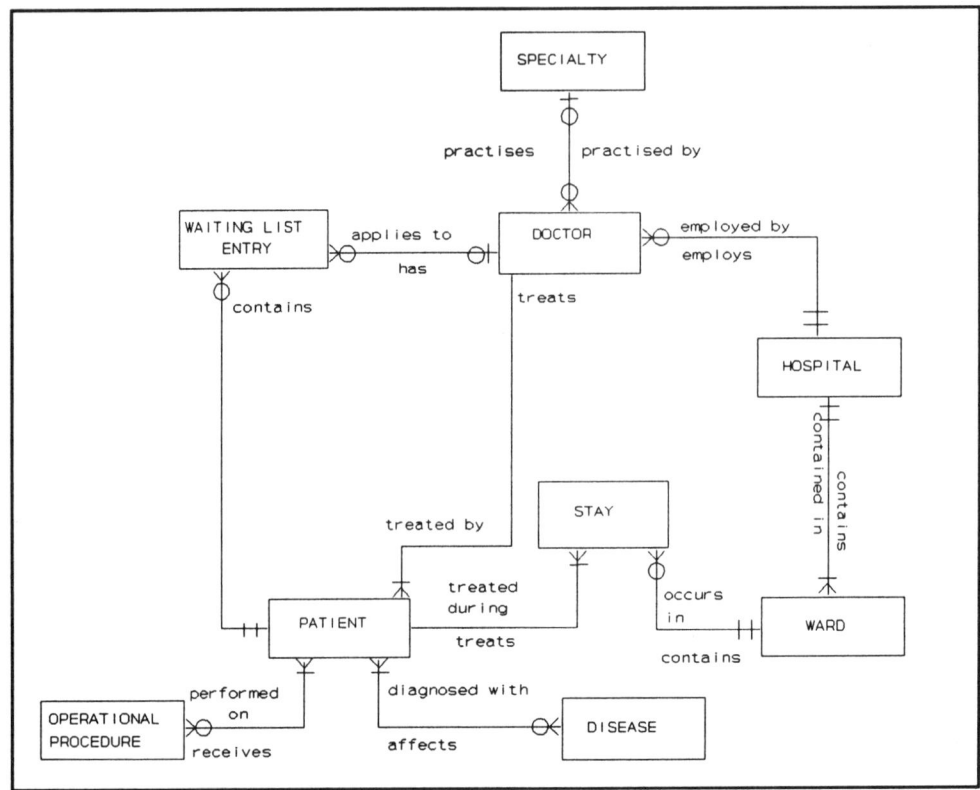

Figure 8.3 High-Level ERM

expanded and refined using the information that has been gathered in user interviews, together with the participation of user team members and, eventually, the User Liaison Group in formal and informal reviews. The final deliverable is an ERM that contains all relevant Entity Types, Relationships, Attributes, and Properties fully named and defined. A summary of this process is illustrated in Figure 8.4.

8.2.1.1 Objectives

A fundamental tenet of the IE approach is that the basic data structures that underpin a business remain relatively stable over time. It is, therefore, essential to have a clear representation of those data structures that is independent of how they are used or applied in a particular system or situation. Modelling the data by means of an ERM is the key means of representing that underlying structure.

The ERM allows both analysts and users to view and review the data structures of a particular Business Area in a format that is standard and mutually comprehensible. In order to do so, it is necessary for all participants in Data Modelling to be aware of the conventions used. These are explained in section 8.2.1.2.

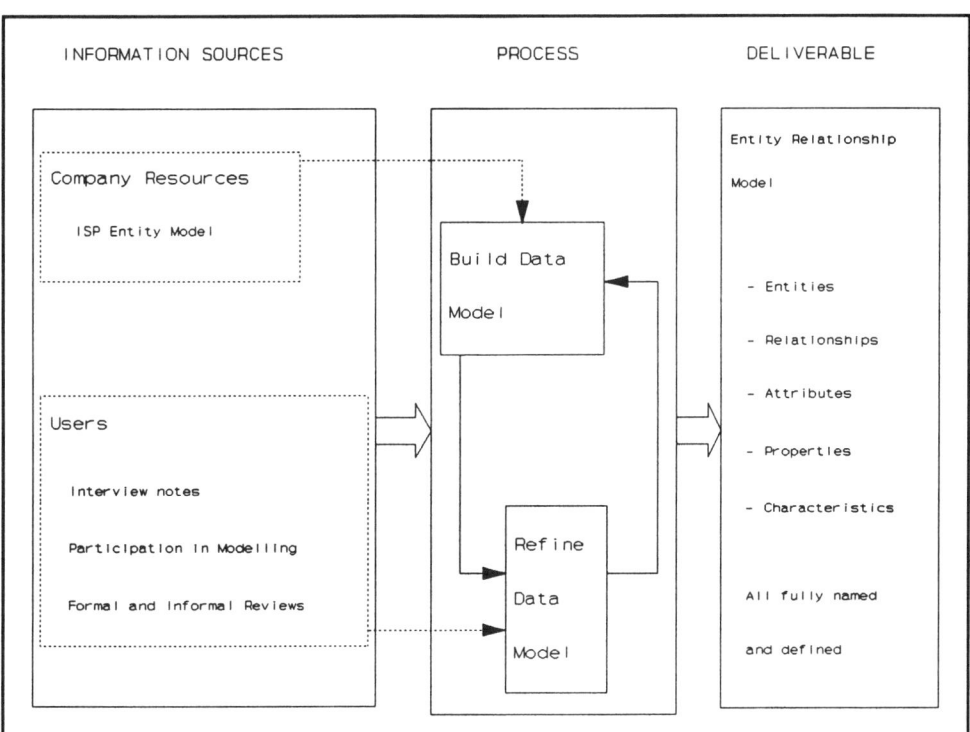

Figure 8.4 Building a Data Model

8.2.1.2 ERM Concepts and Conventions

Entity Type

The fundamental unit in an ERM is the Entity Type itself. This is a collection of types of people, objects, organisations, concepts or things that are of meaning to the business, for example, EMPLOYEE, STOCK ITEM, CUSTOMER COMPANY, UNIT OF MEASUREMENT, or PLAN. An Entity Type is represented by the convention shown in Figure 8.5. Each Entity Type may have many occurrences: an occurrence of the entity type EMPLOYEE may be "John Smith", another "Kate Brown". It is essential that there is a clear **Definition** for each Entity Type identified. Examples of Entity Type Definition have been given in Example 7.1 and Example 7.2.

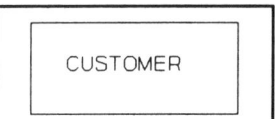

Figure 8.5
Entity Type

The business will also need to hold information about the **Properties of an Entity Type**. These will include details about the following:

● **Volumes:** What are the maximum, minimum, and average number of occurrences of a particular Entity Type; is there likely to be growth or diminution of these numbers over a given time period (per day, week, month, or year); and is there a deviation in these figures based, for example, on seasonal factors such as holidays or climatic variations?

● **Retention:** What are the business rules relating to the retention of the information contained about a particular Entity Type?

● **Ownership:** What business function claims ownership of the Entity Type, or is it shared across business functions? In the latter case, is it possible to determine ownership based on which function is responsible for the Entity Type at different stages in its life cycle? (This can only be determined with accuracy if an Entity Life Cycle Analysis has been undertaken for a particular Entity Type, see section 10.1.4.)

In addition, the business will want to know various things about that Entity Type. The **Characteristics of an Entity Type** that the business needs to know about are called its **Attributes.**   Relevant Attributes about an EMPLOYEE may include SURNAME, FORENAMES, HOME ADDRESS, DATE OF BIRTH, etc. Furthermore, the business will need to know about the **Properties of each Attribute** it is interested in. Such Attribute Properties include:

● **Optionality:** Is the information contained in an Attribute always required by the business?

● **Definition:** What is the business meaning and function of this Attribute?

● **Characteristics:** What sort of information does the Attribute consist of: is it Numeric, Alphanumeric, Alphabetical, Textual, etc? How many characters/digits does the Attribute consist of? If it is numeric, are there decimal places involved, and if so, how many?

● **Type:** Is the Attribute itself *basic*, is it *derived* from other attributes (AGE can be derived from DATE OF BIRTH), or is it *designed* (a code or combination of coded elements)?

● **Default Value:** Is there a usual default value for the Attribute in question?

● **Validation Rules and/or Valid Ranges:** Are there rules that determine the validity of the Attribute? Does it have to fall within a certain range of values?

A good I-CASE tool should allow for the recording of all the information that has been described above pertaining to both Entity Types and Attributes, although the actual method of recording it may differ. Where an I-CASE tool does not have a specific place for recording the information, this is probably because the information is not used in the design and construction of a system, and it may point towards a potential weak point in the tool itself. For this reason, it is recommended that such information is recorded as part of the Definition, and that chosen key words, eg. RETENTION PERIOD or DEFAULT VALUE, are capitalised in the Definition at the head of a paragraph so that this information is easily accessible, for it will be required at various stages in the project life cycle, and particularly to aid in the design process.

Relationship

A relationship that links two Entity Types indicates an association between them that is in accordance with a business rule. Such a relationship is represented by means of a line that joins the two entity types as is shown in Figure 8.6.

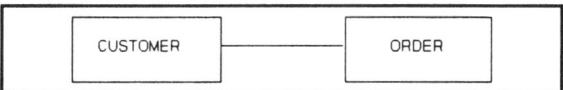

Figure 8.6 Relationship

Each relationship has a name that explains the business association between the two Entity Types that are linked. The relationship is named in both directions as is

illustrated in Figure 8.7, and the general convention is to read the relationship in a clockwise direction. It is essential that the relationship makes sense in business terms, and so vague names such as "has" or "owns" should be avoided (unless, of course, in the latter case, the relationship is one of owning).

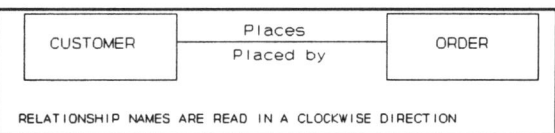

Figure 8.7 Naming Relationships

There are two additional aspects of the relationship that are usually depicted. The **Cardinality** of a relationship shows whether an occurrence of an Entity Type is related to one or many occurrences of the other Entity Type. This is often shown using the conventions illustrated in Figure 8.8.

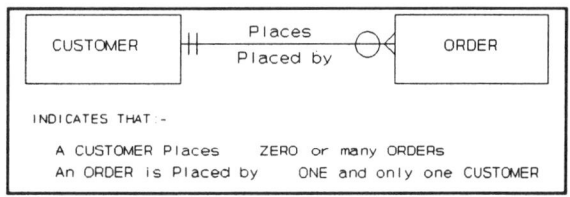

Figure 8.8 Cardinality

The **Optionality** of a relationship defines whether the relationship shown is optional or mandatory, and the conventions commonly used to depict optionality are illustrated in Figure 8.9.

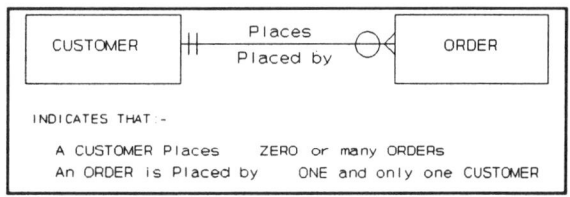

Figure 8.9 Optionality

At times it may be desirable to show the **Exclusivity** of a number of optional relationships, where only one may occur at a time. This is depicted using an arc such as is shown in Figure 8.10. The exclusivity arc is a pictorial way of showing a business rule that governs a particular grouping of relationships. Further details of such rules, and indeed of any rules that govern when optional relationship occurrences do or do not occur, can be captured in textual format in the relationship descriptions of many I-CASE tools.

One-to-One Relationships

A one-to-one relationship tends to be very rare, and should be carefully examined by a team that identifies one. They should initially determine whether the two entities so linked do in fact differ from one another: are they not actually the same thing? If it is clear that they are different, then it is necessary to determine whether the relationship is genuinely one-to-one.

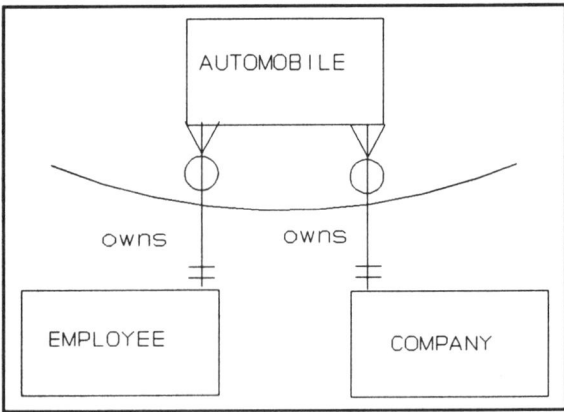

Figure 8.10 Exclusivity of Relationships

In a project that the author was involved in the analysis team had identified the one-to-one relationship illustrated in Figure 8.11. The Business Area had to do with the Development of Products in a Petrochemical company, and the Entity Type definitions indicated that the Entity Type PRODUCT SUBSTANCE was the usually liquid, often oily, substance that was usually stored in a tin, drum or tank. The FORMULATION was the recipe for that substance. The team first had to determine whether they were the same thing or not, and it soon became clear that

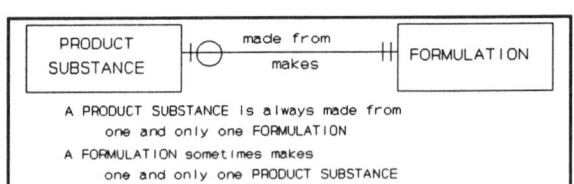

Figure 8.11 One-to-one Relationship

we could put occurrences of each Entity Type side by side and that they were different: the PRODUCT SUBSTANCE made your hands dirty and oily, whereas the FORMULATION existed quite comfortably on a number of sheets of paper, and could be stored in a ring-binder file. The next question to be settled then was whether the relationship really was one-to-one. This required the team to review its business understanding of the relationship thoroughly with the users. The question asked was whether a slight change in the FORMULATION meant that the PRODUCT SUBSTANCE changed significantly enough to bring about another occurrence of the PRODUCT SUBSTANCE. It was analogous to asking a chef the following question: if you bake a chocolate cake using a recipe that called for 4 eggs and then find it possible to vary the recipe by adding one more egg and baking the cake, do you get a chocolate cake as a result, or is there a significant enough difference between the two cakes to decide that they were something different? In the case of the project, the users were unanimous: even the slightest variation in FORMULATION could (and probably would) change the PRODUCT SUBSTANCE significantly, and every such change would result in the creation of a new PRODUCT SUBSTANCE. The one-to-one relationship was retained in the ERM.

Many-to-Many Relationships

Any many-to-many relationships that exist in the ERM need to be reviewed carefully. It is often necessary to resolve such relationships by identifying an additional **Associative** Entity and relating it to the two original Entity Types in the manner illustrated in Figure 8.12.

The main reason for this is that many-to-many relationships often conceal business information that is actually contained in the "intersection entity". In the example shown, the Entity Type ASSIGNMENT is of meaning to the business in its own right, and it

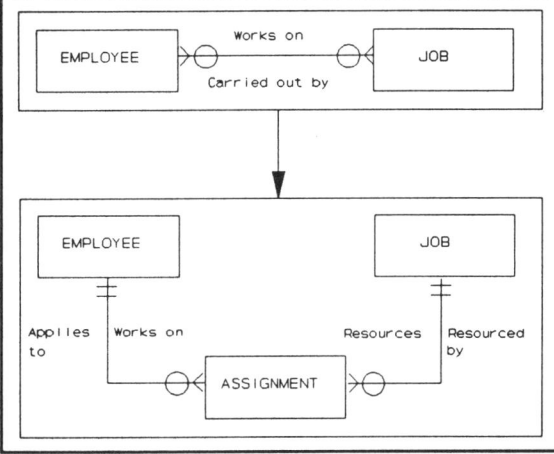

Figure 8.12   Resolving   Many-to-Many Relationships

contains Attributes that are of importance to the business such as START DATE and END DATE.

Some schools of thought advise the resolution of many-to-many relationships as part of the analysis activity. However, one should not lose sight of the fact that this is a Business Model, and an Associative Entity that serves no **business** purpose has no real place in the model:[2] it often does nothing more than confuse users. Such many-to-many relationships are resolved later in one of the first steps of the BSD process - and besides, many I-CASE tools will automatically bring about their resolution in order to effect a preliminary database design. The point is that resolving many-to-many relationships because their physical implementation is difficult is not a business consideration, and should not be undertaken until the design stage: we are involved in BAA with logical data models, not databases, and technical issues should not obscure business ones.

Entity Subtypes and Supertypes

There are a number of instances where a business views and/or relates to an Entity Type in different ways dependent on particular characteristics of that Entity Type. For example, the Entity Type PERSON will be viewed differently in a Business Area that

---

[2] Such an Associative Entity will have **no** attributes.

covers Travel Reservations dependent on whether that person is a TRAVELLER or an EMPLOYEE. In such cases, PERSON is referred to as an **Entity Supertype**, which contains the **Entity Subtypes** TRAVELLER and EMPLOYEE. Furthermore, if we need to be able to distinguish between PERSONs based on the Attribute SEX (for example in order to ensure that single TRAVELLERs who are not paying a supplement are accommodated with

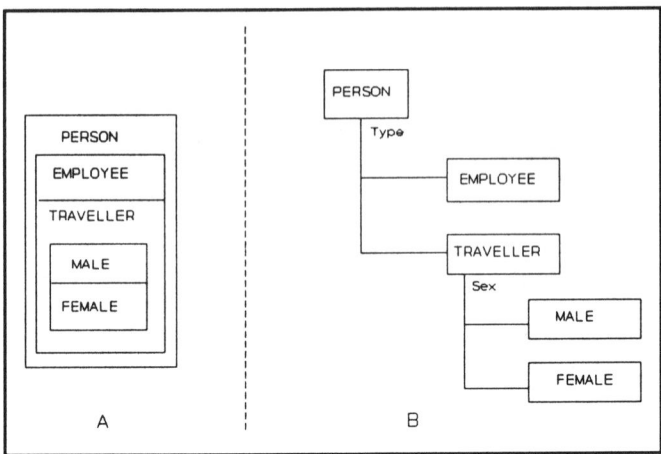

Figure 8.13 Entity Subtype

another person of the same sex), then the Subtypes MALE and FEMALE are of relevance to the business. In this case, the Attribute SEX is known as a **Qualifying Attribute**, and the subtypes MALE and FEMALE are **exclusive**. The conventions used to illustrate the Entity Subtypes discussed above are shown in Figure 8.13.

All Entity Subtypes inherit the Attributes of their Supertype. What distinguishes them is that they may have Attributes or Relationships or both that are unique to the subtype from a business perspective. A TRAVELLER may travel to or from a TRAVEL LOCATION, but we would only be interested in these relationships for an EMPLOYEE if we **also** viewed them as a TRAVELLER (because they had made a reservation through the business); conversely, we may be interested in the SALARY AMOUNT of an EMPLOYEE, but such information about TRAVELLERs is irrelevant from a business perspective.

Not all I-CASE tools support the concept of Entity Subtypes. When they do not, Subtypes have to be modelled as though they are Entity Types in their own right. A way of avoiding the repetition of shared Attributes (and hence denormalising the business data model) is to link each subtype in a one-to-one relationship to its supertype, but this is clearly only a compromise of expedience.

Some I-CASE tools use the convention in Figure 8.13B showing the relationships at an Entity Subtype level, and the diagram itself is called an Entity Horizon Diagram.

Recursive Relationships

Occasionally, an Entity Type may have a relationship with another occurrence of itself. Such a **Recursive Relationship** is illustrated in Figure 8.14.

A commonly found instance of a recursive structure is the many-to-many relationship shown in Figure 8.15, which shows the "Bill of Materials/Part" (BOMP) structure, and its resolution.

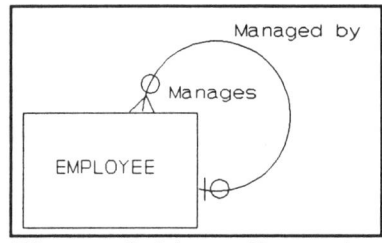

Figure 8.14   Recursive Relationship

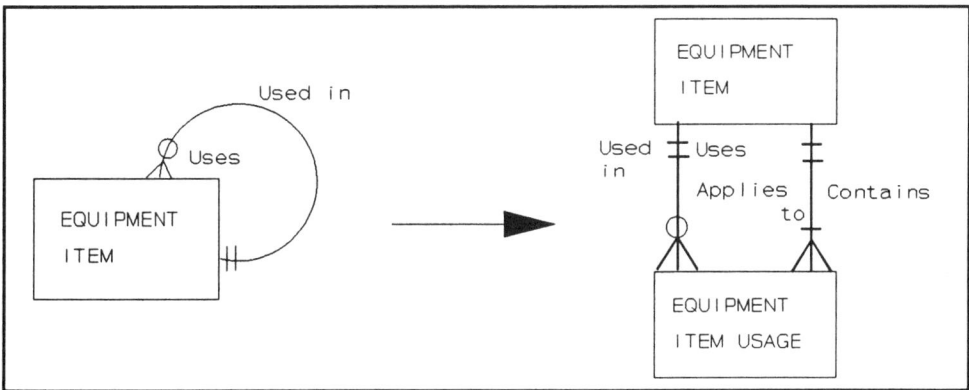

Figure 8.15 Bill of Materials/Part Structure

8.2.1.3 Common Problems Encountered in Building an ERM

It is not possible to construct a viable Business Area model without building an ERM of the data underpinning the business. The process of Data Modelling usually begins with the high-level data model that has resulted from the ISP (or from the BAA scoping exercise). This model forms the basic skeleton to which flesh is added through the information gathered in interviewing senior users, and in formal and informal reviews with the team's Font of Business Knowledge, and the User Liaison Group. This process means that the data model grows and improves through an iterative process of build and review, build and review.

When is the data model then complete enough to proceed with the next step? This is a question that has vexed a large number of IE projects.[3] One of the most common symptoms of "paralysis through analysis" is the data model that is never complete enough. A project manager should realise that a data model will **never** be perfect, and should prevent any attempt on the part of a project team to waste time getting the model right. What is required is a first-cut model that has identified all the major data entities and relationships required to support the Business Area, and is populated with all the obvious attributes that the users need. **One of the major objectives of Interaction Analysis - the understanding of how each Elementary Process identified interacts with the data model - is to identify missing Entity Types, Attributes, and Relationships.** It is a waste of team effort to try to achieve perfection when the data model (no matter how good or complete) will inevitably be thrown into confusion (and indeed initially be destabilised) as soon as Interaction Analysis proper begins. A good project team will expend the twenty percent of effort required to achieve an eighty percent correct ERM, and then move on: the BAA process itself will take care of proving the data model. (Unless, of course, a decision has been taken not to undertake interaction analysis, in which case a significant risk is being added to the project, as there is no way of rigorously ensuring that the data model is correct.)

A strong and effective project leader should use the reaction of users to the data model as a barometer, and, where a team is overanalysing the ERM, enforce closure of this activity and allow the team to move on: the risks of doing so too early are minimal if the project leader is sensitive to the users, and applies measured judgement and common sense to the data model itself.

8.2.2   Normalisation and Canonical Synthesis

Once the main Entity Types have been identified, they need to be populated by Attributes. A major principle underlying the ERM concept is that any element of data that has been identified should occur once, and only once, in the overall data model. To ensure that this is the case, the elementary rules of data normalisation, which are familiar to all data modellers and data administrators, need to be applied particularly in assigning the Attributes that have been identified. These basic rules are described in section 8.2.2.2.

Application of the principles of normalisation can be of particular use when analyzing and deriving the underlying (and often hidden) data structures of an existing system or computerised application package. In this case, each user view that exists in the system is normalised, and the resulting normalised data relations are then combined using some simple, but effective rules, a process known as Canonical Synthesis. These principles are explained in section 8.2.2.4.

---

[3] This issue has already been discussed to some extent in section 7.4.2.

8.2.2.1 Objectives

Why do we bother to normalise data in the first place?

Normalisation allows us to be certain that any Entity and Attribute that we have identified appears once and once only in the Data Model. It also assists us in determining that an Attribute, once identified, is placed correctly in the entity to which it belongs.

The fully normalised data model, while facilitating further logical analysis, also has implications for any systems that are ultimately designed based on these structures. Firstly, the overall integrity of the information contained in the model is assured, and that principle can more easily be transposed into a database design even where controlled redundancy may be required because of performance considerations. In all cases, database design based on a normalised data model should result in a simplification of the resulting physical data structures. Lastly, fully normalised data allows for the manipulation of whole sets of data using a single command, rather than the manipulation of each occurrence of the data through an individual command. Relational data manipulation languages such as SQL have enabled this to occur: it is thus possible with one command to increase, say, the credit limit on all customers whose accounts are over ten years old and who live within the London postal area by £100.

8.2.2.2 The Rules of Normalisation

For the purposes of achieving an ERM that is sufficiently normalised so as to identify the main business entity types and ensure that they are correctly populated with attributes, normalisation to the level known as Third Normal Form (3NF) is recommended. Additional levels of normalisation are well established principles of data modelling, and, once the ERM has reached a good state of stability, it should be checked by a data modelling specialist for instances of fourth normal form and beyond. It is recommended that this sort of check takes place as part of the BSD activity of establishing a first-cut logical database design (see section 12.3.1).

The objective in normalising a data model to 3NF is to ensure that each attribute in an entity type is **functionally dependent** on the key of that entity type, and only on the key of that entity type. Another way of understanding the concept of functional dependency is to consider the question, "Does the value of attribute A uniquely determine the value of attribute B at a given point in time?" If the answer is yes, then B is functionally dependent on A. So, for example:

Salary is NOT functionally dependent on Grade.
(There is a range of salaries for each grade.)

Grade IS functionally dependent on Employee Number.
(An employee is only one grade at a given point in time.)

Salary IS functionally dependent on Employee Number.
(An employee earns a particular salary at a given point in time.)

In order to illustrate the principles behind reaching 3NF, an example based on an existing Sales Order Form will be used. The form is shown in Figure 8.16 on the next page.

Initially a list of the attributes contained in the form is drawn up and an identifying attribute or key is signified by underlining it as is shown in Figure 8.17.

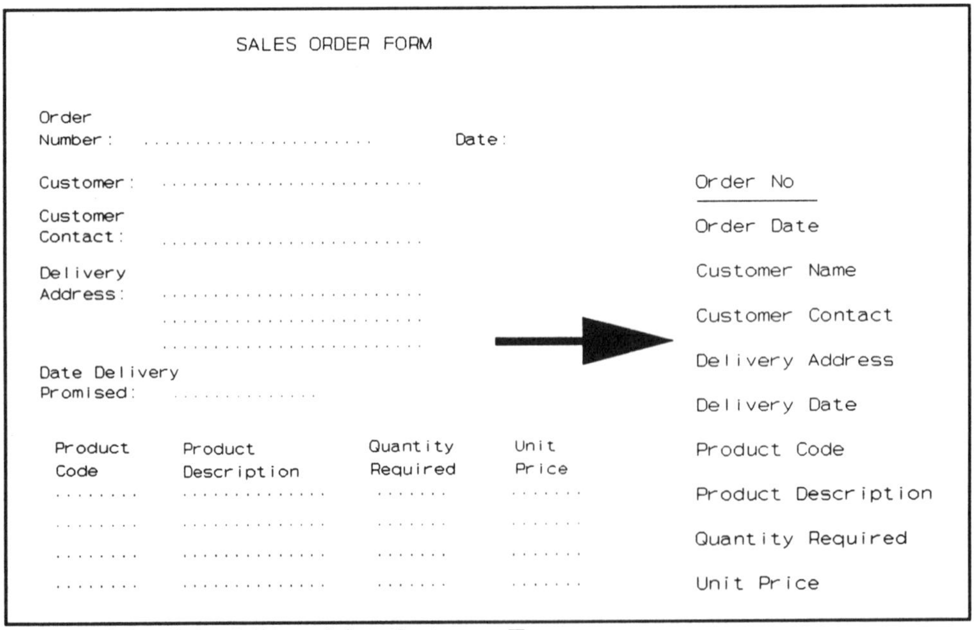

Figure 8.17 Initial List of Attributes on Form

```
                          SALES ORDER FORM

      Order
      Number:  ........................       Date:



      Customer:     .........................

      Customer
      Contact:      .......................

      Delivery
      Address:      .........................

                    .........................

                    .........................


      Date Delivery
      Promised:             .................


       Product       Product        Quantity      Unit
       Code          Description    Required      Price

       .........     ................     .......      ........

       .........     ................     .......      ........

       .........     ................     .......      ........

       .........     ................     .......      ........
```

Figure 8.16 Sales Order Form

The single, unnormalised relation (grouping of data) is then brought to First Normal Form (1NF) by removing those attributes that form repeating groups. As is illustrated in Figure 8.18, in doing so, the original identifying attribute is carried forward, and the attribute which further identifies or qualifies the repeating group is also underlined. The two identifying attributes for this new relation form a compound key to it.

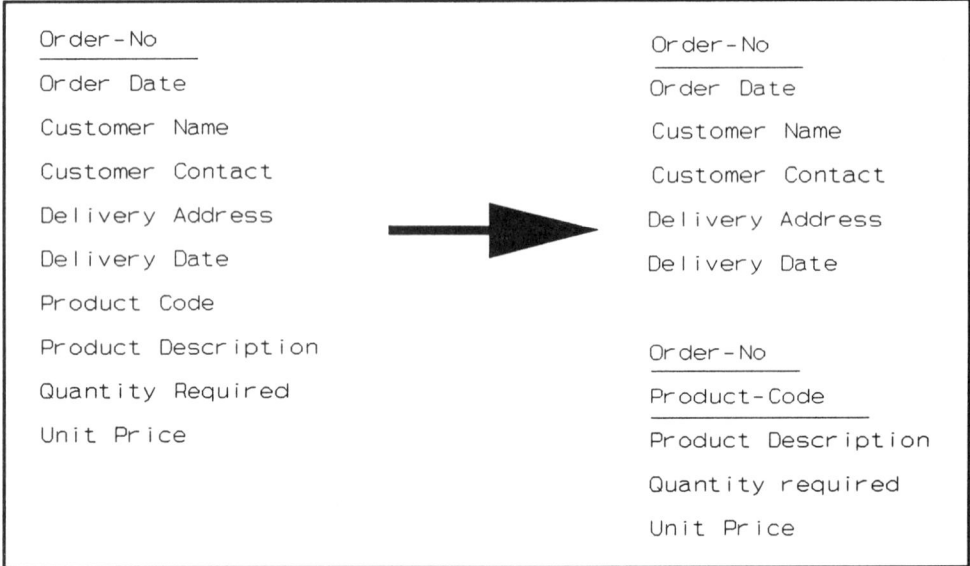

Figure 8.18 First Normal Form (1NF)

Second Normal Form (2NF) is reached by removing the attributes that are dependent on part of the key from any relations with a compound key. As is shown in Figure 8.19, a new relation is created and its identifier is underlined.

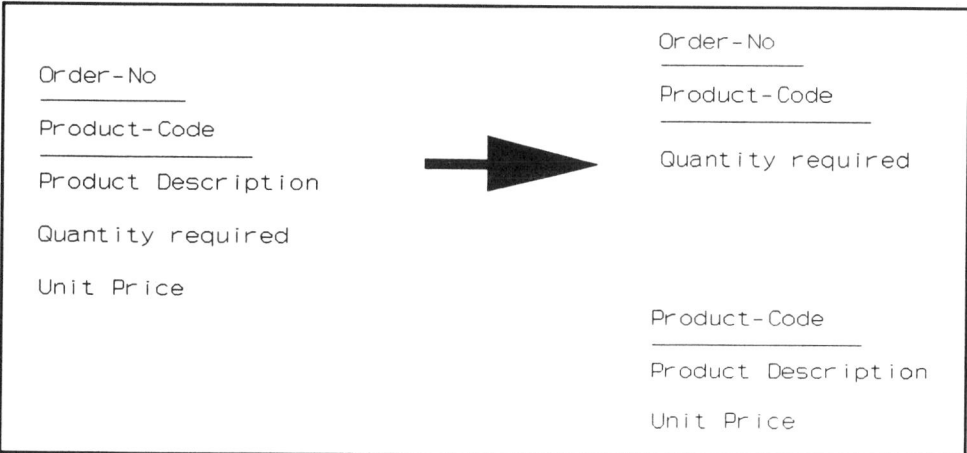

Figure 8.19 Second Normal Form (2NF)

Finally, to bring this set of relations into 3NF, all non-key dependencies are eliminated. Each relation is scanned and it is determined whether any non-key attributes in the relation are dependent on any other non-key attribute in the relation.

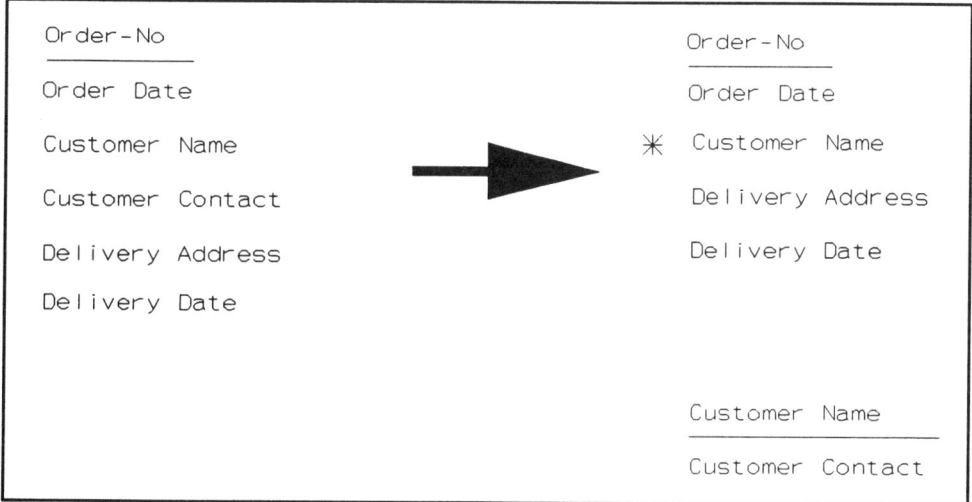

Figure 8.20 Third Normal Form (3NF)

As is shown in Figure 8.20, a new relation is created, but the key to this new relation is **retained** in the original relation and marked with an asterisk. Such a non-key attribute in a relation which forms the key to a different relation is known as a **foreign key**.

A summary of the process of normalisation to Third Normal Form is shown by means of a typical 3NF sheet in Figure 8.21.

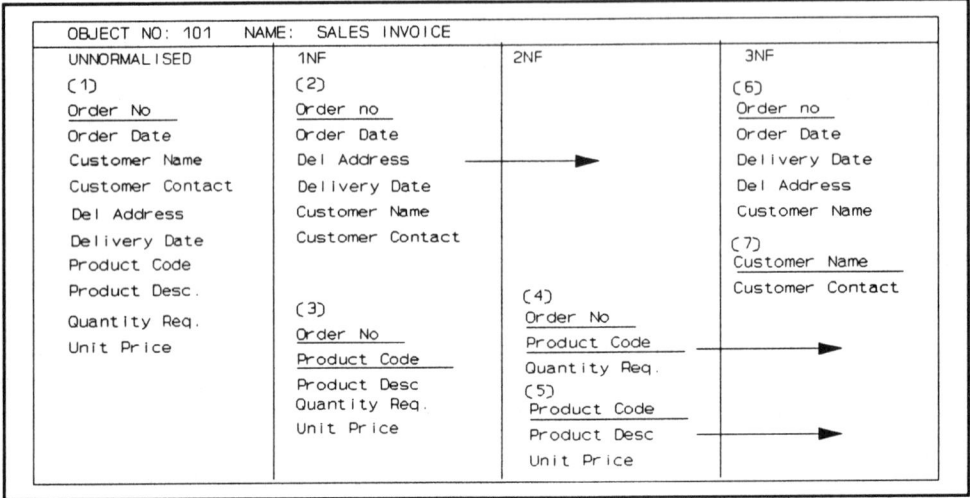

Figure 8.21 3NF Sheet

In order to check whether a particular relation is normalised, a useful set of questions to ask is:

> *Is each attribute in the relation dependent on:*
>
> | | |
> |---|---|
> | *The KEY?* | *(1NF)* |
> | *The WHOLE KEY?* | *(2NF)* |
> | *and   NOTHING BUT THE KEY?* | *(3NF)* |

8.2.2.3 Applying the Principles of Normalisation

Where an ERM has been created top-down as discussed in section 8.2.1, it is necessary that each entity type is fully populated with the attributes that uniquely qualify it.

The sources of these attributes vary, and can include the users themselves, existing systems, and business documentation. Existing manual systems hold a potential treasure trove of attributes in forms and reports, while with computerised systems (including packages) the attributes may also be found in screens. Business literature such as procedure manuals and technical documentation may also be the source of attributes.

The principles of normalisation can be formally applied to a judicious subset of such documentation in order to ensure that the entity types identified are correctly populated with attributes. Even in the case where (realistically) such an exercise is undertaken in a more haphazard way, applying the normalisation "test" described on page 136 can help to ensure that the task is undertaken with a reasonable amount of accuracy and rigour.

Normalisation can also be used to achieve a quick understanding of the data elements in an existing system, whether that be manual, a bespoke computerised one, or a computerised package. Where it is necessary to understand the **logical structure** of such data elements, then the series of rules known as canonical synthesis (see section 8.2.2.4) can be applied in order to derive the logical ERM starting "bottom up" with the attributes. An ERM that is constructed for a current system in this way can then be compared with the top-down ERM that has been built as part of the BAA data modelling exercise. Differences between the two logical models need to be analyzed: they may point to gaps in the business knowledge on the part of the BAA team, or they may result from areas of the current system that are outside of the scope covered by the BAA.

8.2.2.4 Canonical Synthesis

The term "Canonical Synthesis" sounds as if it has been invented by technicians in order to lend an air of mystification to a comparatively simple set of processes. By definition, a canon is a simple set of rules, and so Canonical Synthesis is the combining or synthesising of a number of normalised relations according to those simple rules in order to derive a view of the logical structures underpinning a set of data relations.

Indeed, the rules are very simple to understand and to apply. Once the scope for the exercise of consolidation has been established, they are:

1. Normalise the individual user views of the data that have been chosen. This process has been fully described in section 8.2.2.2.

2. Combine all normalised relations which have the same identifier or key.

    The easiest way to achieve this is to start with the user view that has the most relations, and use this as the base into which other user views are added. For each relation in the view to be combined with the base view, check whether a relation

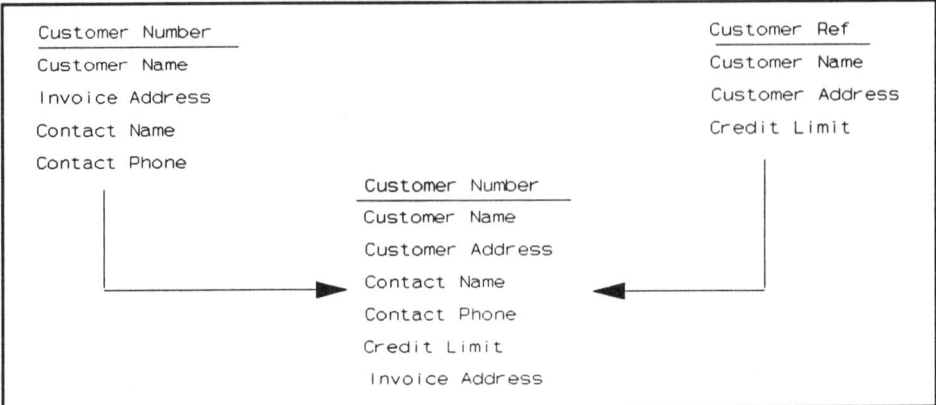

Figure 8.22 Combining Normalised Relations

exists with the same key attribute(s) as in the base view. If so, merge the attributes into the existing relation; if not, add the relation to the base view. As is shown in Figure 8.22, this process is not entirely mechanical, because business knowledge and some common sense may be required in order to detect attributes which are the same thing, but are named differently in the two user views. The key attribute CUSTOMER NUMBER is, in reality, the same as CUSTOMER REF, but this fact may not be immediately apparent in many cases.

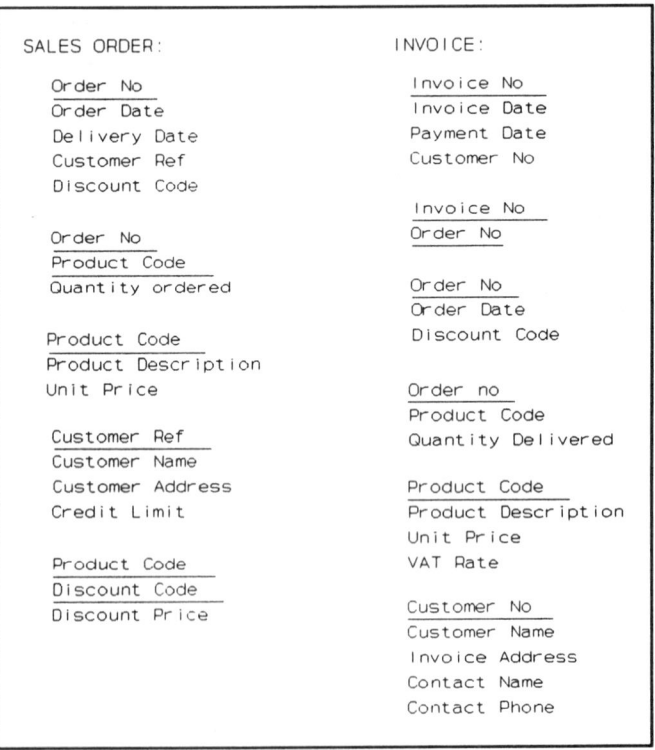

Figure 8.23 Sales Order and Invoice

To illustrate this principle, Figure 8.23 contains the relations resulting from the normalisation of two user views: Sales Order and Invoice. The combination of these normalised views results in the set of relations shown in Figure 8.24.

A last word of caution is called for: in combining normalised relations we can be reasonably sure that they are in 2NF, but we need to check in every case that we have not introduced part-key dependencies.

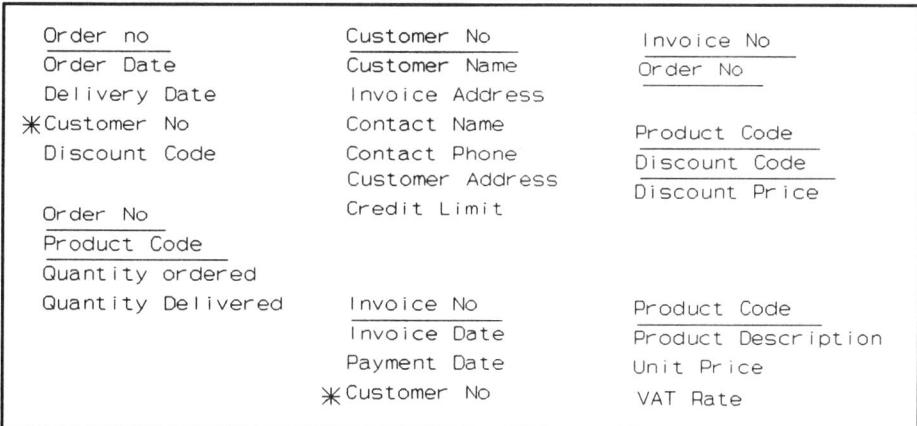

Figure 8.24 Combination of Normalised Views

3. For each relation in the consolidated set of normalised relations, we now create an Entity Type, give it an appropriate name, and show both its key attributes and the foreign keys it contains. Figure 8.25 applies this rule to the set of relations shown in Figure 8.24.

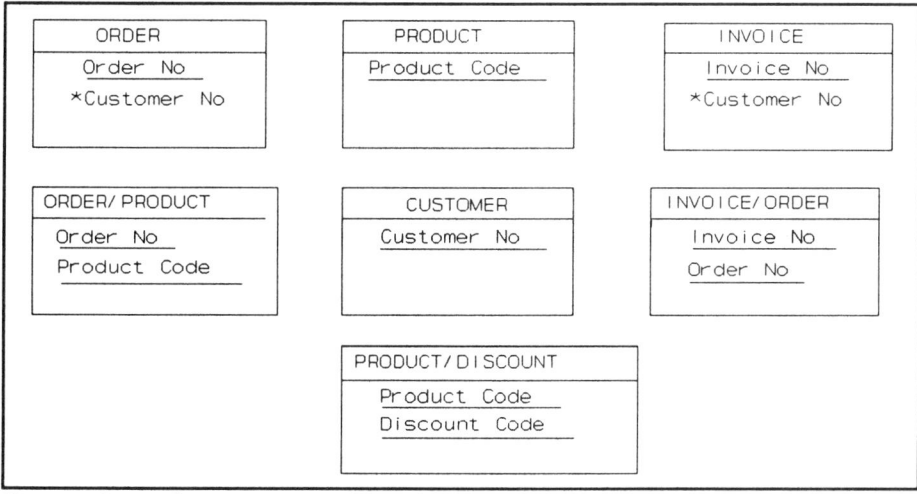

Figure 8.25 Creating Entities from Relations

Note that where a compound key exists, the naming convention commonly used is to concatenate the elements of the key as in the entity type name ORDER/PRODUCT.

4. For each attribute that is part of a compound key, check whether a corresponding entity type exists; if not, create one. In Figure 8.26, for the entity type PRODUCT/DISCOUNT, a corresponding entity type of PRODUCT exists, but the DISCOUNT entity type has to be created.

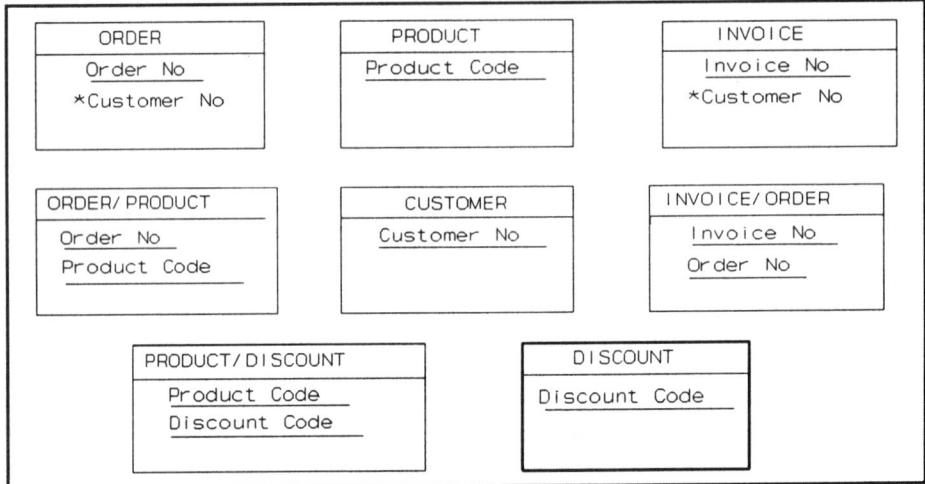

Figure 8.26 Creating Entities for Compound Keys

5. For each foreign key in an entity, create a one-to-many relationship with the many on the side of the foreign key entity as is shown in Figure 8.27.

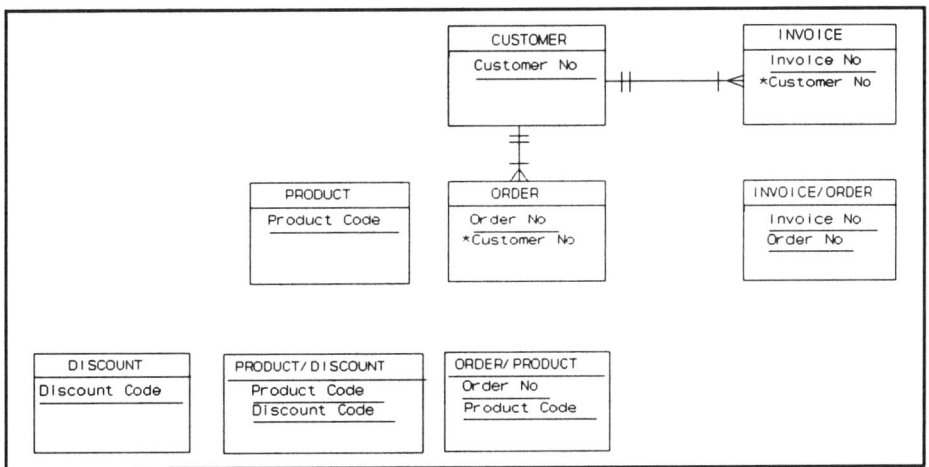

Figure 8.27 Creating Relationships for Foreign Keys

Note that **only cardinality can be determined, not optionality.**

6. For each compound key, create a one-to-many relationship from the part-key to the corresponding entity that has the part-key as its identifier. The many side of the relationship is placed on the side of the compound key, as is shown in Figure 8.28, and again it is not possible to determine optionality.

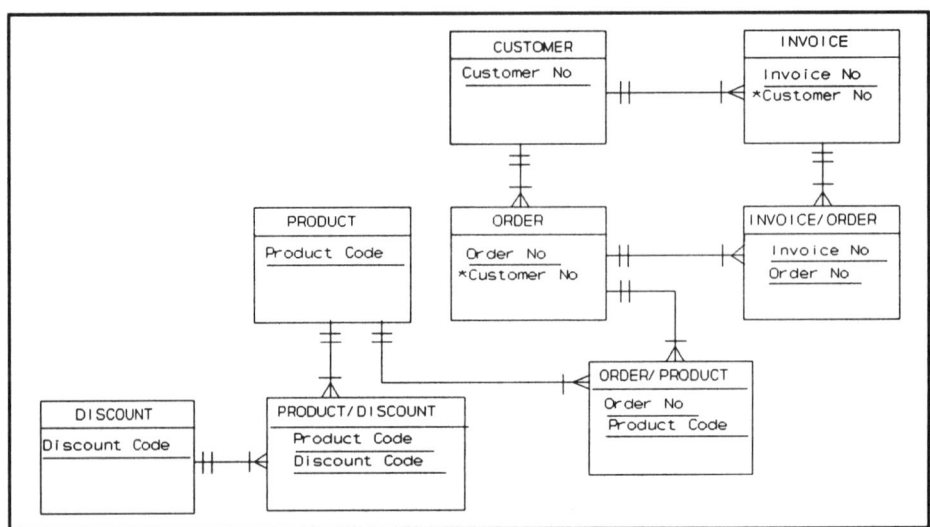

Figure 8.28 Creating Relationships for Compound Keys

Of course, where such a derived ERM has been created in a suitable CASE tool, the entities thus created are populated with the attributes that were originally assigned to each normalised relation in the consolidated set of relations (shown in Figure 8.24).

***

Having dealt with the techniques related to data modelling, it is now time to turn our attention, in the next chapter, to the modelling of processes.

Chapter 9   The Main Techniques and How They Fit Together (2)

The first stage of BAA involves building an initial Data Model in parallel with a Process Model. In this chapter, the main techniques for process modelling will be examined in detail.

9.1   Techniques for Modelling Processes

The main reason that we analyze the business processes within a Business Area is in order to build up a logical model of **what** the business does as opposed to **how** those activities are currently being performed. The understanding that we form of the business operations within a Business Area is derived in a top-down manner through the systematic decomposition of functions into processes, and processes into elementary (or lowest level) processes. The technique of Process Decomposition used to derive an initial view of the functional structure of a Business Area is discussed in section 9.1.1. Initially we want this view of the activities to be unconstrained by considerations of interaction with data precisely because such issues together with factors such as the current organisation structure tend to cloud the underlying functional structure of the Business Area when viewed as a "system" that is dependent on various sorts of information.

As part of the modelling of processes, we become involved in confirming our understanding of the business itself by reviewing the relationships that the elementary processes have with one another. The most effective way of doing this without introducing the consideration of data is by looking at the dependencies that processes have upon one another. The process and techniques used in analyzing process dependencies are discussed in section 9.1.2.

The technique known as Data Flow Diagrams is familiar to many analysts, and is also used to understand the relationships between activities within a Business Area. As the name implies, it introduces questions of the interaction between activity and data, and for this reason is discussed in section 10.1.1 under the broader grouping of Interaction Analysis Techniques.

9.1.1   Process Decomposition

The primary technique that is used to identify the activities that occur within a

Business Area is Process Decomposition.[1] The emphasis in applying the technique is to identify **what** the business does within the scope of the Business Area, and not **how** the business is currently doing those activities. Where an ISP Functional Hierarchy exists, it provides the starting point for this activity; in other cases, the Functional Hierarchy constructed with a view to scoping the BAA is the starting point. Such a first-cut, high-level hierarchy may look like the one shown in Figure 9.1.

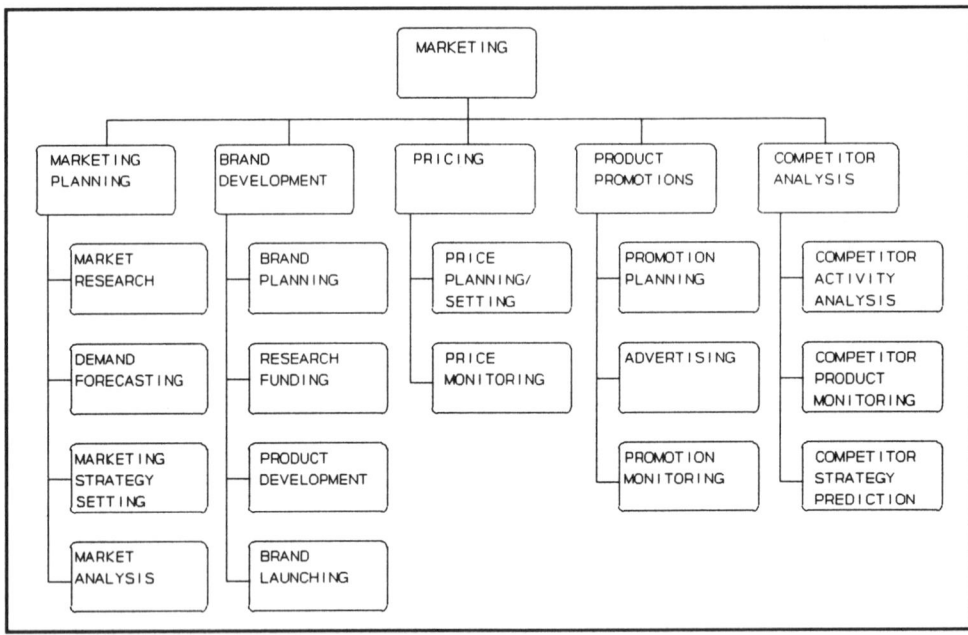

Figure 9.1 High-level Functional Hierarchy

In all cases, it is not simply the shape of the hierarchy that is important, the **definitions** underlying the activities represented play a crucial part in creating and checking the decomposition. The principle underlying the process is simple:

● Starting at the top level activity (most likely to be a function) define a further set

---

[1] While at BAA level we are mainly concerned with decomposing processes and with identifying elementary processes, we will actually begin applying the technique at the level of functions. Functional decomposition has been used as part of the ISP activity (see section 4.2.2) in order to understand the functional structure of the overall business. The principles underlying both Functional Decomposition and Process Decomposition are the same, and in some texts they are generically referred to as Activity Decomposition.

of activities which **together** *completely* **perform the activities of this function.** In this process, the definitions of activities higher up in the decomposition may be adjusted, which will inevitably have an impact on the subsequent decomposition of **that** higher level activity.

● For each new activity identified and defined, define a further set of activities which **together** *completely* **perform these activities.** Continue this process until the **Elementary Process** level has been reached.

Some working definitions of the concepts **Function, Process,** and **E l e m e n t a r y Process** are called for. By convention, all activities are depicted in the same way by means of a soft box as shown in Figure 9.2.

A *Function* occurs at the highest level of business activity and represents a group of business activities which support an

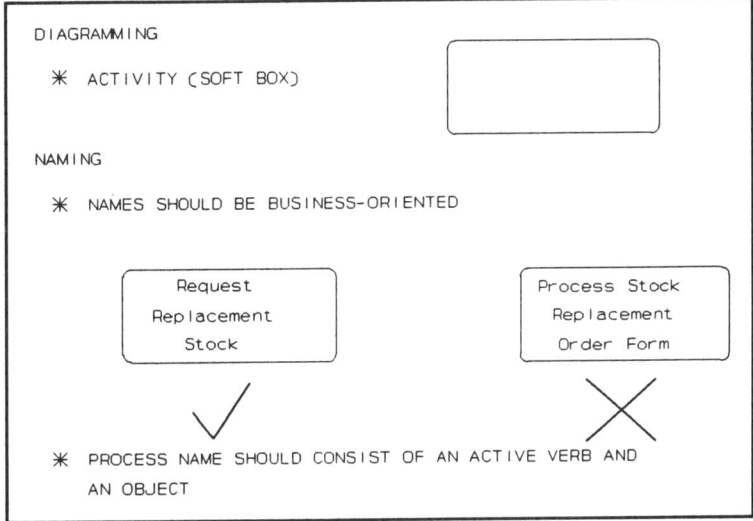

Figure 9.2 Conventions for Showing Activities

aspect of the business **independent of organisational structure.** A Function may be further decomposed into other Functions or Processes.

A *Process* is a business activity which results in the transformation of data. If answers can be provided to the questions "How often?" and "By whom?" the activity is performed, it is a Process rather than a Function. For example, **Purchasing** or **Acquisitions Planning** are Functions, whereas **Prepare Purchase Order** or **Issue Acquisitions Plan** are Processes. As these examples show, processes are named by a verb followed by a direct object; with functions, the naming is less direct and often contains a participle (verb with the -ing suffix). In either case, the name should reflect what the activities does, and should avoid names that reflect the specific way in which the process is currently being implemented. An example of the correct naming of processes is given in Figure 9.2.

An *Elementary Process* is a process, the execution of which performs a logical unit of work in measurable unit of time. As a result of the execution of the elementary process, the integrity of the data model is maintained. Figure 9.3 illustrates the effects on the data model of decomposing the elementary process Raise Purchase Order to sub-elementary level.

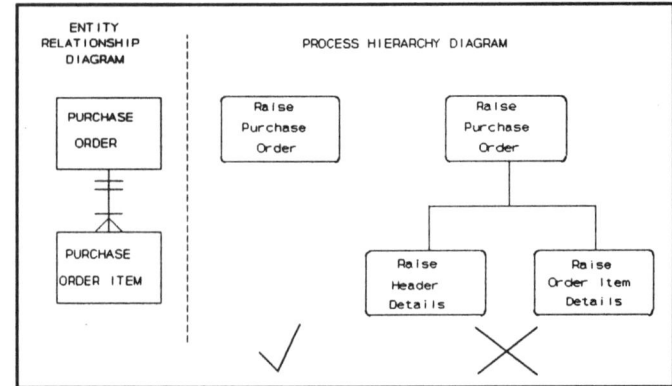

Figure 9.3 Elementary Process and Integrity of the Data Model

The results of the process decomposition can be depicted either in an indented list (Figure 9.4), or by means of a Process Hierarchy Diagram (PHD), which is also known as a Process Decomposition Diagram. This may be shown using a variety of conventions, some of which are shown in Figure 9.5.

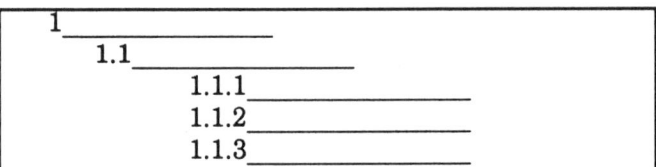

Figure 9.4 PHD as an Indented List

It is important to remember that a process decomposition, particularly in an I-CASE environment does not exist in isolation: depending on the conventions in use and the techniques that have been automated, the PHD interacts either with the Process Dependency Diagram (PDD) or the Data Flow Diagram (DFD) as Figure 9.6 illustrates.

By adding a new process to the PHD, consistency of the model demands that the new

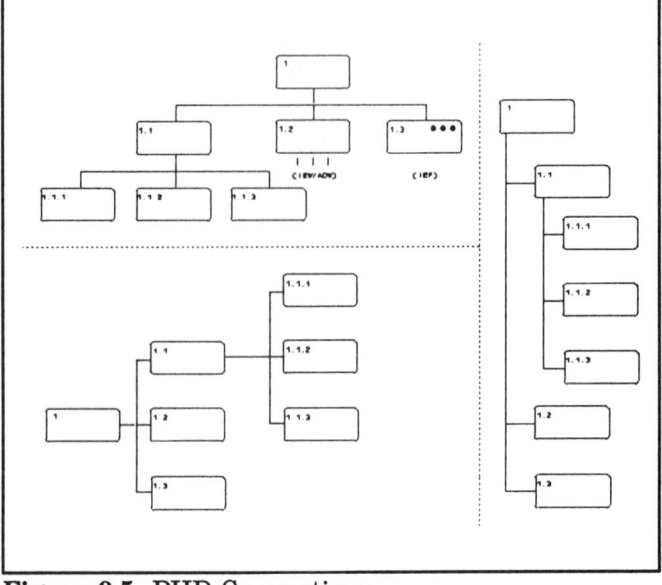

Figure 9.5 PHD Conventions

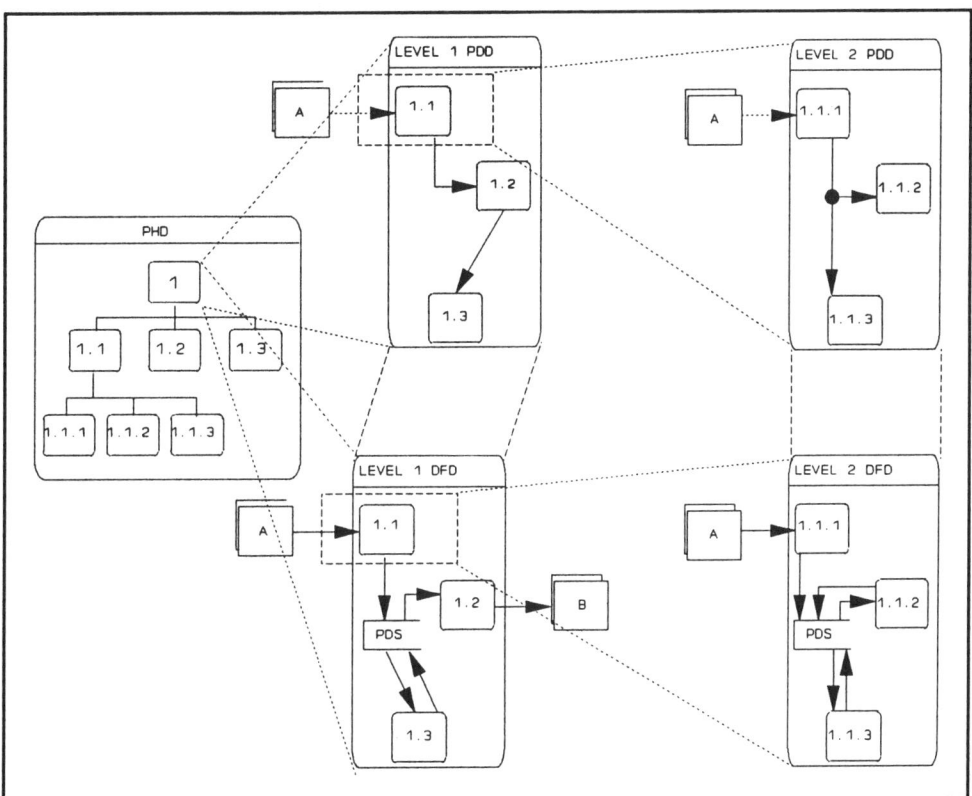

Figure 9.6 Interdependency between PHD, PDD and DFD

process is also reflected in the corresponding PDD or DFD. (Any effective I-CASE tool should ensure that such consistency is automatically maintained.) In a project environment, complete and accurate process decomposition to the elementary process level is achieved through a series of iterations between the PHD and the PDD/DFD as is illustrated in Figure 9.6. Each iteration between PHD and PDD/DFD increases the understanding of the elementary processes involved, resulting in a refinement in their definition.

Some Guidelines

It is impossible to come up with an accurate process decomposition immediately: the reason the activity is being undertaken is to facilitate the building up of an understanding of the underlying business structure. Even after a series of iterations between PHD and PDD/DFD have taken place, some areas of uncertainty will remain. These will include questions over the division of a process into elementary processes that may or may not logically do the same thing. In Figure 9.7, Process Order has been decomposed into Process Standing Order, Process Regular Order, and Process

Emergency Order. At first glance, these "elementary processes" seem logically to be identical, the division between them being based only on the **type** of ORDER being created. A great deal of time can be lost over arguments such as these, particularly where there is no obviously "better" solution. A canny project

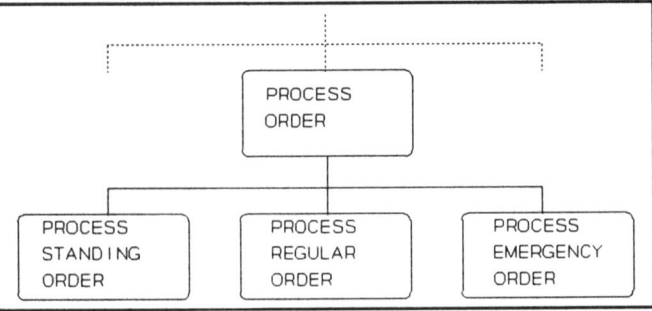

Figure 9.7 Decomposition of Process Order

manager should put pay to the argument by encouraging the team to move on, for techniques that will later be employed will settle the matter unambiguously: Entity Model Views (section 10.1.2) for each process will determine whether they "see" the same Entities and Attributes, while Process Action Diagrams (section 10.1.3) will determine and define whether they perform in the same way against the data model. If the processing differences are slight (accessing or updating a few different Attributes, for example), then the processes are the same, and the issue will be resolved by the business reality that is reflected.

The main purpose behind the PHD is to allow the major elementary processes to be defined. Once this aim has been achieved **to the satisfaction of the users**, the team should move on.

Additional general guidelines that will help in reviewing a PHD include:
- No activity may decompose into only one activity; and
- A decomposition into more than around five to seven activities should be examined closely.

Remember that the order in which activities appear in a PHD is not related to the order in which they are executed. Convention suggests that it is easier to understand a PHD where a sequence from left to right follows execution sequence, but the true dependencies of one activity upon another are shown in the PDD.

Lastly, not all legs of the Process Hierarchy need be decomposed to the same number of levels: the cut-off point remains the Elementary Process, no matter where on the hierarchy one occurs.

9.1.2   Analyzing Process Dependencies

Whereas the PHD allows us to identify the business activities within a Business Area, a Process Dependency Diagram (PDD) shows the dependencies between them.[2] A dependency exists when a process requires an event to occur (a time trigger), information to arrive (a data flow), or for data to reach a particular status (a status change) before the process can execute.

PDDs are particularly useful in helping us to refine our understanding of the processes that have been identified by consciously considering the dependency relationships that exist between them. By building a first-cut PHD, we have taken a view of what it is that the business does. PDDs allow us to refine that understanding **without introducing the issue of data interaction prematurely**. As a result of this refinement of our business understanding, process definitions are tightened up, and the overall functional structure of the Business Area is better reflected. This inevitably means that the PHD will change, and this iterative relationship between PHD and PDD is illustrated in Figure 9.6. The consistency between PHDs and PDDs is usually enforced by the I-CASE tool that implements their use.

9.1.2.1 Drawing up a PDD

PDDs can be constructed at any level of the hierarchy shown in the PHD. At the level chosen, all the activities (processes and functions) under the "parent" activity will appear in the PDD (see Figure 9.6). For each activity in the PDD, one needs to consider:
● What "triggers" the activity off?
● What is the activity reliant upon to make it work?
The answer to these questions may imply three different types of "triggers", which are discussed next, together with the conventions for depicting them.

Data Flows

A process may be activated by the arrival of information **from outside the Business Area**. This is shown by means of a **data flow** into the process from an **external entity** (also sometimes termed an external agent) as is shown in Figure 9.8. The convention used in PDDs to depict the process is the same "soft box" used in the PHD. The external entity is a double box (the same convention is used in Data Flow Diagrams see page

Figure 9.8 External Entity

---

[2] Although the name Process Dependency Diagram implies that they can only exist at a Process level (and it is at this level that we are primarily concerned in a BAA), the technique may be applied at a functional level as well. Process Dependency Diagrams are also sometimes referred to as Activity Dependency Diagrams.

159), while the data flow is a line labelled with the name of the flow, and with an arrow at the end showing the direction of the flow. In order to distinguish a flow containing data from a "pure" dependency,[3] the author has chosen to use a dotted line for data flows. (In some I-CASE tools, such distinctions are made by means of colour.)

The processes within the scope of the Business Area are contained within a boundary box, and data flows clearly cross the boundary box from external entity to process.

Interactivity Dependencies

Direct dependencies between processes are shown by a line connecting the processes with an arrow showing the direction of the dependency. Such dependencies imply a **status change** on the part of an entity, which is a trigger for the dependent process. In Figure 9.9, the process, Schedule Order, is dependent on "Order is Current." (Orders are only scheduled when they are "Current," not when they are already "Scheduled," "Cancelled," or "Delivered" - other potential statuses of the entity ORDER.) The order reaches the status "Current" as a result of the process, Take Order.

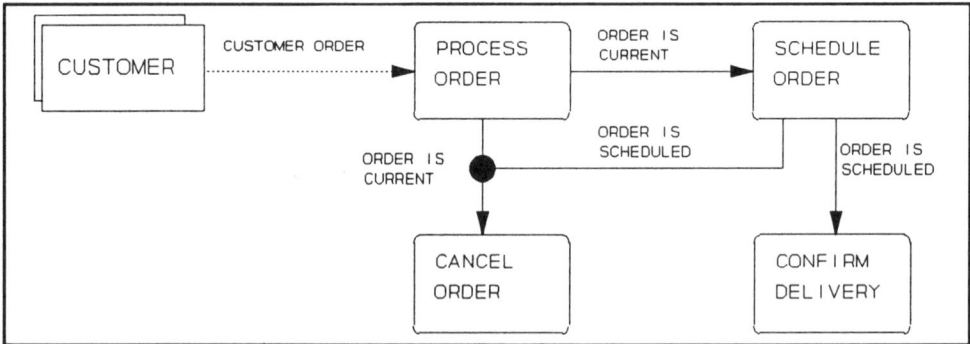

Figure 9.9 Order Processing PDD

Time Triggers

A particular process may be triggered by the passing of a particular point in time: the process, Pay Wages, will be executed at the end of a month. Such a temporal dependency is shown in Figure 9.10, where the time trigger

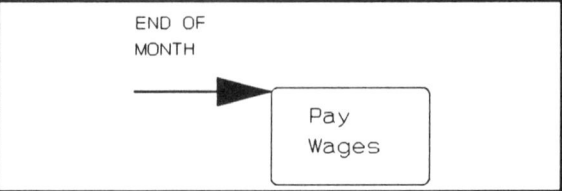

Figure 9.10 Temporal Dependency

---

[3] There is a difference between them in the type of information they contain.

is shown by means of a large arrow which contains a textual description of the event.

9.1.2.2 Types of Interactivity Dependencies

The simple type of interactivity dependency described above may appear to imply a straight sequence of activities or **Sequential Dependency** such as is shown in Figure 9.11.

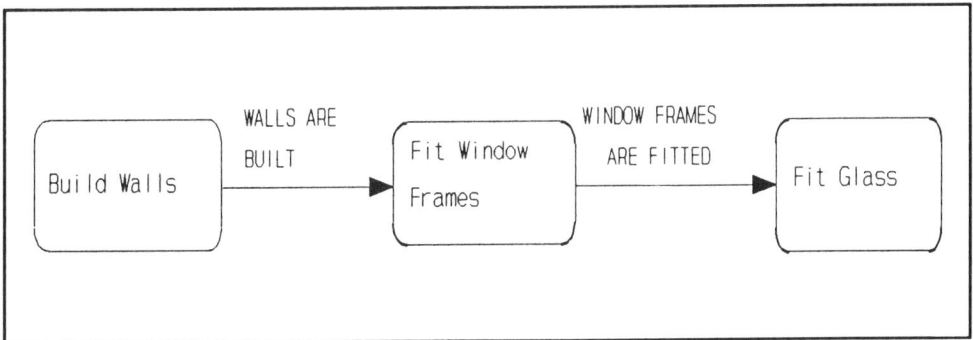

Figure 9.11 Sequential Dependency

However, the conventions used in PDDs can model much more complex dependencies, some of which will be illustrated and discussed.

A **Parallel Dependency** is present where two or more dependent activities require data to reach a state that is set by a prior activity. As Figure 9.12 illustrates, **both** activities may take place in parallel.

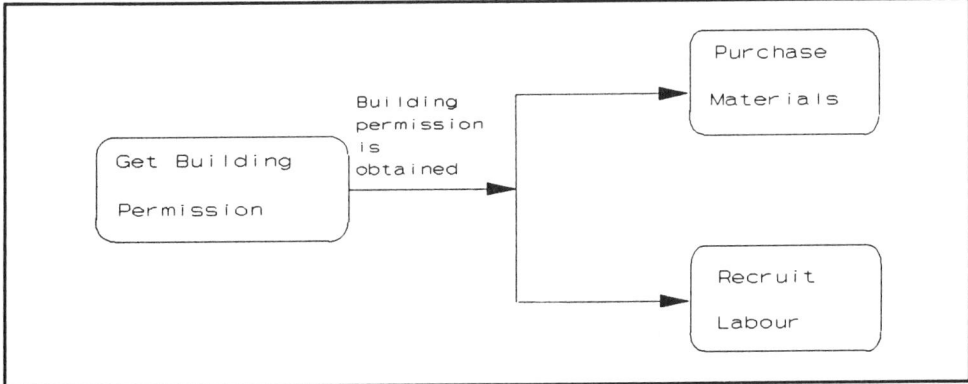

Figure 9.12 Parallel Dependency

By comparison, a **Mutually Exclusive Dependency** is present where two or more activities require the data to be in a state that is set by a prior activity, **but only one is executed.** The conventions for showing this are illustrated in Figure 9.13.

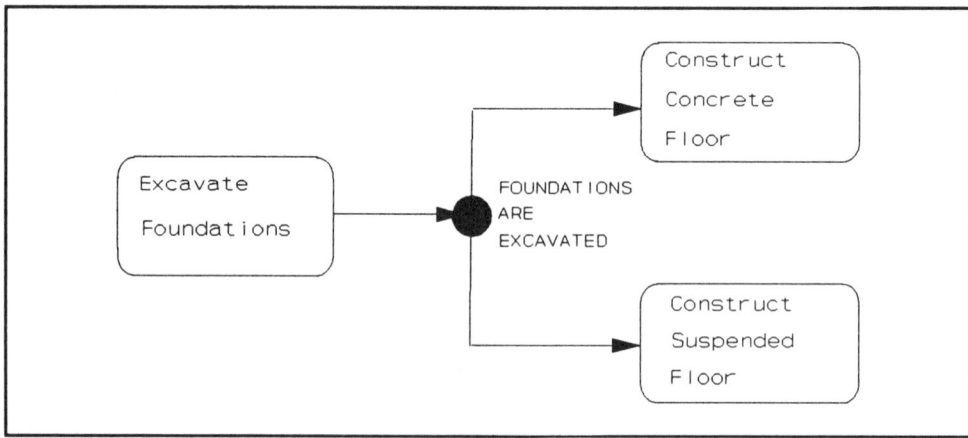

Figure 9.13 Mutually Exclusive Dependency

Optional Dependencies may exist where a process can be triggered off by more than one event, but **only one of the events is necessary** for the process to execute. In Figure 9.14, the process, Admit Patient (to a hospital), occurs either when a scheduled

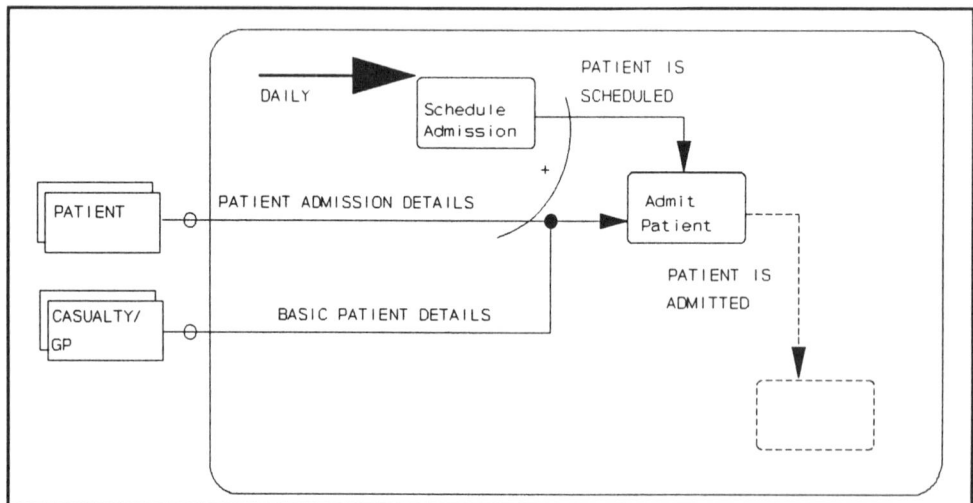

Figure 9.14 Optional Dependency

patient arrives or when an emergency patient arrives. In both cases, the arrival of the patient represents an arrival of information (data flow) albeit from different sources. As the content of the flows are possibly different, it has been chosen to represent them separately. However, the scheduled patient's arrival also implies that there is prior knowledge about the patient (the PATIENT is "Scheduled"), as is shown in the extract from a PDD in Figure 9.14. Note that the optional dependencies (in this case data flows) are signified with an "o" at the start of the line. The fact that the patient must **both** be scheduled **and** arrive in order for Admit Patient to execute is shown using an arc and a "+" sign.

A **Recursive Dependency** may occur where an activity is followed by one or more executions of the same activity. For example, the performance of an EMPLOYEE who is a MANAGER can only be appraised once all the MANAGER's LINE STAFF have had their performance appraised. The conventions for showing this situation are illustrated in Figure 9.15; it is clear that the recursion in the dependency mirrors a recursive relationship in the ERM.

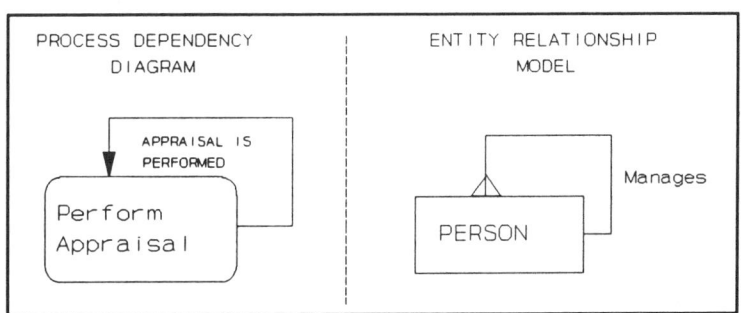

Figure 9.15 Recursive Dependency

9.1.2.3 PDD Guidelines

For analysts familiar with Data Flow Diagrams (DFDs) (which are discussed in section 10.1.1), a first cursory glance at PDDs may give the impression that they are nothing but DFDs without the Data Stores (which are discussed on page 159). However, as should be clear from the distinction made in section 9.1.2.1 between dependencies on information, and those on data reaching a particular state, PDDs contain a different set of information about the interrelationship between processes than DFDs do. The strength of the PDD is that it does not allow the extraneous issue of data interaction to be introduced into the analysis process too early.

In reviewing a PDD it should become clear that each activity identified in it must have at least one trigger. If the "firing off" of the process cannot be linked to some triggering event, then the analyst is forced to ask the question, "What does this process really do?" In this way, PDDs challenge the analyst's awareness of the business, and also facilitate the ability to identify genuine elementary processes. Furthermore, the business knowledge that is helping the analyst to determine that a process exists is unambiguously documented in the form of a dependency: the source of all such dependencies must not only be identified, but also defined and labelled. Data flow dependencies must reflect the nature of the data that is triggering the process off; pure dependencies are labelled to reflect the entity involved, and the status change it undergoes; and temporal dependencies are labelled with the time event that activated the process.

Where PDDs are constructed at various levels in the processing hierarchy (see Figure 9.6), data flows and dependencies that cross boundary boxes must be consistently reflected at each level of PDD.

It is possible to leave PDDs out of the analysis process, but the quality of the activity decomposition will be adversely affected as a result. Not all I-CASE tools support the technique; for those that do, they can be extremely useful and add value to the process of analyzing process. In all uses of a technique though, it would be wise to follow a simple rule of thumb, "Exploit the strength of the CASE tool, be aware of its weaknesses, and understand the risks involved in avoiding them." If the I-CASE tool does not support PDDs then it may be useful to construct them manually if there are parts of the Business Area in which complex dependencies exist. In the development of a new chemically based product, for example, the "Proposed" PRODUCT SUBSTANCE can only become "Branded" after undergoing a large series of tests, some related to its environmental effects, other to its laboratory performance, and still others related to its field trials. Then there are issues related to the branding, packaging, and marketing of the product, and its formal endorsement by major industrial users that may also determine whether and when the product will finally be marketed. Such a complex set of dependencies can only ever be fully reviewed with users using a PDD, and getting the dependencies right will have a significant effect on the shape and performance of any future system designed to support this part of the business.

***

Having analyzed the business area in terms of both data and processes, the BAA team needs now to turn its attention to the interaction between these elements of the overall business model. The techniques used in interaction analysis and in checking the resultant model form the subject of the following chapter.

Chapter 10　The Main Techniques and How They Fit Together (3)

The purpose behind analyzing the interaction between the data and process models is to expose any gaps in the analysts' understanding of the business area, and any deficiencies in the abilities of the business model to support the business. As a result, the initial stages of interaction analysis can be fraught with difficulties as models, hitherto perceived to be accurate, are mercilessly exposed by being exercised in minute detail. Generally though, after the initial chaos, the smooth flow of the project is restored.

It is important that detailed checking and confirmation of the model takes place in parallel with interaction analysis. The main techniques for performing these two tasks are the subject of this chapter.

10.1　Interaction Analysis Techniques

Having firmly established the functional structure of the Business Area, and isolated the elementary processes within it, it is time to turn to a consideration of how data and process interact. A number of techniques that assist in achieving that understanding are discussed in this section.

One such technique that is really a legacy from methodologies that are primarily process driven in their analysis emphasis is the Data Flow Diagram which is discussed in section 10.1.1.

While in theory each elementary process has access to all of the global pool of data represented in the ERM, in reality each elementary process sees only a circumscribed subset of the data. This view of the data is known as an Entity Model View, and techniques for analyzing and representing them are discussed in section 10.1.2.

The details of the actual processing each elementary process performs against the data model is detailed in a formal specification known as a Process Action Diagram which is designed to capture business logic and rules in an unambiguous fashion. Process Action Diagrams are discussed in section 10.1.3.

Each major entity contained within the scope of the Business Area has its own life history, or subset of its life history that is of interest to the business. The techniques for analyzing and diagrammatically presenting that Entity Life Cycle are discussed in section 10.1.4.

10.1.1 Analyzing Data Flows

Data Flow Diagrams (DFDs) are a technique used for modelling the information flows between business activities. At the highest level, the DFD documents the relationship that the Business Area has with its external world - the world that is outside of its scope, but from which it receives a flow of information, and to which it returns information.

The DFD can also be used to document the relationships that exist between processes in terms of the data that "flows" between them. In applying the DFD to this task, it is a top-down approach that involves the decomposition of the business activities and as such has a significant impact on the decomposition of activities (see section 9.1.1).

In general, DFDs are a useful diagrammatic technique which facilitates the achievement of a common understanding between users and business analysts.

10.1.1.1 Problems with Data Flow Diagrams in an IE Context

Within the IE context of attempting to construct a logical model of the Business Area, there is a fundamental conceptual problem with DFDs. We have constructed a data model which reflects the structure and content (entities and attributes) of information that is required to support the Business Area. Conceptually, all information resides **in the data model**. An elementary process will transfer data to and from the model, but it will only "transfer" data to another elementary process **via the data model**. So, data does not flow from one process to another, and the concept of a Data Flow Diagram in this context is really a misnomer.

There are a great number of potential dangers in the use of DFDs in an IE context. Firstly one should recognise that data **does not flow through a business**. This concept arises from representing a paper-based flow of control through a business, which may or may not still occur in some business areas. Where it does, analysts certainly do not want to replicate it. The danger with using a DFD to document such flows is that thinking may be circumscribed by **how things are currently being done**. Secondly, at this stage of the BAA process the team is attempting to understand the business process involved in a business area **independently of data**, and the DFD can introduce issues of data too early in the process, thereby constraining both their understanding and thinking. At worst they can end up replicating all the structural problems that are intrinsic in the current business system because their "analysis" of its processes in the DFD mirrors it too closely **in structure**.

Despite this fact, it is necessary for us to consider DFDs seriously because **they are used in specific applications of IE theory (i.e. in specific I-CASE tools)**. Furthermore, they are familiar to a generation of analysts for whom "structured analysis" is almost synonymous with DFDs - analysts who, like the author, were fostered on a solid, process-driven approach to systems analysis.[1] Where a chosen I-CASE tool is particularly strong on DFDs, it would be foolish to ignore its point of strength, but the project manager needs to be aware of the potential pitfalls of using DFDs. In reviewing DFDs, users themselves will often tend to fall back on the familiar, and a technique that can easily lapse into a replication of current practises may be used, or even manipulated by them to do so. To counter such possibilities, a project manager needs to ensure that DFDs are reviewed critically by both QA staff and by senior analysts (the process co-ordinator role) who are comfortable with the IE analytic thrust, and aware of the potential problems that may be lurking within a DFD.

Despite these comments, DFDs do play a clear role where the analysis of existing systems is undertaken. They are particularly strong at recording exactly **how** a specific system (manual or computerised) operates. If the intention of the analyst is to gain such understanding, then DFDs are a useful tool.

The discussion of DFDs below is based on a conventional approach to DFDs, but incorporates some suggestions that may assist in using them in a BAA context.

10.1.1.2 Data Flow Diagramming Conventions and Practices

DFDs can be constructed for any level in the PHD. The highest level DFD, often referred to as the **Context Diagram**, shows only the Business Area and the flows of data it receives from the world outside of its scope, and a simplified example of a context DFD is shown in Figure 10.1, where the scope is clearly not that of a complete

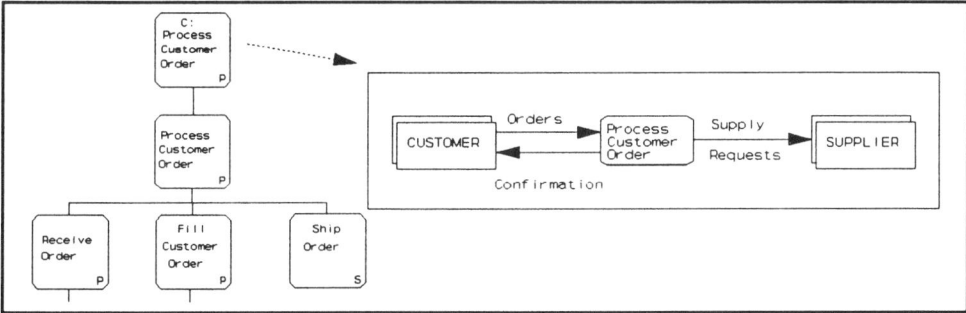

Figure 10.1 Context Data Flow Diagram

---

[1] Experience tends to show that the learning curve for analysts wishing to adopt IE principles is often significantly higher for those with previous experience of analysis. It can take a good systems analyst around six months to become a competent IE Business Analyst. Inexperienced graduates do not appear to have as many preconceptions to unlearn, and are productive a lot sooner.

Business Area.[2]

At the next level down (sometimes called the **Level 1 DFD**), the DFD contains all the processes that appear in the next level of the PHD. This is shown in Figure 10.2, where it should be noted that the data flows into and out of the level 1 DFD are consistent with those shown in the context DFD. In a similar way, a process within the level 1 DFD can be decomposed to a further level until the bottom level of the PHD is reached. Elementary processes are **not** decomposed into DFDs.

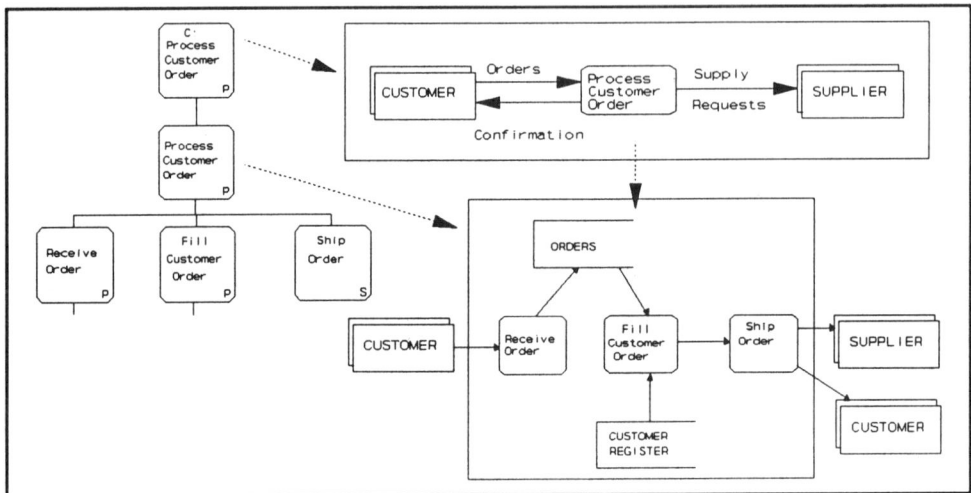

Figure 10.2 Level 1 Data Flow Diagram

Where DFDs are being constructed for BAA, the minimum set recommended is a context DFD, together with a set of DFDs at the elementary process level.

The basic components of the DFD and the conventions used for showing them are briefly discussed next.

The *Process* itself is shown using the same "soft box" convention used with PHDs (see Figure 9.2). Each process shown must have at least one input and one output. A process that does not have an incoming data flow has no incoming information that it can transform, and so is either inadequately defined or understood; a process with no

---

[2] The example shown uses a convention required by some I-CASE tools of requiring an artificial context level process to be introduced. This is signified by prefixing the process name by "C:" (for "Context"), and then decomposing it to a single process without the "C:". The convention has been retained as it makes the point more clearly.

outgoing data flow represents a black hole down which information disappears.

The *Data Store* is shown in Figure 10.3 and is used to represent a collection in any form of any type of data that is stored either permanently or temporarily. The

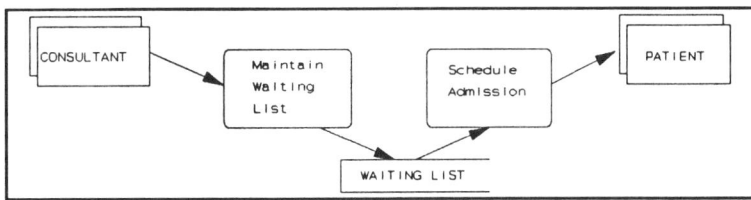

Figure 10.3 Data Store

data store has a name assigned to it, and data flowing between processes will usually go via a data store, unless the processes are synchronous.

It is important to understand that in a logical model of the Business Area, the concept of a data store is just a convenient device for grouping data items that are stored and/or accessed together. **The data store may have no actual existence as such: it is a grouping of data comprised of Entity Types and Attributes that are already defined in the data model.**

In an IE context, it has been found useful with some CASE tools to represent a single common data store, which maps to the full BAA data model, on any non-context DFD. In this case, all data flows between processes via the data store. Any data flow that has to go directly from one elementary process to another will imply that one or other of the elementary processes (or both) has been defined at a sub-elementary level and needs to be carefully reconsidered. In order to establish the specific subset of data that the processes uses, the concept of the Entity Model View, which is discussed in section 10.1.2, is used.

An *External Entity* (sometimes called an External Agent) is the source and/or recipient of a data flow that is outside of the boundary or the Business Area being considered. It may represent a person (Customer),

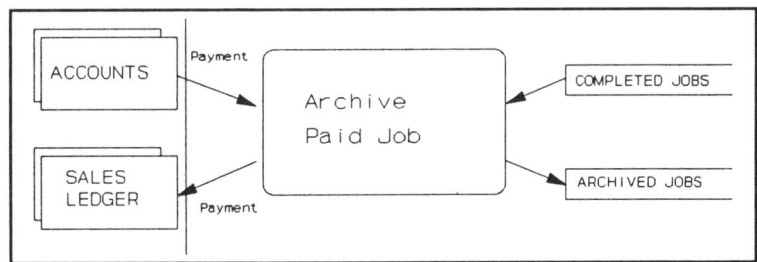

Figure 10.4 External Entity

business (Supplier), or system (General Ledger). The convention used for representing an external entity is shown in Figure 10.4.

The *Data Flow* is represented by a line with an arrow indicating the direction of flow. Each data flow shows the transfer of one grouping of data (eg. customer information,

invoice) in one
direction such as is
s h o w n   i n
Figure 10.5.

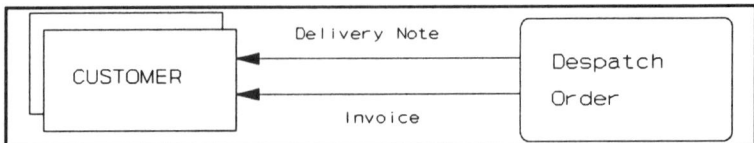

Figure 10.5 Data Flow

Lastly, Figure 10.6
shows the *Boundary
B o x* ,   w h i c h
represents the scope
of the process that
t h e   D F D   i s
documenting.   Not
all I-CASE tools that
support DFDs show
the boundary box.

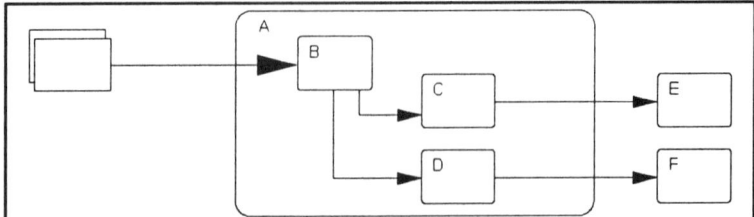

Figure 10.6 Boundary Box

10.1.1.3 General Data Flow Diagram Guidelines

A DFD with more than around 5 to 7 processes becomes difficult to read due to the
number of data flows involved. Try to review the decomposition of processes if a large
number of sub-processes result, and be careful in placing data flows to maximise
legibility.

Make sure that all data flows are connected at both ends: a data flow should have both
a source and a destination. Similarly, data stores must have both input and output
flows (when the data store is viewed across a complete set of DFDs). If this is not the
case, then the implication is that data placed in the store is never used, or data
somehow reaches a store in order to be used by a process. Both these cases indicate
some flaw either with the modelling itself, or with the business knowledge that was
the basis for the modelling. In the same vein, a process must have at least one input
and one output flow.

All data flows move to and from data stores and external agents via processes. Data
may, however, flow directly from one process to another if there is no time delay
between the execution of the two processes.[3]

It is essential that the DFDs are reviewed with users in order to ensure that the
analysts' understanding of the business is sound: ideally a user representative on the

---

[3] However, see the author's comments on direct flows of data between processes
when using a single data store to represent the whole data model (page 159).

analysis team should play a leading role in the construction of DFDs.

10.1.2 Entity Model Views

In theory, each process identified can have access to any entity and attribute that is contained in the data model. The technique of defining an Entity Model View (EMV) allows us to determine precisely which entities, attributes, and relationships the process interacts with. We are particularly concerned with the EMV for an elementary process, though it is, of course, possible to produce an EMV for a higher level process. (By this token, the EMV for the Business Area is the data model, for it contains all the entities, attributes and relations in the corporate data model that the Business Area "sees".)

It is possible to identify three types of EMV.

An *Import View* describes the data that enters the process from the outside. This is analogous to an external data flow into the process, and should be shown as such both in the PDD and the DFD that contain the process.[4]

An *Export View* describes the data that the process presents to the outside world. In a DFD this will correspond to a data flow from the process to an external entity. (There is, however, no analogous flow in a PDD.)[5]

The *Entity Action View* describes the direct interaction that the process will have with the data model: which entities, attributes, and relationships it will access to read, create, or to amend. Figure 10.7 shows how the three types of EMVs described relate to the elementary process.

When constructing EMVs in the context of Data Flow Diagrams, it is important to note that EMVs can be constructed not only for the process as a whole, but also for any data flows shown, and also for external entities and for data stores. It becomes obvious that the sum of the EMVs flowing into and out of a process represents the overall EMV for that process. If the convention described on page 159, of using a single data store to represent the data model, is applied, then the entity action view for a process is the

---

[4] In an elementary process that is eventually implemented as an on-line procedure, for example, the Import View will map directly onto a screen that is used to create and/or update information held in the system.

[5] In an elementary process that is eventually implemented as an on-line procedure, for example, the Export View will map directly onto a screen that is used to report on information held in the system. This may be a read only screen, or a screen that presents information held in the system for update. In the latter case, attributes for which update is permitted will also be found in the Import View for the process.

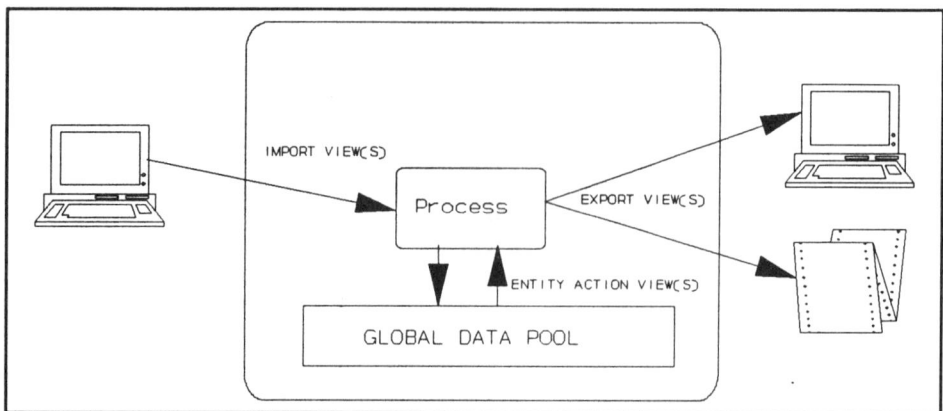

Figure 10.7 Entity Model Views

sum of the data flows into and out of the data store **from that process**. (Again, there is no analogous construct in the PDD.)

In describing all EMVs a clear distinction should be made between those attributes in the EMV that are **mandatory**, and those that are **optional**. The EMV may be represented as a subset of the overall ERM. This is illustrated in Figure 10.8. In this representation, the attributes relevant to the view are contained within the EMV, and usually can be accessed as such.

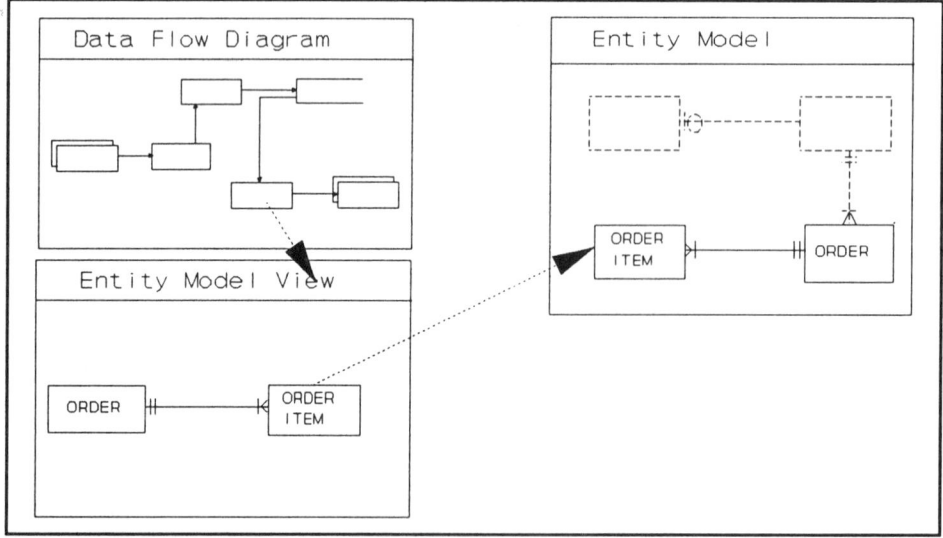

Figure 10.8 The EMV as a Subset of the Entity Model

```
Process            CONTROL_DIRECT_DEBIT_EXCEPTION

Import Views
   View IN of entity PAYMENT
      Attributes:
              BACS_PROCESSING_DATE
              DIRECT_DEBIT_EXCEPTION_VALUE
   View IN of entity PAYMENT_IN
      Attributes:
      Optional      INCOMING_NAME
              INCOMING_VALUE
              INCOMING_BANK_ACC_NO
              INCOMING_BANK_SRT_CODE
              DIRECT_DEBIT_INSTRUCTION_NUMBER

Entity Action Views
   View ENTITY of entity PAYPOINT
      Attributes:
              NUMBER
              START_DATE
              END_DATE
              TYPE
   View ENTITY of entity PAYMENT_FILE
      Attributes:
              IDENTIFIER
              PROCESSING_DATE
              BACS_PROCESSING_DATE
              STATUS_CODE
              STATUS_DESCRIPTION
              STATUS_REASON_CODE
              TRANSACTION_DATE
              DIRECT_DEBIT_EXCEPTION_VALUE
```

Figure 10.9 Alternative Form of Entity Model View

An alternative form of showing the EMV is shown in Figure 10.9. This is the sort of EMV representation that will be used within a Process Action Diagram (a structured specification for each elementary process, see section 10.1.3) and will ultimately form the basis for code (and screen) generation.

When EMVs are being identified, it is possible to identify additional attributes, relationships, and possibly even entities. These are added to the overall ERM, with the analyst always ensuring that the data model does not become denormalised as new attributes are included.

In explicitly linking each elementary process to the subset of the data model that it "sees", an analyst is forced to refine and redefine the definition of the elementary process itself. In doing so, not only is a clearer understanding of the elementary process itself achieved, a basis is also put in place for the further detailed analysis of **what exactly the elementary process does** in terms of its interaction with the data model. This topic is explicitly dealt with next.

10.1.3 Process Action Diagramming

At the heart of interaction analysis lies the Process Action Diagram (PAD). Its function within the IE context needs to be fully understood, as **the construction of PADs can take up to half the overall elapsed time of a BAA project.** It is particularly important, therefore, that the payoffs resulting from their use and the risks involved in not constructing them (or, alternatively in constructing them in an abridged form) need to be fully appreciated.

Before turning to these issues, it is necessary to understand what a PAD is, and to examine its main conventions.

10.1.3.1 Process Action Diagram Conventions

Basically, a PAD is a structured specification of **the business rules** contained in an elementary process. The overall construct of the PAD follows the basic principles of Structured English, in which a limited subset of the English language is used to specify the sequence of actions that occur in an Elementary Process. The PAD also allows us to express these actions using the three basic structured programming constructs of sequence, iteration, and branch. However, within the I-CASE tool context, the tool itself checks the overall consistency and integrity of the PAD against the contents of the project encyclopedia. In addition to this formal checking (which occurs to a greater or lesser extent, dependent on the I-CASE tool being used) certain diagrammatic conventions are added to the specification to facilitate our comprehension of it. Again, the exact conventions used will depend on the particular I-CASE tool itself.[6] Figure 10.10 illustrates an example of a PAD. In it, a number of the typical diagrammatic conventions are shown. The numbers shown in the figure relate to the following conventions:

1.   The **Title Block** contains free format text that serves as a brief introduction to the Elementary Process that is defined in the PAD. It will generally contain a succinct process definition, some information about the business events that trigger the

---

[6]   Of course, most I-CASE tools are currently directed at one or other target implementation environment, and this environment is likely to influence the nature of the syntactic structures that the tool imposes upon would-be users. For a further discussion of the implications of this fact, see pp. 168 onwards.

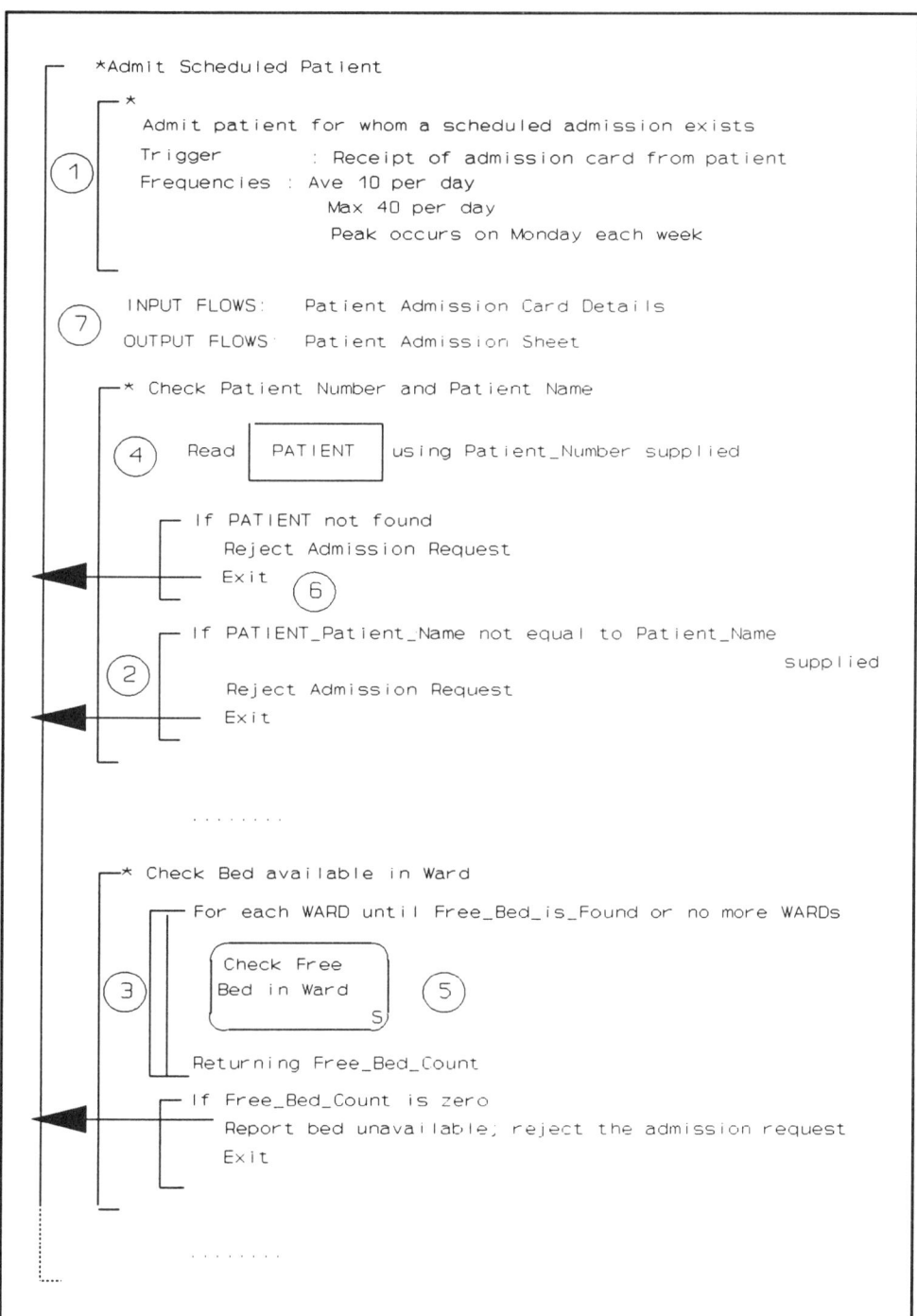

Figure 10.10 Example Process Action Diagram

process off, and some information about the frequencies with which the process is performed as well as key variations in them.

2. The **Selection Block** visually represents the alternative paths to be followed in a branch, or "if" statement, and may also be applied to multi-branch "ifs" and, in some implementations of PADs, to "Case" statements. An example of the latter is shown in Figure 10.11.

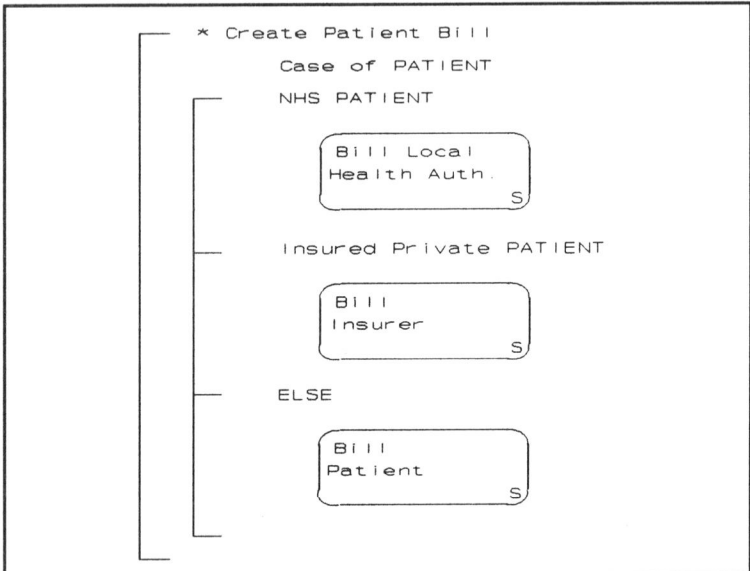

Figure 10.11 CASE Statement

3. **Repetition Blocks** are used to show the extent of the application of a "loop", where a series of actions are repeated based on a condition ("FOR EACH..." or "DO WHILE [statement is true]..." or "DO... UNTIL [statement is true])

4. **Data Access** is highlighted by using the same box used in ERMs to represent an entity immediately following the use of one of a set of reserved words - Read, Create, Update, and Delete. The I-CASE tool will not allow any of these verbs to be used against an entity that has not been defined in the encyclopedia. In some I-CASE implementations, the tool also checks that the unique identifiers for the entity itself have been identified, and/or assigned values. In reading from one entity to another, some tools will check that the relationship that is used for navigation exists.

    The strength of these checking facilities also determines how strict or lenient the I-CASE tool is in enforcing rules. The trade-off may mean that a more rigorous checking of rules imposes very tight disciplines on the PAD writers: their task is then made much more complicated **if** the overall quality of the model - particularly the data model - is poor.[7] The I-CASE tools that check PADs more rigorously also generally have the ability to generate various checking matrices automatically (see section 10.2), and this will increase the overall quality of the analysis being done.

5. **A Process Action Block (PAB)** is a self-contained specification of a piece of business logic that is used in more than one context. It may contain a simple set of business rules such as the allocation of free stock to a customer's order, or may in reality be a complex algorithm in its own right such as the measurement of bulk liquid stock in a container before and after delivery occurs.

    The PAB is referred to in the PAD using the "soft box" convention associated with processes. In some I-CASE tools, the box itself can be "exploded" out to reveal the detailed logic it contains.

6. The **Exit** construct gives a visual representation of where the flow of logic goes to in the case of some or other condition being fulfilled.

7. A representation of the **Entity Model View** is also an intrinsic part of the PAD. This may take the format of a brief description of the input and output data flows, such as is shown in Figure 10.10, or may be a full ERM description such as is shown in Figure 10.9.

The PAD constructs that have been described, and their exact implementation, are highly dependent on a particular CASE tool. As a result, we need to consider questions like the purpose behind constructing PADs, whether they are required for all elementary processes that have been identified, and to what level of detail and rigour they need to be described.

10.1.3.2 Why Bother with PADs?

There are two main reasons for the formal construction of PADs: they unambiguously describe the business logic that underlies an elementary process, and, in achieving this description in terms of the business's interaction with the information contained within the data model, the PAD allows us to exercise and cross-check the data model itself. Both of these are fundamental issues relating to quality: in describing business logic in a formal way that unambiguously reflects an understanding of it, flaws and faults in that understanding can be identified and rectified. At the same time it is possible to ensure that the correct information structures are in place to enable the process to execute. When we consider the question of the level of detail appropriate to a PAD, it will become evident that this issue is really a question of the granularity of the quality checks that we wish to put into place, or to make an intrinsic part of the

---

[7] See also page 169 where the use of PADs in verifying the data model is discussed.

analysis process.

There is a further dimension to the question of whether or not a PAD should be written and the appropriate level of detail it should contain, and that has to do with the question of whether the PADs will be used merely as a description of the business rules, or if it will be the basis from which automatic code generation will take place.[8] If code generation via the PAD is envisaged, then it is essential to describe the logic fully and in accordance with all the syntactic rules that a particular CASE tool imposes. This is undertaken precisely because the capturing of full details at this stage prevents additional analysis of the business at the design stage. However, it should be noted that the mechanisms of PAD "coding" bear a close affinity to programming, and some organisations have found it more appropriate to postpone the encoding of PADs to the BSD stage when the detailed specification of system procedures through Procedure Action Diagrams (see sections 12.3.3 and 12.3.4) is combined with the rigorous analysis and definition of business logic. In such a case, the conscious decision has been made to combine two related activities: the major risk that this imposes upon the analysis then relates to the checking and confirming of the overall business model. In order to minimise this risk, it is then necessary at least to describe the high-level effects that the process will have on the data model so as to be able to construct a Process to Entity CRUD Matrix, the full implications of which are discussed in section 10.2.1.

In recognising that major aspects of code generation are determined from the PAD, it becomes reasonably obvious that the syntactic structures and rules that a particular CASE tool may impose upon the construction of PADs is likely to bear a strong affinity (and even resemblance) to the target environment. A PAD that will ultimately generate CICS DB2 code will be quite different in structure to the equivalent PAD designed to generate ORACLE SQL*FORMS.[9] (This should not be the case in theory, but the general statement does reflect the current state of the art.)

A major benefit of constructing PADs in detail is the rigour with which they allow the interaction with the data model to be checked. However, the more rigorous the on-line checking a CASE tool applies to PADs, the less flexibility do they afford to would-be PAD writers. In some projects, PAD writers have resorted to constructing the skeleton

---

[8] It should be noted that the PAD (or the business logic it contains) needs to be incorporated into a Procedure Action Diagram (PrAD) for ultimate code generation. The PrAD is basically a specification of the **system** procedures that will support the elementary process, and contain elements such as screen handling, and the processing of error conditions.

[9] This is certainly the current state with the leading I-CASE tools. However, it is recognised that the future application of some intelligent processing to the translation from PAD to code is likely to change the physical constraints described.

and basic details of the PAD manually (often in a word processor) and later coded them up in the CASE tool.

Whatever mechanism is used, and no matter what level of detail is deemed to be appropriate, the PAD can be seen to be a useful tool in the checking of the data model. When a PAD is being written, it is essential to have a copy of the EMV for the elementary process on hand. Then, as the business logic is being recorded, the EMV is annotated and manually cross-checked against the process. In this way, the subset of an ERM is subjected to an extremely thorough scrutiny with a view to establishing whether all entities have been identified, whether the necessary relationships to support the process's navigation through the data model are in place, whether identifying attributes are in place and alternative identifiers are marked as such, and lastly whether all necessary attributes required to support the process have been defined.

At the most basic level, though, this process involves simply ensuring that the required navigation through the data model is possible. Figure 10.12 shows how the EMV is marked up (by hand) in order to check it against the PAD shown in Figure 10.13 (1) - (2). The marked-up ERM is sometimes referred to as an Entity Action Diagram, and, though it is useful as a working document, it is of no real benefit to designers, and should not be "dressed up" as an end-of-BAA deliverable.

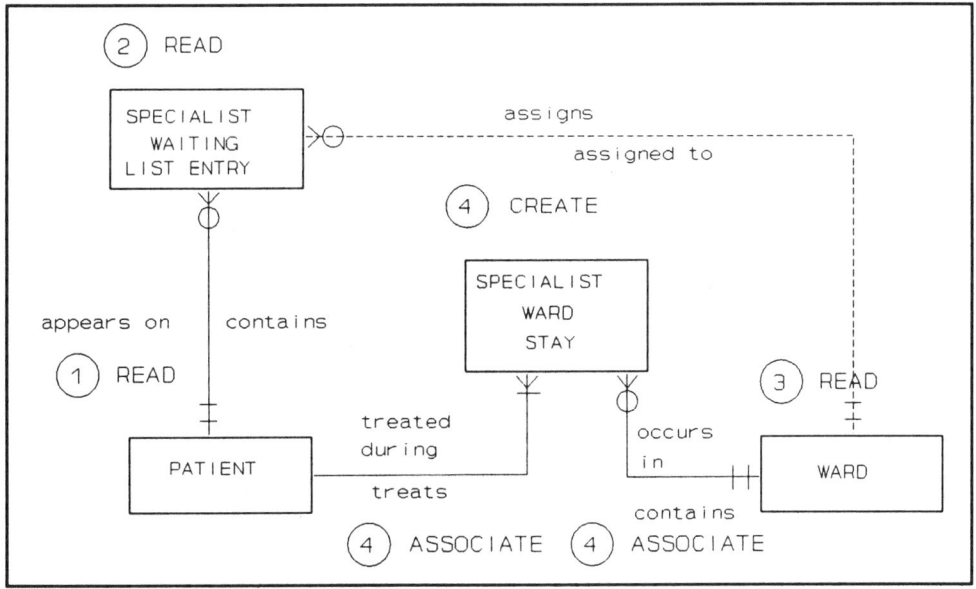

Figure 10.12 Marked-up EMV for an Elementary Process

The information recorded in the PAD and Entity Action Diagram need to transferred to a matrix, a row of which summarises each elementary process's interaction with the

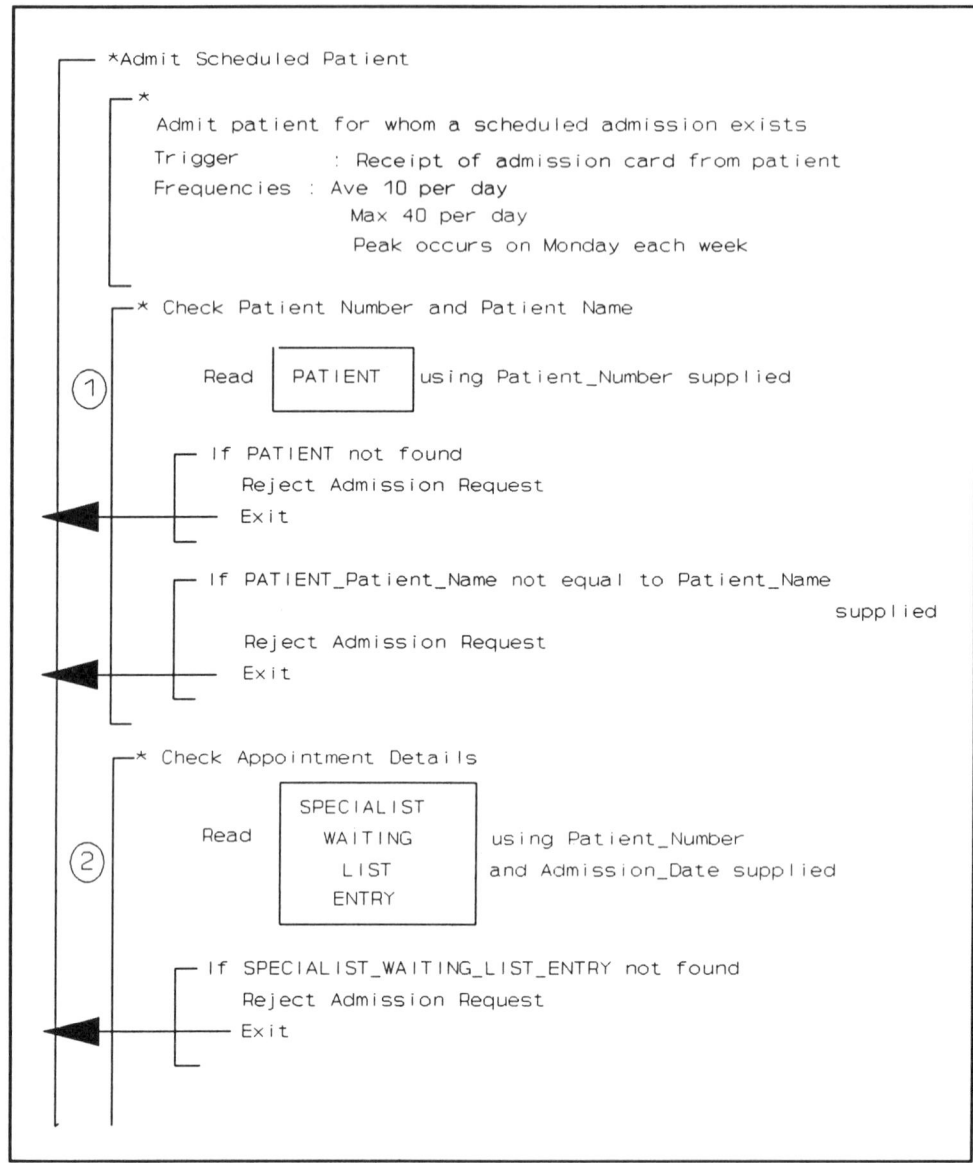

Figure 10.13 (1) PAD Cross-referenced to EMV (Figure 10.12)

data model. The matrix maps the process against each entity it interacts with, using the letters C, R, U, and D to indicate whether the process Creates, Reads, Updates, or Deletes the entity in question. The uses of such a CRUD matrix are explained further in section 10.2.1.

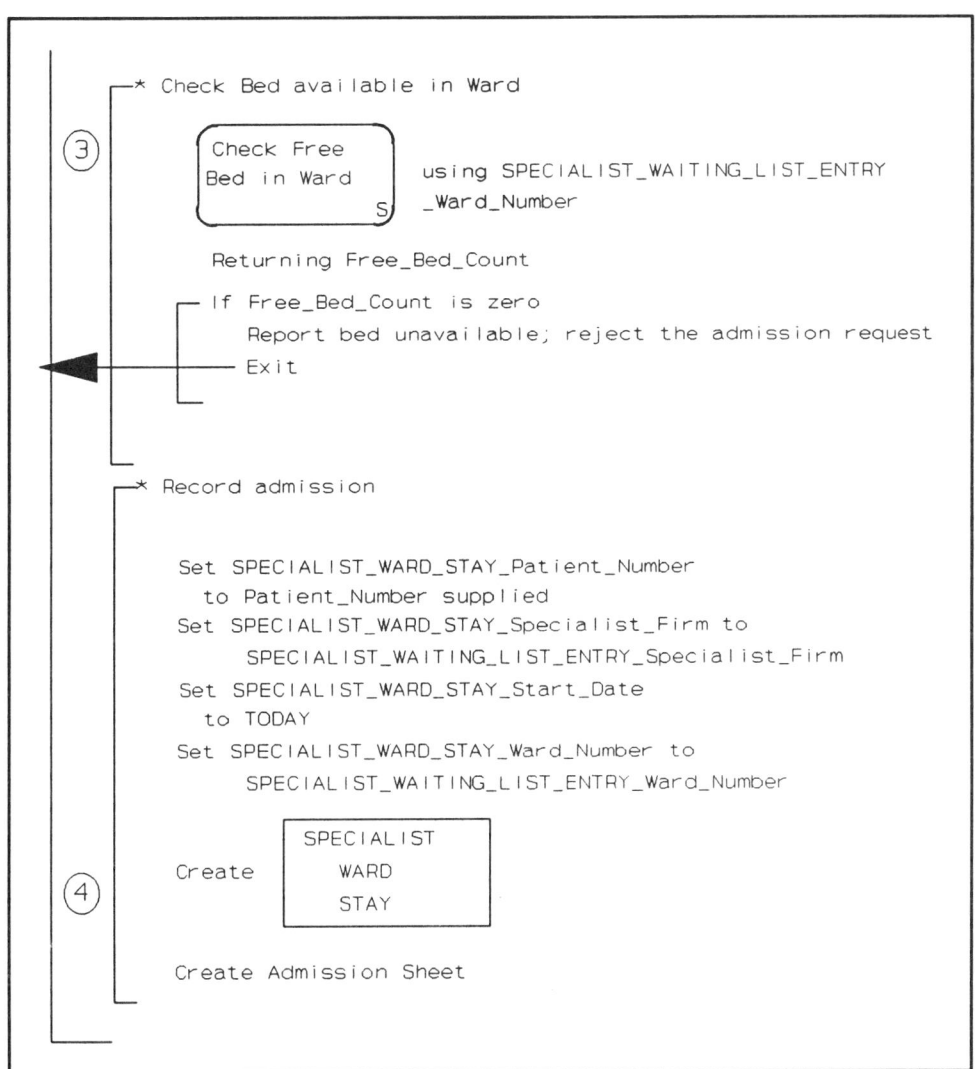

Figure 10.13 (2) PAD Cross-referenced to EMV (Figure 10.12)

From this discussion, it must be evident that the very least that can be expected of a PAD is that it provides a formal definition in outline of the business logic that the elementary process executes, and that it is supportive to the less formal and rigorous prose **description** of the process recorded within the CASE tool. The least then to be expected would be a skeleton PAD that looks something like the one shown in Figure 10.14. A more thorough version of the same PAD is given in Figure 10.13.

A final question that needs to be addressed is whether it is necessary to write any form of PAD at all for every elementary process that has been identified. The theoretical

```
*Admit Scheduled Patient


    Admit patient for whom a scheduled admission exists
    Trigger          : Receipt of admission card from patient
    Frequencies : Ave 10 per day
                   Max 40 per day
                   Peak occurs on Monday each week


  *  Check Patient Number and Patient Name
       Reject Patient if not found

  *  Check Appointment Details
       Reject Patient if no Appointment found

  *  Check Bed available in Ward
       Reject Patient if no Bed is available


  *  Record admission
       Create Patient Admission Sheet
```

Figure 10.14 Skeleton Process Action Diagram

answer is, of course, yes. However, the reality of deadlines, and the need to use scarce analytic resources most effectively, mean that in practice it will only be necessary to write PADs for those elementary processes that are likely to be computerised, **and/or** for the subset of elementary processes where it is perceived that the real business benefits will be derived as a result of the introduction of a computerised system.

There are some risks involved in leaving some elementary processes out: these are that those processes not subjected to rigorous analysis may contain important data interactions that will improve the quality of the underlying data model. Here the risk is probably minimal: is it worth undertaking a large amount of work for a small return in quality? Almost certainly not. The second area of risk is that priorities may change, and what is seen as an area of little benefit to the business today may not be seen in that light in some future period. The practical focus, however, should be on deriving real benefits **now**, and some of the stability analysis undertaken as part of the checking of the model (see section 10.2.3) will indicate whether it is necessary to undertake any additional speculative analysis. In such a case, the users will be firmly in the driver seat, and should ensure that the analysis does not merely become an academic exercise.

10.1.4 Entity Life Cycle Analysis

The analysis of the life cycle of the main entities within a Business Area is a useful aid both in achieving a better understanding of those entities' roles within the Business Area, and in understanding the overall business model where a large number of complex transitions in entity states occur. Entity Life Cycle Diagrams (ELC) present the "life history" of the entity in question in a diagrammatic format, which allows gaps in the processing model to be identified. Furthermore, where an entity's processing occurs across the boundaries of a number of Business Areas, an ELC for the entity can make sure that the exact processing boundaries are unambiguously defined and understood by all participating analysis teams.

The main objective behind analyzing entity life cycles is to understand the life history of the entities that are key to the Business Area being analyzed. As a result of this process, the analyst can ensure that all changes of state that affect the entity are identified, and that the processes that effect the status changes are identified. As the status change of a particular entity often acts as the trigger for another process, there is a clear affinity between the ELC and the PDD in which such status changes are shown as dependencies (see section 9.1.2, especially page 150).

ELCs are only drawn up for those entities that are of central business importance to the Business Area being analyzed. The user representative is the best person to identify such entities. An initial ELC should be drawn up which identifies all the statuses that the entity can reach, and all valid transitions from one status to another. Such an ELC is shown in Figure 10.15 where the basic conventions used in ELCs are shown.

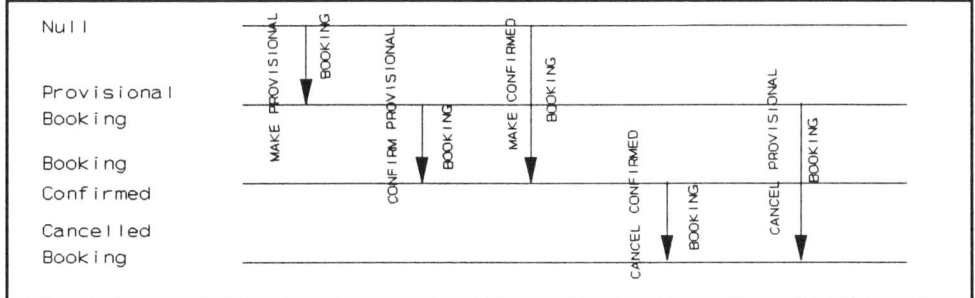

Figure 10.15 Entity Life Cycle Diagram

Each valid state that the entity can be in is represented by a horizontal line. The null state represents that state from which the entity comes into being in terms of the scope

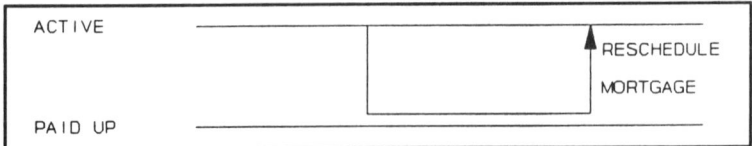

Figure 10.16 ELC Showing No Change in State

of the Business Area.[10]   The transition from the null state represents the "birth" of the entity from our perspective, and the state it is "born into" is known as the start state. An arrow is used to represent the change in state, and the event which drives that state change forms the label for the arrow. Any state which does not result in a further state change (i.e. that does not have an arrow leaving it) is known as an end state. As is shown in Figure 10.16, major events that act upon key entities may not result in a state change.

Once an ELC has been drawn up for all key entities, and the results have been reviewed with the users, each ELC can be used to further check the interaction analysis and growing understanding of the Business Area processing. Where PDDs have been drawn up, at an elementary process level, each inter-process dependency should map to a state change on an ELC unless, of course, it affects an entity for which an ELC has not been drawn up. If there are a large number of such cases for a single entity, then this indicates that an ELC **should** be constructed for the entity. It is then possible to ensure that for each state change shown on the ELC, a process can be identified that effects that change, and this fact can be confirmed at high-level by reference to the entry for that process in the CRUD matrix, and in detail by examining the PAD that defines the process.

From this description, it should be evident that the ELC is a useful technique for achieving a focused understanding of key parts of the Business Area, and then for checking that the relevant entities are fully processed as a result of the interaction analysis that has been undertaken. ELCs are easy and swift to draw up, and a useful aid to both analysis and the checking of the integrity of the overall business model.

10.2   Confirmation and Checking of the Business Model

Although questions related to the confirming and checking of the Business Model are here discussed formally and separately within the context of the techniques that are applicable to BAA, this does not imply that such quality checking only takes place at this stage in the BAA process. The construction of a quality plan as an intrinsic part of the overall project plan was emphasised in section 6.5.2, and the idea of building quality into the BAA process was addressed there. As a result, quality checking, and

---

[10]   Where the ELC is being used to co-ordinate the entity across a number of Business Areas, the transition from the null state represents when the entity comes into being **for the whole business** not just for a particular Business Area.

specifically some of the techniques that will be discussed in this section, **should be an ongoing and intrinsic part of any BAA project.** Any team that waits until the end of the project before it checks its work is courting disaster. However, there should, in addition, be a formal confirmation and checking of the overall model at this stage as part of the final wrap-up of the project: there is no sense in being careful and disciplined all the way through the analysis, only to destroy the overall integrity of the model through carelessness as the pressures to complete become intense.

Confirming and checking the model imply that three aspects of the overall model have to be reviewed. These are its overall correctness, its completeness, and its stability in the light of known and foreseen changing business needs.

10.2.1 Completeness Checking

In checking that the model is complete, there is a need to ensure that all the processes, entities, attributes, and relationships within the Business Area have been found and are fully defined.[11] Furthermore, it is necessary to ensure that each entity (and, depending on the granularity of the quality check, attribute and relationship) is created, updated, or deleted.[12]

Completeness checking can be a fairly mechanical activity, and there are three main techniques that can aid the analyst in this task. Many I-CASE tools have a suite of analysis reports that highlight anomalies with the business model. These always include the ability to list what is in the model and to check visually, for example, that each entity or attribute has a definition.

I-CASE tools that are generally non-methodology specific will allow analysts to enter almost anything into the supporting database or encyclopedia. It is then necessary for the analyst to run a series of consistency checks that will highlight potential problems with the model. I-CASE tools that are more specifically focused on IE will usually enforce many of the rules on-line. So, for example, it will not be possible to identify an attribute without specifically assigning it to an entity. Even these I-CASE tools, however, have checking and analysis reports which will highlight inconsistencies and areas of incompleteness in the model. Where the I-CASE tool is going to be used for code generation, it is essential that the model is brought into a state that is sufficient for the tool to do its work. In other cases, the project manager may consciously decide to allow the anomalies to remain either because they will be specifically addressed in the design phase (in which case this fact should be recorded as part of the project control mechanism) or because a transition will be made into a different design and

---

[11] The scope of such completeness checking is determined by the concluding scope of the BAA project, which may no longer be the complete Business Area.

[12] As we shall see, where this is not the case, anomalies must be accounted for.

build environment where other rules of consistency and integrity may apply.

A second source of completeness checking lies in comparison checks which can be made with parts of existing systems, be they manual or computerised. Points at which comparisons may effectively be made include:

Business Model	Current System(s)
Entity Relationship Model	Canonical (Derived) Model
Elementary Process	Procedure Program
Entity Type	Record File Table
Attribute	Field Column

In making such comparisons, any differences that are encountered may not necessarily indicate a flaw in the analysis, for they may show up expected differences with a flawed system, the scope of which may overlap with, but still differ from the Business Area. All such differences should, though, be analyzed and accounted for.

Another simple way of making such comparisons is via the construction of matrices.

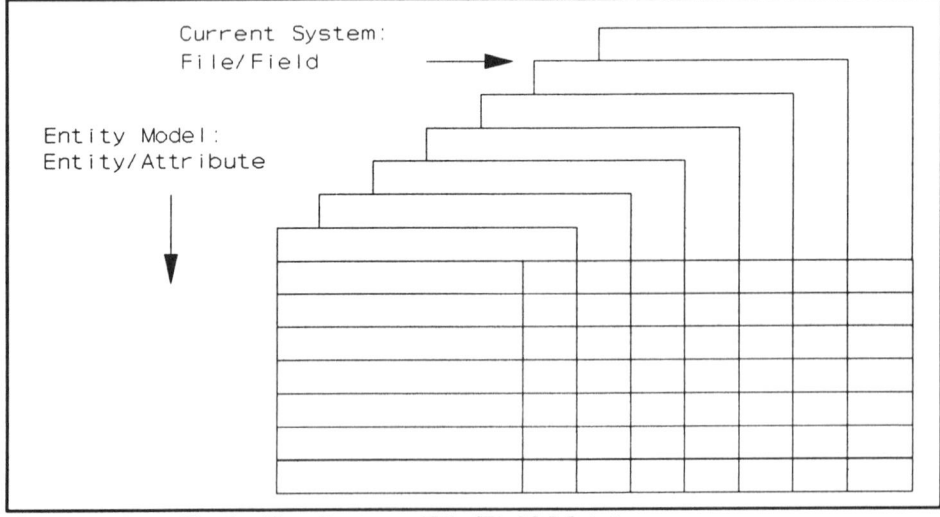

Figure 10.17 Entity/Attribute vs File/Field Matrix

For example, the matrix shown in Figure 10.17 compares the ERM on an Entity/Attribute level with the File/Field structure of an existing system. Such a matrix can easily be used to highlight significant points of difference. It does, however, have a very practical additional use in that it formally maps the Business Area model to an existing system. This mapping could then be used as a means of:

● Ensuring, where a current system is going to be replaced as a result of the BAA initiative, that the Business Model does contain within it all the data elements that were involved in the old system. The matrix serves as a means for identifying gaps that exist, not only in the analysis itself, but also in the overlapping, but not necessarily equivalent scopes between Business Area and system.

● Identifying and defining interfaces to and from the existing system with any additional systems that grow from the BAA activity. This assumes that the existing system is to remain in place, or will be minimally affected directly by systems arising from the BAA.

● On the same assumption, the matrix can form the basis for the re-engineering of the existing system. This can prove to be of particularly valuable assistance with poorly documented and structured current systems that are causing maintenance problems. In one such case, where no money was available to redesign a functional system that was adding value to the business, but that was proving costly and troublesome to enhance, the mapping between the system and the BAA model served as the means for adding value to system releases. Not only could the additional functionality be provided, with the matrix mapping becoming the key source of information about potential knock-on effects, the system's structural design problems could, where applicable, be slowly remedied without an appreciable additional amount of effort being expended. In a short period, data redundancy within the system was reduced significantly, thereby making the task of the maintenance team a less hazardous one.

An additional form of comparison checking is facilitated by the building up of a **CRUD Matrix**. In its most basic form, this matrix maps the interaction that elementary processes have with entities by indicating whether they Create, Read, Update, or Delete the entities. By means of a CRUD matrix it becomes easy to check the overall business model in two main ways. By reading the matrix horizontally (see Figure 10.18), the analyst can determine whether each elementary process is doing what is expected of it in terms of its interaction with the data model. In an extreme case, if no entries were present for a particular elementary process, then the analyst would clearly have to ask the questions, "What on earth is this process **really** doing? Do we really have a process here?" Similarly, by reading the matrix vertically, the analyst can see a summary of how processes interact with a particular data entity, and quickly determine whether the entity is in fact used within the business area (no interactions against a particular entity should be treated with suspicion), and whether its full life cycle is addressed. If the entity is not created, updated, and deleted in the

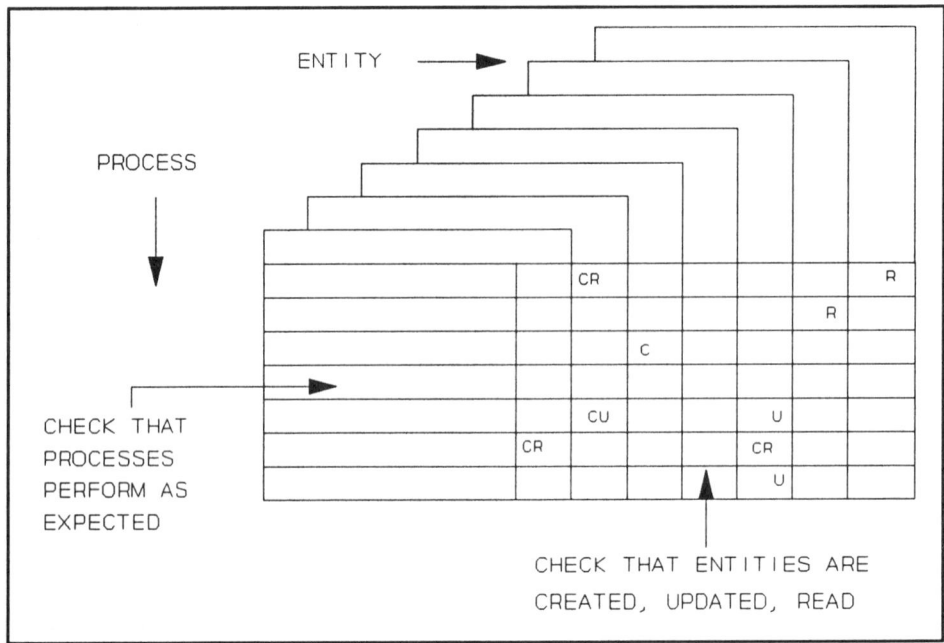

Figure 10.18 CRUD Matrix

business area, the analyst needs to make sure that it is clearly understood where these data interactions take place.

The construction of the CRUD matrix should be an integral part of the interaction analysis. As each elementary process is defined to whatever level of detail is viewed to be appropriate, a corresponding entry in the CRUD matrix should be made. The project manager is able then also to use the evolving CRUD matrix both as a barometer of progress, and as an early warning system of potential problems and gaps in the team's understanding of the business.

It is worth noting that there are no "Ds" in Figure 10.18. This is often a reflection of the fact that the **business** would prefer not to lose any of the information it has gathered. Business procedures, however, do give an indication of the "rules" for retaining "dead" data before it is archived. Such archiving procedures are where, in terms of the ERM, the deletes occur. Such business procedures are more fully dealt with in the Business System Design Phase (see section 12.3.2.1).

It is also possible to construct additional CRUD matrices and those with similar functions to assist in completeness checking. The most obvious of these is a CRUD matrix that maps Elementary Process to Entity/Attribute in order to check that every attribute described in the ERM is, in fact, accessed. Drawing up such a matrix manually is extremely cumbersome, and so a full version of such a matrix should only be contemplated where it can be automatically generated by the CASE tool being used.[13] Where absolute accuracy with the data model is essential, the construction of such a matrix may prove beneficial.

Even at an entity level, a CRUD matrix can do no more than provide a means for checking that the entities themselves are created, read, etc. What it fails to monitor is the creation and deletion of the relationships between entities. A matrix that maps elementary processes to the relationships shown in the ERM in terms of the interaction between them will show where relationships are broken (Disassociated), made (Associated), and moved from one entity to another (Transferred). Such a "DAT" matrix can improve the quality checking of the analysis work done, but can be cumbersome to create, and is only really viable where it can be generated directly by the CASE tool.[14]

10.2.2 Correctness Checking

There are two key elements to checking that the business model is correct in its representation of the ways in which the business area interacts with information: the first of these is to ensure that the model reflects the users' perception of their business; the second involves applying theoretical checks on the model to ensure that no basic rules have been violated.

The users constitute the key link with the business itself, and it is to them that we turn to confirm that the business model represents their business correctly. The primary responsibility for this lies squarely in the lap of the user team member. It is this person who provides the first assessment of any work that the team undertakes, and who initially reviews any of the project deliverables. It is also through this person that the work of the project team is presented to and reviewed by the broader user community. This takes place through formal walk-throughs of key deliverables with the user liaison committee, a group of users specifically set up as a means of ensuring that the work of the project team is seen by and disseminated to the most influential members of the user community. (For a further discussion of the role played by this group see section 6.1.1.) It is via this group that concerns with the model will initially be raised with the project steering group.

Ultimate responsibility for the work undertaken by the BAA project team lies with the project steering group: it will be up to them finally to approve and accept the team's work. This group will receive formal presentations of key project deliverables from the BAA team.

---

[13] This would also suggest that fully detailed PADs are being written.

[14] Again, detailed PADs would have to be written.

Besides the user checking on whether the business model correctly reflects the business they are engaged in, there are also the formal correctness checks that can be made on the model. The most obvious of these is to check whether the data model has been correctly normalised to 3NF (see section 8.2.2.2). In addition to this, many of the CASE tools will either apply interactive consistency checking to the model as it is being built up, or allow various consistency checks to be run on various parts of the model. **It is strongly recommended that such applicable checks are run, and that the errors located through them are corrected in the model.**

Lastly, it goes without saying that the role of a QA group that functions separately from the project team is essential in ensuring that overall quality standards are being adhered to. This group should interact with the team in accordance with the quality plan that is an intrinsic part of the overall project plan. The QA team's first point of call, should it detect problems or anomalies, should be the project manager, but their ultimate responsibility should be to the project steering group, who should be copied in on all QA checks that they undertake.

10.2.3 Stability Analysis

Although initial interviews with senior management would have focused on both their current and future requirements, it is still essential, at the end of the analysis phase, to check once again that the business model is robust enough to handle changing needs. It is possible that even during the project's short life span, needs and priorities might change: environmental concerns, for example, may have become politically more sensitive; new draft legislation may have been published; or a new corporate strategy, hitherto highly confidential, may now be common knowledge.

It is essential then, at the end of the BAA, to review once again with senior management likely and possible changes in the general business environment, legislation and regulation, competitive pressures, and considerations of a more operational nature. As part of the review, it is necessary to assess the probability of each of these cases occurring: those with a high probability need then to be measured against the business model. In many cases, the data structures will be in place to handle the change; for example, the introduction of a new type of insurance policy may simply mean the introduction of a new entity subtype. The change may, however, be far more drastic, and may require additional relationships, attributes, and processes to be added to the model. In some cases, it may be too early to analyze the precise nature of many of these changes. In such cases, the analysts involved should document their thoughts about the likely effects on the business model. These should include possible different ways of changing the model in the event of certain alternative scenarios becoming a reality.

There is, of course, no point in speculative analysis unless the probability of changes occurring are extremely high, or the competitive edge that may be achieved by having an early system in place is considerable. In all cases, some minor adjustments to the model and/or the documentation of the way in which the model can deal with the possible business changes considered must be recorded. The details of the stability analysis are usually recorded in a separate appendix (see section 7.1.2.15).

***

At this stage of the BAA project, a model should now be in place in which the business users can see their business reflected, and understand how it has been represented. This model should be fully reviewed by them, and by quality assurance personnel both internal and external to the project team.

It is now time to focus our attention on the ways in which the business model, or parts of it, can be transformed into systems that support the users in their business needs. The next chapter will deal with the issues that need to be considered in scoping the design project. These will include how to use the model both as a basis for selecting a package or for building custom systems, and how to use the results of the BAA to communicate the alternative ways ahead to the project steering group.

Chapter 11 Finishing... and Moving On

The business model that has been created as a result of the BAA can be used for a number of purposes. These have been mentioned in sections 5.1, 5.3, and 5.4. This chapter, however, is concerned with using the model as a basis for planning the route ahead. The model (or the most relevant parts of it) needs to be transformed into systems that support the users in their business needs in as efficient a manner as possible. Again, the business considerations need to drive design considerations as much as is practicable. The first set of issues, dealt with in section 11.1, covers how to use the model to assist with the scoping of the design project(s).

A possible route forward could be the evaluation and selection of software packages to meet the users' system needs. Section 11.3 provides a framework within which the business model can be used as the basis for assessing the overall coverage various packages provide for the scoped system, and also presents a summary of the key broader issues that need to be considered before a package solution is chosen.

Section 11.4 examines the uses of the business model and issues that need to be considered in the task of planning for the design of custom systems.

Lastly, the task of communicating the design plan and any alternative ways forward falls on the project manager. The key aspects of this task are discussed in section 11.5 where they are linked to the BAA report, which has previously been discussed in section 7.1.

11.1   Scoping the Business System Design Project

A BAA project will usually cover a broader area in scope than the system(s) that will be designed to meet the most immediate business needs within the business area. It is, however, possible to use the work of the analysis to help the project manager and the steering group to define the scope for the design projects clearly, unambiguously, and to understand what technical trade-offs may have to be made in order to meet the business processing needs. Although the initial emphasis in this section will be on understanding the logical groupings of elementary processes and data in order to define the scope of design projects,[1] the purpose behind doing so is **not** a purely technical one. This structural evaluation assists the manager in making scoping decisions that are **business driven**, but at the same time helps to keep a balanced view on the compromises that are imposed upon neat, logical considerations by business priorities. The same structural considerations will be foremost in deciding how to segment the

---

[1] And often, to confirm the scope of a conceptual system identified during the ISP.

business area into design projects, and how to phase those projects, where more than one project of equally high priority is identified by the users.

The key analysis tool in understanding how system scope within the business area may be determined by common data usage is the Elementary Process/Entity CRUD matrix used in the checking of the model (see section 10.2.1). By clustering this matrix in such a way that the strongest interactions with the same entities (Create, Update, and, where applicable, Delete) are identified, a natural system with strong inner cohesion and minimal coupling to other such "natural systems" is highlighted. This concept is illustrated in Figure 11.1.

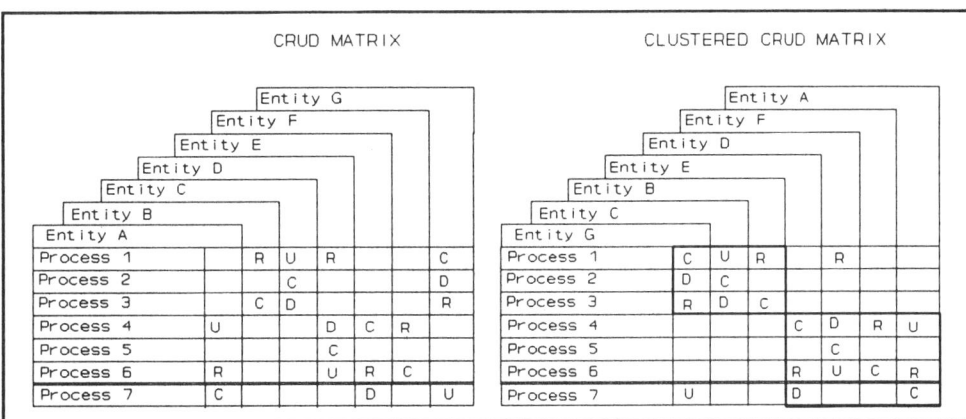

Figure 11.1 The Clustered CRUD Matrix

A good I-CASE tool will be able to run clustering algorithms that will both identify such cohesive clusters, and indicate the ways in which they are coupled with other elementary processes within the business area. For the purposes of this book, it is not necessary to understand the mechanics of such matrices. Suffice it is to say that the project manager can use them, and their output and/or analysis reports to understand what the internal trade-offs are in segmenting a business area in various ways, and in phasing further development work in a particular sequence. These considerations need to be measured up carefully against more purely business considerations (such as are discussed in section 11.4) before final recommendations are made.

11.2   The Consideration of Hardware and Software Environments

Where an ISP has taken place, the organisation's technical architecture will form the primary input to considerations of the most appropriate hardware and software platforms upon which to develop the proposed system(s). There is, however, a broad implication behind this observation that when the ISP is revisited as part of the annual planning cycle, the technical architecture is itself subject to some review and updating.

Usually, a responsible IT department will be watching broad trends and specific developments both in the hardware and software arenas, and their input to the ISP review in this regard is an essential component.

In reality, though, many organisations' technical strategies are a product of their historical IT developments and allegiances, as well as expressions of the technical experience and preferences of senior IT staff. While the emphasis in IE moves the locus for such decisions away from the technicians and towards the business, it is impossible, outside of a green field site, for a new project not to be a prisoner of the organisation's IT history. Despite this observation, it is possible, especially with highly competitive IT initiatives, for the needs of the business to lead to a change in IT direction. It is important to remember, however, that any venture into unfamiliar ground for an organisation represents an increased level of risk for the projects affected. This will be particularly acute where the new ground is right on the leading edge of technology.

In more conservative environments, the hardware and software direction may be predetermined and not open for discussion. In such a case, the constraints imposed by these technical decisions will limit the types of system solutions that can be proposed, and even the approach to be used in finally constructing them.

The BAA project will have allowed those participating in it (including the senior managers on the project steering group) to have gained a much clearer insight into the business processes contained within the business area. This enhanced understanding may provide a strong business impetus for a particular type of system solution. For example, where a key part of the computerised system will be dealing with a business need to analyze large amounts of data and to ask many "what if" questions, an organisation that wants all computing to be centralised may be persuaded to offload this aspect of the system to powerful workstations so that the processing power (and in this case the data) can be found and manipulated where it is needed by the business.

The sorts of technical considerations relating to hardware and software that will come into play, and some of their broad implications for system development, should be briefly reviewed by the project manager, as they will have an effect both on the types of systems that can be developed, and upon the approach used to build systems. What may be advantageous in one context could become a serious handicap in another: using a 4GL for system development may speed up the production of systems, but may place serious performance constraints on aspects of those systems. Technical directions must address and meet business needs and, in effect, be driven by them.

In choosing a hardware and software platform for a particular system, projects are seldom given *carte blanche*. It is seldom that a new system or set of systems will not have to interface with existing and operating systems. More often than not they will have to be produced on already purchased equipment. Where a project manager is considering implementing either 4GLs or code generators, some of the issues that should be examined are summarised in the following table:

4GL	Code Generator
Supporting Tool Set Does the 4GL provide a full supporting tool set to facilitate its use? (For example, screen painters, test harnesses, etc.)	**Completeness** Is the code that is generated complete? Can it be compiled, or is it just a skeleton that requires adjustment?
	Quality What is the quality of the code produced? Does it perform as specified? Does it require manual intervention, or is the underlying specification (PAD) corrected?
Performance How well does the 4GL perform against the business requirements? Is it interpretive, or does it have a compiled run time version?	**Efficiency** Is the code that is produced efficient? Can it be compiled and run as generated in both on-line and batch environments? Does it require additional code (ASSEMBLER, SQL, etc.) to be embedded into it for efficient and effective operation?
	Maintaining the Code Where does maintenance occur? Is the code itself adjusted, or is the base model changed and new code then generated from it? In the former case, can the generated code be understood and maintained by a programmer?
Portability Where relevant, how portable is the 4GL code and resulting system across operating environments?	**Portability** Where relevant, how portable is the code generated across operating environments? Can the code itself be compiled and/or generated into different operating environments?

Licensing	Cost
Can one buy a run-time only licence, or is one forced to purchase a development licence for each operational site?	In considering cost, is there a single one-off cost for the generator? What do maintenance charges include? If more than one copy of the generator is required (for example in a PC environment), is a discount offered?
Lock-in Will the 4GL lock developers into one environment?	**Lock-in** Will the code generator lock developers into one environment?

11.3   Evaluating and Selecting Software Packages

In many organisations, the preferred approach to systems development is to implement software packages where a suitable one is available. Unless the organisation's complete business needs can be addressed by a single family of packages, it is likely that packages from one supplier will have to interface and interact with packages from another. It is also realistic to assume that in most environments some custom built systems will be in place or will be built. The latter case is especially true where an organisation is using computerisation to gain some sort of competitive leading edge.

The BAA deliverables can be effectively used in the assessment and selection of packages. The business area model provides a comprehensive description of what it is the business does, and, as such, forms an excellent basis both for package selection, and, ultimately, for the control of an operational environment that may consist of a mix of old systems, a selection of packages, and some home-grown systems built within the framework of the ISP architectures. Where an IE approach to systems development has been adopted, the haphazard selection of packages will undermine the underlying principle afforded by an architectured approach. Using the BAA model for package selection helps to ensure that any systems that are implemented fit in to the overall corporate framework. In fact, the business models (particularly the evolving corporate data model) become the fundamental point of reference for system integration and the interfacing of disparate systems.

How can the BAA process be used where a software package is the preferred solution? Not surprisingly, very little changes, and this means that even if, in the end, no suitable package can be found, the basic BAA model still exists, and it can be used to drive the custom design process, as is further described in chapter 12.

In the approach discussed in this section, the emphasis will be placed on how to modify the normal BAA process in order to use the business model for package selection. A detailed description of all the issues underlying the selection of packages will not be undertaken.

Two fundamental approaches can be adopted in package selection in the context of a BAA project. In the overview shown in **Figure 11.2**, the assumption is made that all aspects of package evaluation will be undertaken by the BAA analysis team. This approach will initially be discussed, and then consideration will be given to ways in which the **package vendors themselves** can be involved in the process.

In all cases, step one ensures that part of the project scoping exercise involves a definition of any technical considerations that will constrain the selection of packages. As discussed in section 7.2, the broad area of business functionality to be addressed by the BAA project is unambiguously defined in an initial ERM and PHD, ideally passed on to the project team as part of the ISP process. These deliverables are supplemented by a scope statement which should include any hardware and software constraints that will limit the nature of any packages that the team may investigate. Of particular interest are the following questions:

● Is there a predetermined hardware and software environment that any package must fit into?

● Is there a predetermined hardware and software environment that any package must interface with?

● Is a particular DBMS targeted for the software package?

Before the BAA team begins any detailed investigations or modelling, it should initially establish whether any packages exist that fall within the functional and technical constraints imposed upon the project by the scope statement. The answer may be "none," in which case the normal BAA process can be followed. Where such potential packages do exist, initial contact should be made with the suppliers so that information about the packages can be obtained, and a base list of potentially suitable ones can be drawn up. Pragmatically speaking, if there is only one entry on the list, and it seems to provide wide enough coverage, it may make sense to get information from reference sites immediately. This may also prove to be the expedient way ahead if the package itself is an acknowledged industry standard. In most cases, though, an initial base list of suitable packages will be the interim deliverable, and the normal work of BAA will proceed.

The first part of the BAA process[2] results in a reviewed first-cut ERM and PHD (supplemented by a PDD or DFD). In effect, this allows the team to gain a more detailed understanding of the business rules and information requirements within the business area. This understanding has been formalised into the business model so that each entity type identified has a formal definition, its attributes have been identified and defined, and the relationship existing between entities has been

---

[2] See section 7.3.1.2.

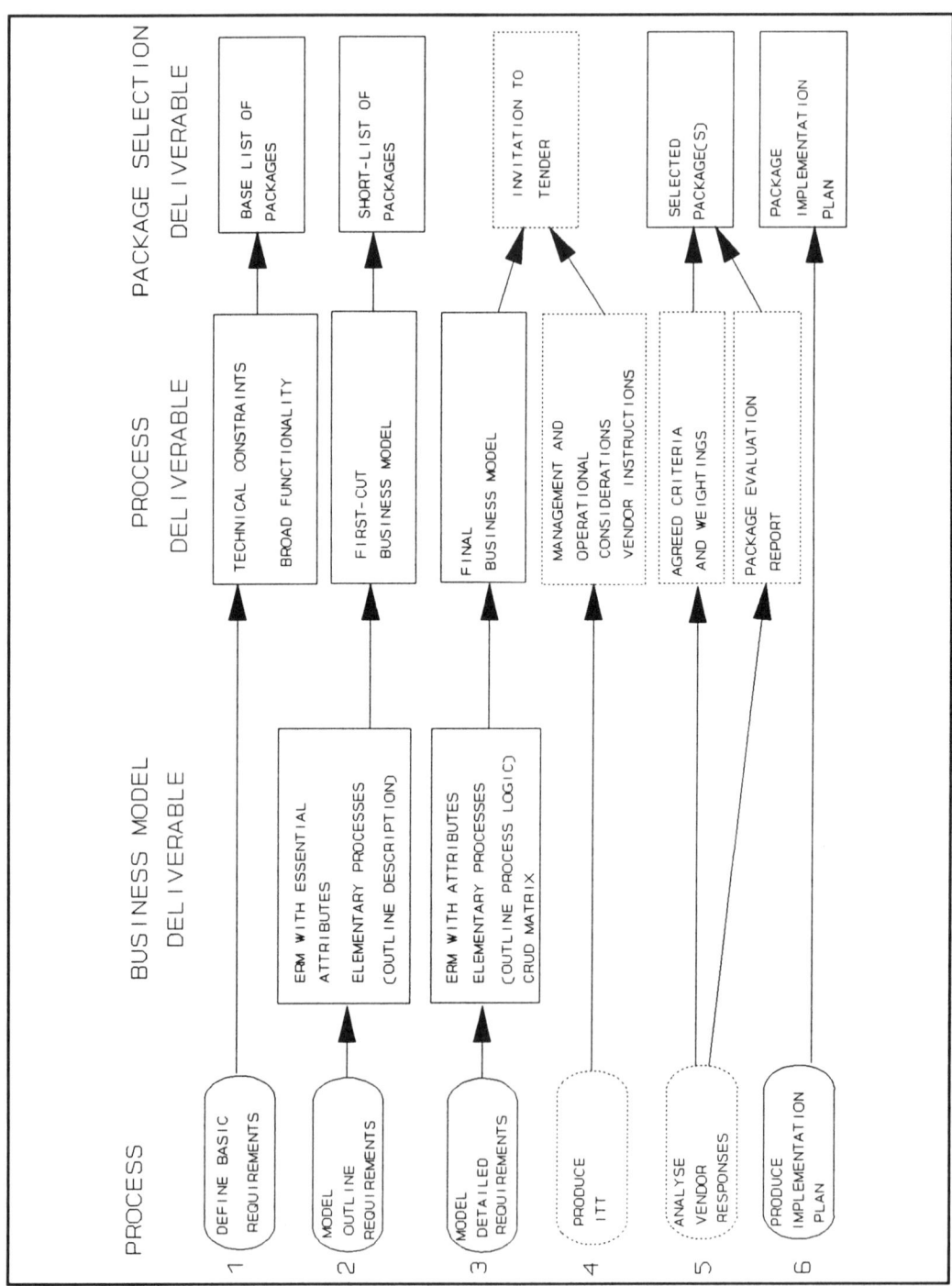

Figure 11.2 An Overview of the Package Selection Process

determined. At the same time, the elementary processes within the business area have been identified and defined, and their dependencies have been formally described (or, where DFDs have been used, their interconnection in terms of "data flows" has been formally documented). This information should, in itself, be enough to form the basis for a formal or informal Preliminary Package Requirements Specification which will allow the base set of packages identified in step one to be pared down to a short list of serious contenders. At this stage it is advisable to eliminate packages which do not contain **all** the main entities[3] and the **essential** business processes. Where it is difficult to determine whether a package procedure is the equivalent of, or covers part of a business process[4] (there may not be a direct one-to-one mapping), the expected effects of the business process could be used as a firmer basis for comparison. The aim of this second step is to eliminate from consideration any package that has a poor fit with the overall business requirements. The basis for such a decision should be that the package contains less than eighty percent of the information **and** functional coverage. Additional reasons for rejecting a package at this stage may include the following:

● There appear to be potential difficulties with interfacing the package with current systems or with the current operational environment.[5]

● The response from the package vendors has been poor. This may indicate future poor response to operational problems and issues.

● The quality of the package documentation is poor. This may indicate sub-optimum quality of software, and/or potential difficulties with its implementation.

● The vendor's financial stability and/or reputation is poor. In the former case, future maintenance and package support may be threatened. In the latter, the quality of the package itself, and of support for it, may be questionable.

As a result of this shortlisting exercise, it is possible that a single package may emerge as the only one that meets the business requirements, or that no packages do so. In the latter case, the BAA can proceed with a view to custom building the required

---

[3] The package will represent some sort of physical implementation of the business model if it indeed covers the business area or part of it. The "entities" contained in the package may not be immediately recognisable as such, but the entity definitions in the business model should allow the team to establish if, for example, what they have called CUSTOMER is, in fact, what the package calls "Client".

[4] i.e. What Entity Types it Creates, Reads, Updates, and Deletes.

[5] The relevance of this point to each project may differ, depending on particular circumstances.

systems. In the former case, judgement will have to be applied in the specific case as to whether to begin planning for package implementation, or whether further analysis needs to be done. The need for any further work will clearly be driven by a need to assess, minimise, and control risk.

The third step in package selection is to go ahead with interaction analysis, in order to verify the overall business model so that any final selection of package(s) from the short list can be based on a stable and proven business model. Where it is clear that a package solution is likely, it is not necessary to write fully detailed PADs. What is required from the interaction analysis - and hence from the PADs - is that the data model is proved to be complete enough (in terms of attributes and relationships) to be able to support the business processes identified and defined. Moreover, the elementary processes themselves need to be understood in sufficient detail so that they can be unambiguously described, and verified with the business users. From the business model, it should now be possible to define the detailed business requirements that the package should cover unambiguously. In order to finalise the scope for package selection, any processes and entities that are not essential to the current and anticipated user requirements[6] are marked as such.

Where the BAA team will themselves undertake the detailed package evaluation, they can now separate the two dimensions from the CRUD matrix that they created in order to verify the model, and use them as the basis for two new matrices: one will formally map the BAA Entities (and Attributes if such granularity of detail is required, though at this stage this is unusual) against the package "entities" or equivalents (probably files or tables); the second will form the basis for a formal comparison of the BAA elementary business processes with the procedures implemented in the package. It will now be up to the team to fill in the details of these matrices, and use the matrices to determine the extent of functional coverage and potential interfacing problems to and from the package. Also key to the team's work will be the analysis of "gaps" and omissions in the package based on the information that is summarised in the matrices. Problem areas with each package will have to be investigated, and their impact on the business assessed, before a formal recommendation for or against a particular package can be made. Where a package is recommended, included in such an assessment will be a strategy (including cost estimates) for overcoming any gaps in the package. **Developers should be very wary of tampering with proprietary packages. This is euphemistically called "package tailoring," but it can cover over a series of problems that a package solution was intended to avoid. At the worst end of the spectrum, developers in effect create their own version of a package which is not automatically compatible with new releases. Every time an enhancement to the package is released, a major in-house "updating exercise" is fired off. The long term costs of this route can completely override the benefits ostensibly gained from installing the package in the first place.**

---

[6] See section 10.2.3 where Stability Analysis is discussed.

A further word of warning about the installation of packages, particularly where they have to fit into an already complex operational environment. Every interface to and from a system, be it package-built or home-grown, represents a potential system in its own right. **Interfaces can be complex systems, and this is particularly the case where the interfaces are not simple.** It is extremely unlikely that any package that is bought into an organisation will conform fully to the organisation's system and information architectures. **Unless a BAA model or corporate data model of some sort is used as a basis for the definition of clear and clean interfaces, such interfaces can become complex and potentially costly systems in their own right. Again, the potential benefits from buying a package could be thrown away by the cost of constructing and maintaining interfaces. Ironically, in an environment that lacks the controlling "common denominator" of a corporate data model, the more packages bought in, the more potentiality for complex interfaces is being created.**

Of course, what can be broadly described as functionality and data coverage are not the only areas that need to be considered in selecting packages. A number of additional factors play a role, and these together constitute the package selection criteria. In consultation with all interested parties (hands-on users, management, operational staff, auditors, etc.), these are weighted to reflect the comparative importance of the criteria so that a well-considered selection from among the candidate packages can be made.

Additional technical factors which may be of relevance include the following:

- The extent to which the package conforms to the company corporate data model.[7]
- The extent to which the package conforms to, or allows conformance to, company standards (naming conventions, coding structures, etc.).
- Whether the way in which the package procedures implements actual business procedures implies that the business will have to adjust the way it operates.

Those who will have to use the system operationally will consider the following issues:

- How usable is the package in the business context? In order to assess this, operational staff may wish to try the package either at the vendor's office, or at a customer reference site.
- What sort of operational support is offered by the package vendors in the form of "hot lines," etc.? Is such support directed only at the IT technical staff, or are the needs of business users also taken into consideration?
- What is the quality of the system documentation? Is it directed at all levels and classes of potential users?
- How reliable is the system? At this stage, customer reference sites may be the only reliable source of such information.

---

[7] Non-conformance may imply more complex interfaces.

- Does the package meet company standards for backup and recovery?
- Does the package meet company standards related to audit and the security of information systems?

In addition to these aspects, management will wish to consider factors such as:

- What sort of reputation does the package vendor have in the marketplace? Is the vendor financially stable?[8]
- What are the contractual arrangements for the use of the package? Where, for example, the package is a PC-based one, are licences necessary for each PC, or is a site licence possible? What are the costs of the package? Are bulk discounting arrangements negotiable?
- Does the package have a future development plan that drives future releases of the product? Is it possible to influence the content and/or priority of such future enhancements? What is the mechanism for doing so?[9] Is there any large, powerful user of the package who may exert a strong influence on the direction the product may take? Is this factor likely to compromise any business gains envisaged by implementing the package?
- What is the overall quality of the package documentation like? Is this confirmed by the quality of any presentation that the vendor makes in the course of its sales effort? Sloppy documentation, poor responses to requests for information, and low quality sales presentations may be early indications of the overall poor quality of the product and its support.
- What sort of time scales are envisaged in the implementation of the package? How committed are the suppliers to this process? Who will be providing initial training and support? Is this part of the overall contractual obligations on the vendor's part?

Before any final recommendation for a particular package takes place, it is strongly recommended that potential users of the package be given an opportunity to try it. This should, if possible, include seeing the package in operation in a live situation and giving users the opportunity to talk with actual users of the package. In this context,

---

[8] Potential buyers of a package do not want unwittingly to find themselves reliant for support and future enhancement on a company that is financially unsound. The net result of such a situation may involve the users in the acquisition of the vendor company in order to ensure that the package continues to be maintained and enhanced. If a major factor in the decision to purchase a package was so that these responsibilities were off-loaded onto the suppliers, then the purchasing company may be worse off as a result than if they had built the system in-house!

[9] Quite often, the means for influencing such decisions is through a product user group. In such a case, it is often worthwhile finding out how responsive the suppliers are to the user group, and who its current members are.

"users" will include computer operations staff, if this is applicable. Live operational site can prove particularly useful as a basis for measuring and predicting performance of the system in its envisaged operational context.

For all packages that are serious contenders, the vendors should be given the opportunity to make a formal presentation of the package to potential users and their management. It is at such presentations that particular problem areas can be fully addressed and aired.

In various organisations, some sort of Package Evaluation Report will result from these investigations, and this will be used as the basis for the Project Steering Group to make its final decisions. Figure 11.3 summarises the inputs to the Package Evaluation Report.

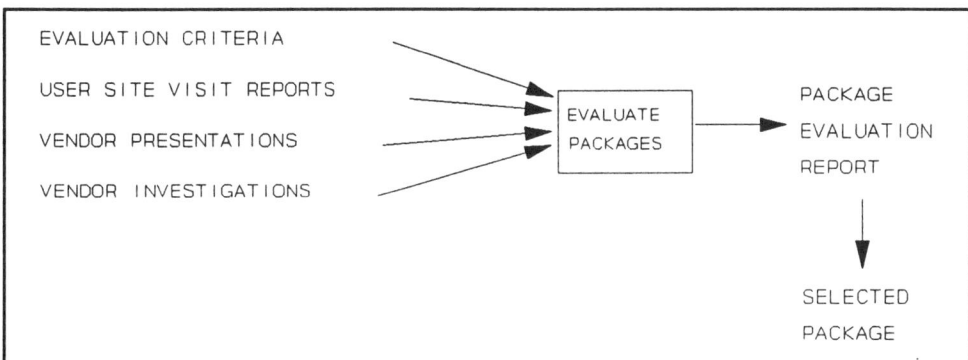

Figure 11.3 Inputs to the Package Evaluation Report

A lot of detailed package assessment work can be off-loaded onto the vendors themselves. As the detailed business model is a reflection of what the business does, it, or an appropriate subset of the model, can form the basis for an invitation-to-tender document that is presented to all vendors of packages that have been shortlisted. The vendors can be asked whether their package can meet the business requirements contained in the model,[10] and, if not, to highlight the gaps that exist. They can also be asked to quote, on a fixed price basis, for amending their product so that it meets fully all the requirements expressed in the business model. In this way, the experts on the package can carry out their assessment of its conformance to a set of unambiguously expressed requirements, and their response can become the basis of a

---

[10] It will probably be necessary to explain to the vendors that their package is considered to be an **implementation** of all or part of the business model. It is not necessary that, for example, the package should directly reflect the structure of the data model. It should, however, implement all (or some) of the model.

legal obligation on their part.

As a general rule, a package should not be tailored to meet requirements **unless the package suppliers are prepared to do the tailoring.** In such cases, only essential features should be added, and the specification of those changes and additions must be very tight (the basis for these should be the business model itself). A fixed price contract to incorporate the changes is strongly advised. All such changes should be fully documented, and that documentation must be part of the final deliverable. It is quite possible that, where there is mutual benefit to be gained from such an arrangement, the changes will become part of the standard package. However, changes that are intended to gain an organisation a competitive edge may be explicitly excluded from the standard package.[11] In order to ensure that the changes do indeed meet specific needs, would-be users should maintain a close involvement and, even (where time is a critical factor), tight control over the changes, reserving the right to review them, and accept or reject them based on pre-agreed criteria.

Once a package has been finally selected, a full implementation plan for the package needs to be drawn up. Factors that will have to be taken into consideration include the following:

- Does data have to be captured and/or converted? If so will the procedures to do so have to be constructed, or are they integral to the package?
- Interfaces to existing systems will have to be considered. Do these have to be constructed?
- User training will have to be put into place.
- Test and acceptance criteria have to be drawn up, and the system will have to be brought into an operation state that allows it to be fully tested against real, operational data, and against actual performance requirements.

11.4   Planning for the Design of a Custom System

The design scope for building a system can be strongly influenced by a number of factors that may force the project manager to consider different approaches to the sequencing of the design effort from those that would be "ideal" if merely considering the logical (data-driven) issues discussed in section 11.1. Available resources may mean that certain options are simply not possible: pressing business opportunities may mean that time is of such importance that overall long-term functionality is sacrificed for the short-term gains; or the people may not be available with the expertise required to do the job, and this may enforce a package solution **even where no package is deemed to be ideal** (see also section 11.3).

It is important that the design alternatives that are considered, and especially those

---

[11] No doubt, in such a case, the pricing of the changes will reflect their exclusivity.

that are eventually presented to the Project Steering Group, are dictated by business considerations. It is business considerations that should be the driving factor, not technical ones. However, a solution prompted in response to real business needs may require the use of a new, less proven, technical environment, and/or the acquisition of scarce technical skills in order to meet the business need. In **all cases, the costs of** such decisions need to be carefully **weighed** up against the potential **benefits to be** derived for the business, and these costs need to be made explicit so that a **business decision** can be made (see further section 11.4.1). Where a particular design approach either increases or diminishes the risks involved in the project, **these also need to be spelt out clearly in terms that business-oriented users can understand.**

In order to assist the Project Steering Group in reaching an informed decision, a cost/benefit analysis of all suggested alternatives must be undertaken. This is dealt with in more detail in section 11.4.1. A further means of assisting the group to make decisions may involve prototyping aspects of the system in order to illustrate different environments graphically (for example the difference between a "dumb terminal" and an intelligent workstation using WIMPS), or in order to give potential users a "feel" for the type of system that they are committing themselves to. The use of prototyping at this stage of the project has a clear and specific purpose and carries some potential risk. Both of these issues are more fully discussed in section 11.4.2.

11.4.1 Cost/Benefit Analysis

Each organisation has its own format and standards for the calculation and presentation of a cost/benefit analysis. These standards should be adhered to as much as possible, for an IE approach does not in any way change the basic elements of such an analysis. What it does add is some formal connection of the cost and benefits to those that were expected from the ISP.

An important starting point for the gathering of information relevant to a cost/benefit analysis is the Information Strategy Plan itself. In it, a series of business justifications for the development of systems was supported by a number of matrices upon which that justification was based. The BSD planner should now revisit those matrices (more specifically those sub-sets of them that relate directly to the business area that has been analyzed) in order to relate the scope of potential systems that have been identified directly with the original business goals, opportunities, and critical success factors (CSFs) that were the reasons for examining this area of the business in the first place. In addition, the problem areas and inhibiting factors that envisaged conceptual systems were intended to address should also be formally examined. The stability analysis undertaken as part of the confirmation exercise (see section 10.2.3) should have determined the extent to which these areas, as addressed in the ISP, are still relevant. Where priorities have changed, the project manager should have obtained a good insight into current problems, opportunities, and CSFs, and their relative importance. These factors are key elements in building up a business case for or against a particular design approach.

It is possible in some I-CASE tools to update and expand the relevant sub-set of the important ISP matrices to reflect both the current understanding of business needs, and the enhanced understanding of the business area. Thus, for example, where CSFs were previously linked to either Functions or High-level Entities, they can now be related directly to Elementary Processes and Entity Types (or even Subtypes). In this way, the granularity of the matrices becomes finer, and it is focused in at the lowest levels **relevant** to the business. The determination of costs can then be related to a specific set of elementary processes and the entities required to support them, while, similarly, the business needs for, and benefits to be derived from, such a constellation of processes and data can be determined. It is important that the technical viability of such a clustering is considered, as well as the (possible) additional technical costs that such a clustering may impose upon the design effort. This is where the simultaneous work undertaken as part of the overall assessment of BSD scoping based on data interaction (see section 11.1) is of particular importance. Similarly, a business clustering of processes and entities may impose technical challenges, or encounter technical constraints that have to be taken into account when considering alternative hardware and software environments (see section 11.2).

Once all the business and technical issues have been isolated, it is necessary to quantify for each **viable** design project the following estimated figures:

- Short term benefits, based on business needs, opportunities, and assumptions;

- Longer term and probable benefits, based on many of the assumptions made in the ISP as modified to reflect current business strategy, thinking, and understanding; and

- Likely costs, based on whatever methods the organisation currently uses to estimate IT projects.[12]

An evaluation of the various options for the design project can now take place using the calculation parameters for the cost/benefit analysis as a basis. These can now be applied to the various options raised in considering many of the business and logical

---

[12] The problems with estimating costs of IT projects are legion, and they become particularly intensified where new technology and approaches are being applied. A sensible approach would be to estimate based on current organisational guidelines and practises, and then to make adjustment for risk and learning curves where new approaches are being adopted. It is unrealistic to expect immediate massive productivity gains from a new set of approaches coupled with a different set of hardware and software tools. The new developments however need to be closely monitored in order to determine whether expected productivity gains **are** being realised as projects progress, and more projects come onto stream using IE principles and a suitable supporting tool set.

issues discussed in sections 11.3 and 11.4 in building up a case for presenting to the steering group fully and objectively the options open to them.

11.4.2 The Role of Prototyping at the End of a BAA

The BAA model clearly encompasses **a business perspective** on an area of the business. In doing so, it focuses on information needs and processing requirements. Any **system** that is designed to support that area of the business will need to take into account **how** the business operates both currently and in terms of foreseeable business changes. As such, it will have to be transformed from a model that describes the business from a business point of view, to one that describes a business system from the point of view of potential system users and those who will have to construct the system to operate on a given hardware and software platform. The process of moving from a Business Model to a Systems Model (described in Chapter 12) is not one of simply adding more detail to the BAA model: it is a process of **transforming** the model into something different. As a result, there are some potential problems in building any sort of system prototype based simply on the BAA model.

On the other hand, there are some very powerful reasons for attempting to do so at this stage.

11.4.2.1 The Use of Prototyping in the BAA Phase

The strongest argument for attempting to build a narrowly circumscribed prototype at the end of the BAA is to add some real meat to the skeleton that the business users have up to now had to contend with. Some I-CASE tools introduce limited prototyping capabilities at this stage, specifically in order to fulfil this purpose. In many cases, the BAA prototype is a form of confidence building exercise that is undertaken both to re-instil a sense of commitment and enthusiasm on the part of business users, and to give them a demonstrable deliverable that is easier to sell up the line than a set of models, no matter how good that set may be. The prototype thus becomes a means for winning users' confidence and support for the ongoing design project.

Any prototype produced should at least have as a goal the ability to give end users of the system a preview of the "look and feel" of the envisaged system. Within this context, prototyping may even be used to demonstrate, albeit in a cursory fashion, the different types of functions and dialogues that the system may contain. A more focused use of prototyping, best employed in an area of the business that has never before been computerised, is the development of a specific dialogue or set of dialogues in order to refine some of the users' specific requirements - but here, the border with design proper has clearly been crossed, and the project manager should be aware of some of the potential hazards this may present (see section 11.4.2.3).

There is also a strong argument for developing some tightly circumscribed prototypes upon different hardware/software platforms **in order to illustrate them** to would-be users.

In all these cases, the project manager, steering group, and broader user community involved in viewing the prototype, must be clearly appraised of the limitations and constraints of the prototyping exercise itself.

11.4.2.2 Limitations of the BAA Prototype

Any dialogue that forms the basis for a prototype at this stage will not be based upon final screen layouts: screens are only likely to contain a representative subset of the relevant data in order to fulfil their purpose within the dialogue. No real data will be displayed, although some sort of dummy data, especially tailored for the prototype demonstration, may be present, depending on the tool used to create the prototype. Similarly, most prototypes will not be supported by an actual database.[13] As a result, the prototype will not accurately demonstrate potential system performance. Lastly, a prototype is unlikely to contain any error handling.

While the limitations mentioned are probable, the actual nature of the prototype will be determined by the purpose behind prototyping itself. The topic of prototyping in the BSD phase is more fully addressed in section 12.2.3, while potential pitfalls in beginning prototyping as part of the BAA are dealt with in the following section.

11.4.2.3 Potential Dangers

The key to successful prototyping at this point in an IE project is the management of user expectations. This will firstly need clear objectives for undertaking the exercise to be spelt out and agreed. Secondly, the scope and limitations of the prototyping exercise need also to be documented and agreed **and then properly controlled and managed.**

The main danger of developing any prototype at this stage is that users will either be disappointed by the result, or their expectations will be inflated by it. In the former case, the whole credibility of the project can be eroded because the prototype is a pale reflection of what the users were expecting - and, indeed, a pale reflection of the potential system itself. This pitfall is most likely to occur if the medium chosen for prototyping has limited facilities. For example, a CASE tool may allow the EMV for an elementary process to be turned into a screen, or series of screens (as is further described in section 12.3.3), and then for the flow between screens to be illustrated in a fairly basic manner. Users' reactions to this may be, "So what?" and their enthusiasm for the system may be dampened. At the other extreme, where a powerful

---

[13] Where the prototype has been developed specifically to show the capabilities of a software platform, then it is probable that some sort of supporting database will be used.

prototyping environment has been used (usually supported by an RDBMS), the users may become so enthusiastic that they want the system "tomorrow." Here the danger can be that, as a result, the project is *de facto* led into an unscoped design project, or that the prototyping exercise becomes an uncontrolled Rapid Application Development session.[14] In the latter case, again, the project has slipped into the design phase, but without a clear scope or terms of reference.

Lastly, where extensive prototyping takes place (for example, where a number of different environments are being illustrated and contrasted), the real design process, which in itself should involve extensive prototyping, will be delayed, and this may cause some frustration to the wider user community.

11.5   Communicating the Design Plan to Management

Formal communication of the BSD plan to management forms a necessary project check point at the end of the BAA phase and is done so partly by means of the end of BAA report described in section 7.1. It is at this time that formal acceptance of the analysis work by the user community occurs, and it is now that management (usually on the recommendation of the Project Steering Group) decides whether the project should continue, and what the scope of the design project should be.

Although the formal recommendations of the project team are presented to the Project Steering Group at this stage, and via them to senior levels of management, the team's recommendations should not come as a surprise to them. Throughout the course of the project, the steering group should have been kept informed of any problems arising, and any decisions regarding the project's scope should have been referred to them. As the project team builds up an understanding of the business area, any potential organisational issues that arise should also be brought to their attention. It is possible that the encapsulation of business knowledge and structure that the business model represents may throw a new or different light upon the business area as a whole, or may lead to a clearer understanding of it. This enhanced understanding may, as a result, lead to a restructuring of the current business either in terms of business procedures, or structure, or both. In many organisations, both structure and procedures have been inherited from days in which information **and** control were effected by means of paper flows. By comparing the current business procedures with the understanding of what they do (which is contained in the formal definitions that the PADs represent), management can highlight parts of the business which can be effectively streamlined and/or restructured. The potentiality for such changes should be brought to the attention of senior management **as soon as possible** preferably by the team's user representative. A proposed system that is likely to be based upon - or worse, be perceived to cause - significant changes to the business, needs the approval of management, and such changes must result from **business, not technical**

---

[14] For a full discussion of Rapid Application Development sessions, see section 12.2.

decisions.

The organisational impact of any proposed design alternative should have been reviewed with the steering group **before any** such recommendation is made. **This is not the sort of issue to spring upon senior managers at the end of a project.**[15]

Before the formal project steering group meeting, it is advisable to publish a draft report of the team's recommendations. Each design alternative presented should contain a clear statement of the costs and benefits involved, as well as make explicit any organisational impact that the alternative is likely to have. This impact should, of course, be included in the calculation of the cost/benefit figures.

The content of the BAA report has been discussed at length in section 7.1. Its main body contains the management level summary of the Business Area Analysis, and it is supported by a series of appendices in which the full details of the business model are contained. The appendices are really of interest to any project team that is charged with designing systems arising from the analysis.

It is possible that a steering group may ask for aspects of the team's recommendations to be investigated further, or for the draft design plan to be fleshed out in further detail. It is important that the group should have as many facts presented to it upon which to make an informed, business-driven decision as possible.

The steering group's decision may be for the implementation of a software package, or for the development of a custom-built system. In the latter case, a Business System Design project is floated, and the full repercussions of that are discussed in chapter 12.

Where a package solution is chosen, the business model may form the basis for the identification and definition of interfaces to and from the package. Throughout the implementation of a package, whilst the general issues faced by the development team will be non-IE specific (and hence are outside the scope of this discussion) it should be kept in mind that the business model forms a valuable point of reference against which to compare the package itself with existing systems to which it may have to interface.

---

[15] In some IE projects, where the impetus for the use of the methodology has come largely from the IT department, the business effects of the project have been ignored or misunderstood. The result has inevitably been the cancellation of the project, and often, the IE initiative.

What should be reiterated is the need to drive an IE approach to system development from the top of an organisation. Where this has not been fully achieved, it is almost inevitable that an expanding IE initiative will land up in trouble, for its emphasis on systems to support the business must, by definition, both have an impact on the business and be actively supported by business users.

The issues to be tackled in the BSD phase of an IE project are what we turn our attention to in the following chapter.

Chapter 12 Preparing for Completion

Once a BAA has been completed, IE traditionally recognises three further development phases prior to the Transition phase in which the system is migrated from a Test environment into a Production one. Each system that has been identified in the BAA for development progresses through Business Systems Design (BSD), Technical Design (TD), and Construction. Section 12.1 discusses the basic principles that underlie these three IE phases. Technical Design and Construction are generally referred to generically as TD&C, largely as a result of the fact that they are closely aligned in their technical focus upon a specific operational environment and platform. This becomes even more applicable in an I-CASE environment.

In their division between what can be broadly styled as "logical" design, "physical" design, and "coding", these three phases reflect the way in which system development has traditionally been undertaken. However, both the solid foundation that a business model provides for the underpinning of systems, and the advent of a plethora of CASE tools aimed at facilitating Design and automating Construction (Code Generation), forces computing professionals to reassess the design and construction process that they have formerly followed. The issues that IE raise in this regard are discussed in section 12.2, where the potential for the rapid development of a system from the business model is explained.

Section 12.3 discusses the issues that arise in transforming a BAA model into a design specification where a more traditional approach is adopted, whether or not this is supported by the use of CASE tools.

12.1   An Overview of the Concepts Underlying Business Systems Design (BSD), and Technical Design and Construction (TD&C)

The BAA model represents a view of the business **as a system that processes information**. It attempts to show what the business does (in information terms) rather than how it does it. Section 11.1 discussed the part played by this model in the scoping (and hence definition) of potential design projects. The final system scope is represented by the relevant sub-set of the BAA model which is carried forward as the basis for design.[1]

---

[1] In a true I-CASE environment, this transition from the end of BAA to start of BSD should be transparent.

The design process itself is divided into two steps. Business System Design (BSD) effectively transforms the business model into a logical design model for a system. What does this mean in theory? In design, the business model is effectively constrained by two factors: the need for the system to meet specific constraints imposed upon it by **how** the business actually operates; and the need for the system to contain interfaces to its users so that they are able to get information into and out of it. In considering the first of these, it is important to remember that most business procedures are **already constrained by the context within which they operate**. If they are paper-based, then they reflect, in the flow of paper, the flow of the need to know (and very often approve) what is contained on that paper. If they are already computer-based, then the procedures are probably constrained both by the structures that a particular combination of hardware and software imposes as well as by how the system itself was constructed upon that platform.[2] To a large extent, our thinking of computer systems, particularly large ones - and, to date, IE-supporting CASE tools have targeted large mainframe installations - is currently constrained by how "dumb" terminals operate in an environment where the **sequence of operation has to be predetermined**. As long as we know that, in taking an order from a customer, the orders clerk can be asked to enquire whether there is sufficient product in stock, we can write a computer system that interrupts the normal flow of order processing in order to make the enquiry. Such systems, if well analyzed, and **if** the business operational environment remains stable, will continue to keep users happy for a long period of time. If, however, the "interrupt sequence" is not fully understood, or if part of it is seen to be "out of scope", or if it changes over time (customers not only want to know that the item is in stock, but also want it reserved for them), then the computer system requires a rewrite. This usually has meant not just a redesign, but a full run through of the system development life cycle from feasibility study onwards, as the business problem and its impact on the system are not fully understood. (See Figure 12.1.)

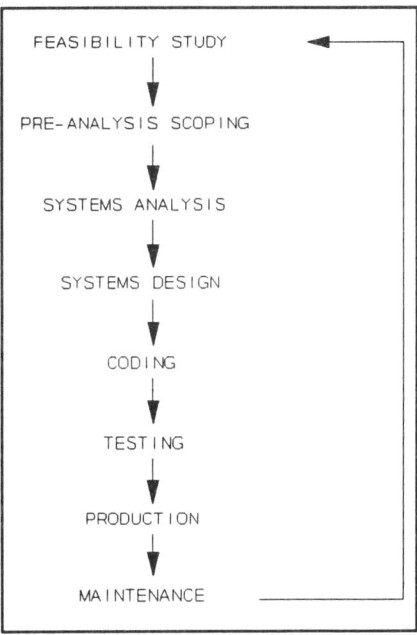

Figure 12.1 Traditional Systems Development Lifecycle

---

[2] As a result, users' thinking about how their business could operate is constrained by what the system can do. Remember, if you can, how difficult it was to make potential users of a computer system think "on-line processing" when all they were used to was filling in forms for data capture and responding to information contained on printed reports.

If, by contrast, the business were to bring "how" it operates into line with "what" it actually does, then the business model itself can form the basis for the generation of systems. This implies a restructuring of business procedures to reflect more closely the structure of the information that underpins them. Putting aside for a moment the internal political waves that this may generate, it is also rather optimistic to hope for total one-to-one mapping between elementary process and business procedure in the foreseeable future for much is ingrained in current operational procedures. We do not operate in a perfect world. Besides, the issue is further complicated by the computer systems themselves. Any application system is developed using, and runs upon, **a hardware and software platform which, in itself, imposes a structure, and hence *modus operandi*** upon such a system. In theory, the physical design (Technical Design) phase of IE takes care of such constraints, but this is not entirely true in practice: **the very syntactical structure of a particular PAD or formal specification implies a type of target environment that may support that structure.** If, in theory, such structures were not imposed upon computer systems by their underlying hardware and software operating systems then there would be no need for a design process: the business model would suffice. **So it is that a particular analysis/design CASE tool will impose some structure and constraint on a resulting system, no matter what vendors claim.**

IE theory implies that the BSD stage involves the purely logical design of a system. There is an extent to which that claim is true: for it is possible to define direct user interfaces in terms of what information is used, rather than how the user interface is to operate. However as soon as prototyping is used, and/or a target environment is implied, then the "purely logical design" becomes constrained by that environment. It is possible to take the product of a BSD and implement it on different environments but, then, all implementations of the system will look the same.[3] Further detailed design work will have to be done to utilise the strengths of each chosen environment, and then the resulting systems will **not** look the same: nor could they. The Technical Design stage of IE is theoretically where the design of the "logical system" is further adjusted to take into account the constraints imposed upon it by the target hardware and software platform. What is likely to be significantly different in different hardware/software environments is the type of user interface possible. So the two design constraints - how the business operates, and user interfaces - are, in fact, inextricably interwoven with one another, and with the target operating platform chosen.

IE theory tends to blur this problem. The division between BSD and TD, though theoretically attractive, is currently impractical. So too is the division between

---

[3] This may be the intention. However, where the environments are radically different, the system throughout will be completely constrained by the most primitive of the environments: a system running on a state of the art graphics terminal will look exactly like the same system running on a "dumb" terminal.

Technical Design and Construction. That the two phases are generally referred to as one - TD&C - tends to confirm their interdependence. The technical design of a system will be strongly influenced by the physical environment it is to operate in, the tools available for the system's construction, and, therefore, the overall approach to building the system. If, at one end of the spectrum, the system is going to be built by an army of coders - precisely the approach IE aims to eliminate - then a clear, formal, traditional technical specification of system and programs needs to be constructed. If, by contrast, the system will be generated, then the computer system that will do the generating will require a complete and unambiguous "specification" of what is required, though that "specification" may never ostensibly be more formal than a series of user interfaces, the business rules involved in moving from one interface to another[4], and the structure of the data that underlies the whole system. Clearly form, content, and process are interdependent.

"Pure" IE theory (if we allow it to exist) speaks of three distinct phases. Practice begins to show that TD&C are closely linked, but that is easy to accept because of their emphases on a physical system and the means of achieving it. What is harder to grant is the close (albeit sometimes unconscious) connection between what we design logically, and the target physical environment. In section 12.2, it will be shown how the sacrifice of the hard separation between BSD and TD allows for the application of a fast path through the BSD, TD&C phases. It is this recognition that allows so called Rapid Application Development approaches to be used within an IE context. In speculating about the future, particularly in section 14.1, where Object-Oriented Analysis and Design are discussed, the future boundaries between analysis and design - BAA and BSD - are further questioned, but for the moment it is necessary to remain grounded in the here and now, for this book is about the real, practical application of IE principles.

12.2 Traditional Design and Construction Approaches versus Rapid Application Development

The traditional approach to systems development using structured methods has placed an emphasis on separating the logical view - usually of a system - from a physical representation of it. While such a distinction has been invaluable, particularly in allowing analysts to understand the nature of the problem they are coming to grips with, when it becomes a dogma it can actually inhibit system development. The author is aware of more than one development site where a great deal of wasted time and effort is spent on arguing about what constitutes a logical representation and what a physical one.

---

[4] This may be in the format of the rules that transform data from an input form to a printed report, or the rules of a dialogue flow that determine the passage from screen to screen.

It is far more important to understand how a logical - or largely logical - model of the business can aid the development process, particularly when that logical model exists within the context of an Information Architecture.[5] Where the organisation is using IE to build up a model and understanding of the business, then the BAA model should constitute that view. It may, in practice, be necessary to freeze such a business model **before** any design is undertaken. The model, or at least the sub-set of it that forms the basis for a business system, provides not only the system's scope; it provides the solid framework for the rapid development of that system. In order to understand how that framework operates, it is necessary to understand a little about how various development environments operate to facilitate the construction process. This is considered in section 12.2.1.

Section 12.2.2 considers how the BAA deliverables can be used effectively to provide the framework and basis for interactive design with the potential users of the system, while section 12.2.3 discuses the nature of the interactive design process itself by considering the role played by prototyping in BSD and beyond.

12.2.1 The Comparative Roles of 3GLs, 4GLs, and Application Generators

Business application systems grew out of the need to segment a business problem into a series of activities performed in a predetermined sequence. 3GLs allowed the coding of this sequence more or less directly, and added various characteristics of data file structuring to their syntax. With the advent of 4GLs, many of the formal sequential constructs associated with programming are hidden from the programmer or user, and are put in place when the 4GL code is interpreted or compiled. What 4GLs tend to allow is the faster construction of systems because they do not require as detailed or rigorous specification of the program logic as a 3GL requires. In many cases this means that systems can be more quickly constructed and/or modified than using a 3GL.

Application generators are computer programs that generate programs and/or systems from some sort of formal structured specification. Sometimes the structured specification comprises diagrams, or diagrams supplemented by text.

A prime rationale for the IE approach has been the automatic generation of systems from complete, cohesive, structured specifications **that in turn fit in with the overall business structure and rationale for the system.** However, this is only now beginning to become achievable. Would-be users of application generators need to be aware of the current limitations of such an approach and cut their cloth accordingly, though there is no reason to doubt that many key systems of the future will be built faster and to a better quality by this method. The key component to this approach is the tight **framework** that the BAA/BSD model can provide, and it is this topic that is further explored in the following section.

---

[5] For a full discussion of the Information Architecture concept see section 4.3.1.

Various issues that need to be considered in adopting either a 4GL or code generator were considered in section 11.2. What needs to be addressed now is the differing impacts such environments might make on the BSD through to Construction end of the IE life cycle, the end where technological issues come to the fore.

Hand coding using a 3GL requires tight, clear, and unambiguous specifications. These can easily be provided by some of the component parts of the IE design models. However, a 3GL environment necessarily implies that a sequence of events needs to be predetermined and specified, and this will have major implications on the structuring and design of systems to meet business needs. How to cope with these issues is more fully covered in section 12.3.2.[6]

Both 4GLs and code generators more readily lend themselves to the rapid development of prototypes than 3GLs, and it is primarily in this role that they can effectively be used in the BSD through to Construction phases. In section 12.2.3, the role of prototyping in the design process is more thoroughly explored.

12.2.2 Using the BAA Deliverables

The business model produced as part of the BAA process is the explicit link to the business and to the architectures produced (and updated) as part of the information strategy planning cycle. It is also the key link forward to systems that will support the business in its endeavours.

That subset of the data model that covers the BSD scope can form a solid basis for the design of a system. Its explicit link to the corporate data model ensures that a common basis to the understanding of information contained in the system is maintained. Nonetheless, design decisions can impact upon the structure of the system's underlying data model: all entry points into the data have to be defined and considered, and the data model may have to be denormalised or adjusted to meet performance requirements. This means that the EMVs of frequently used elementary processes need to be analyzed carefully so that potential system bottlenecks can be identified. The issues that should be considered and the processes involved in moving towards a physical database design are discussed in section 12.3.1.

Where the system will be constrained by its target environment to predetermine the sequencing of elementary processes to meet business needs, the processes themselves will have to be mapped to business procedures.[7] Such procedures will themselves

---

[6] It is not meant to imply that the issues dealt with in section 12.3.2 are only applicable to 3GLs: they may also apply to a varying extent to 4GLs and even to code generators.

[7] This topic is fully discussed in section 12.3.2.

relate to procedure EMVs that are identical in form and content to process EMVs. (For the purpose of design they are identical.) The EMV for each system procedure - be that an elementary process, a subset of one, or a grouping of two or more - can then be structurally analyzed. The results of this analysis, as is suggested in section 12.3.3, can be used to derive the structure and design of on-line dialogues, and also as the basis of screen design. In this context, the business rules contained within PADs help to determine the rules for moving from field to field, and from screen to screen. It should be possible for aspects of a first-cut prototype to be automatically generated from part of the BAA model.

In the case of elementary processes that are likely to be implemented as batch procedures, EMVs similarly provide the basis for structuring the input forms, relating them to the target system data structures, and/or for designing reports. The business rules contained in PADs form the basis for program design and/or generation, and the structure of the EMVs may facilitate the structuring of such batch programs much in the same way as various structured design and programming techniques use data structures as the basis for creating program module structures.[8]

So, it is clear that while the BAA data model provides the fundamental platform for the structuring of a system, each procedure EMV, together with the business logic contained in a PAD, provides the detailed basis for the content and structuring of each business module or unit of the system.

Process Dependency Diagrams primarily illustrate the dependency links between elementary processes. These can be used to help structure the sequence of execution of system procedures once the mapping between process and procedures has been determined.[9] Like DFDs, PDDs can be used to ensure that the inputs to a procedure are identified and defined. DFDs help to ensure also that outputs from process/procedures are recognised and become translated into reports of output screens.

The main relevant BAA components and their links into the design process are shown in Figure 12.2.

12.2.3 The Use of Prototyping in the BSD Phase

The subset of the BAA deliverables that defines the scope of a BSD project also provides a tight framework within which the power of prototyping comes into its own. The major inhibiting factor on this activity is the power and limitations of the

---

[8] For further details see section 12.3.4.

[9] It is, of course, possible to convert the PDD to a **Procedure** Dependency Diagram to make the **system** dependencies more explicit.

prototyping tool chosen.[10] An ideal prototyping tool would be closely integrated with, or connected to, the CASE tool that has been used for the building of the business model.

Ideally, using the framework provided by the model, the prototyping exercise should be directed at constructing a system that can be brought into live operation. Theoretically, any problems with such a system will be sorted out in further controlled iterations through the prototyping process. So the system will be grown or evolved from the solid basis provided by the BAA model, and any change in business requirement, or better understanding of it, will result in the system being adjusted in a controlled manner through the use of

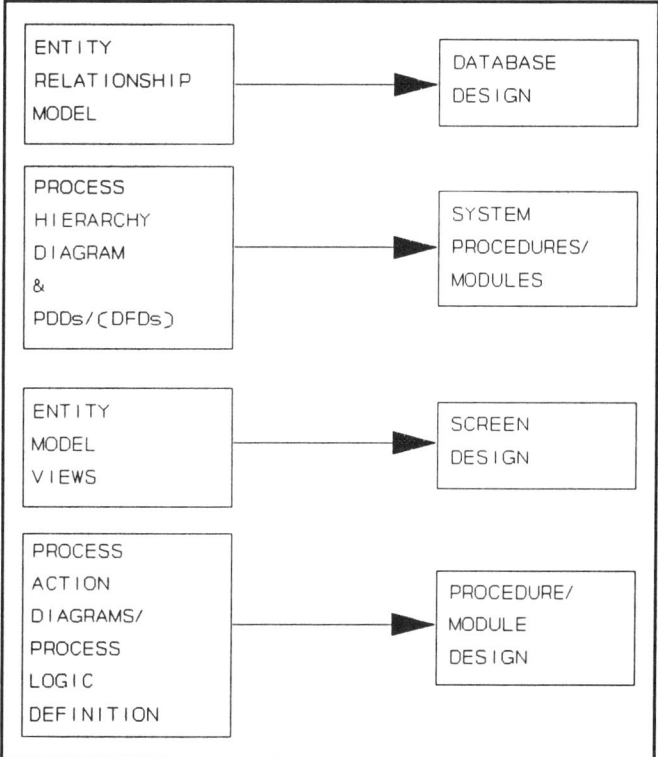

Figure 12.2 The Main BAA Deliverables and their Link into the Design Process

prototyping. This would be possible if the issue of performance did not creep into the picture - and one should not forget that **performance can also be a business requirement**. In order to ensure adequate performance of the system, compromises need to made with the analysis model which generally means that the design data model is denormalised.[11] However, **each such adjustment to the underlying business ERM introduces a design constraint that may eventually inhibit the ability of the system to cope with changes to the business**. This is a reality that will have to be borne in mind as the design process progresses whether or not prototyping is used.

---

[10]   These limitations may also be inherent to the whole design/construction environment, which cannot effectively be separated from the prototyping one in an IE rapid development context.

[11]   The considerations that come into play in this process are discussed in section 12.3.1.

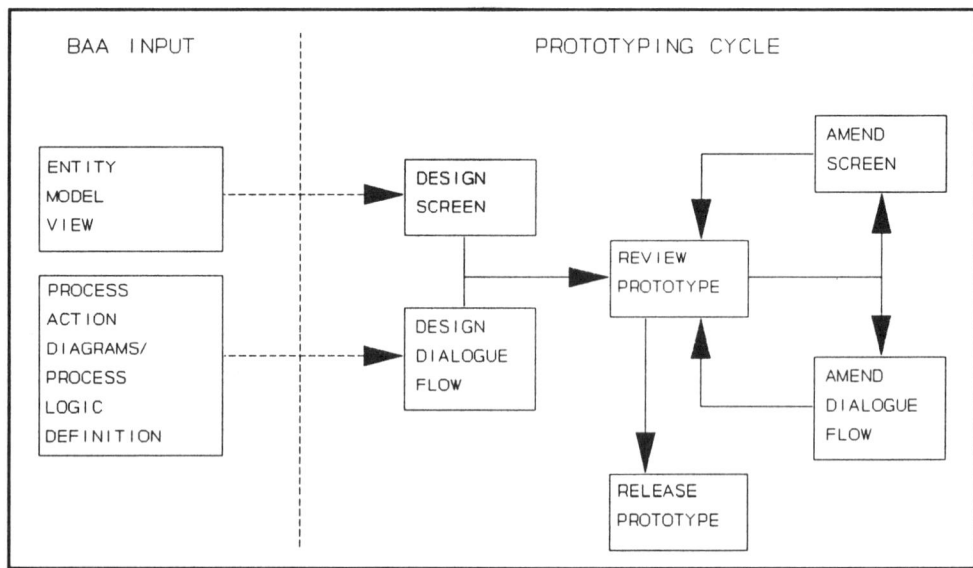

Figure 12.3 The Prototyping Cycle

Before beginning prototyping, it is essential to decide what the purpose behind prototyping is. The ideal prototype in an IE context is one that becomes the live system. The aim then is to use the prototype to **meet** user requirements: each early iteration of the prototyping cycle shown in Figure 12.3 is designed to meet user needs in a narrowly circumscribed context and within a tight time envelope:

- establish the screen design
- confirm the screen design
- establish the dialogue flow based on data structures and/or PAD logic
- confirm the dialogue flow.

Further iterations repeat the refinement of each system procedure until it meets the overall user requirements set out for this development time envelope. What is essential in order to keep this process from becoming locked into an endless loop, are two contexts: a time limit, and a set of requirements to be met within this time span by the first release of the system. In this way, the system will evolve in a controlled way over time. The next release of the system will be dictated by business priorities and needs, and again a fixed time will be allocated to the task, with an agreed set of requirements and objectives to be met.

By contrast, the decision could be made[12] that prototyping be used as a means to agree and establish the users' functional requirements, the prototype then becoming a part of the design specification to be written in a 4GL. In such a case, the prototype will be built on a limited database with no or little real data underpinning it. At its

---

[12] - Or the nature of the prototyping environment chosen may dictate -

most primitive, such a prototype will merely be a set of screens flashed upon a screen in a predetermined order; at its most sophisticated the prototype may be supported by some "real" data that allows it to mimic the characteristics of the envisaged system. This approach to prototyping will still require the developers to consider separately many of the design issues discussed in section 12.3.

Ideally the prototyping tool should be part of the I-CASE environment: it should be driven by the definitions and model contained in the repository or encyclopedia. Furthermore, the prototyping tool should have the following characteristics:

● Automatic generation of a preliminary database from the relative ERM subset of the BAA data model;
● Automatic generation of preliminary procedure screens from the elementary process EMVs;
● Automatic generation of procedure dialogue flows[13] from the structure underpinning the elementary process EMV;
● Integration of the business rules contained in the elementary process PAD into the dialogue flow transition rules;[14]
● Ease of use in adjusting screens, on-line dialogues, and data structures, with the controlled reflection of these changes back into the base model;[15]
● The ability for the prototype to generate an operational system, or for it to be used directly for such a purpose.[16]

12.3 The Design Process

The way in which the process of design will proceed is dependent on the technical platform for which the system is targeted and the software tools available for that chosen environment. The basic issues that have to be addressed in the BSD phase are summarised in Figure 12.4 and are discussed in detail in sections 12.3.1 to 12.3.4. The extent to which any of the steps involved in design will require manual intervention and extensive work will be dependent on the chosen environment and support tools available within it. At one extreme, a primitive 3GL environment will require a maximum of such manual intervention; at the other, a design tool set that is based

---

[13] See section 12.3.3.

[14] *ibid.*

[15] It may not always be desirable that **design** elements be rippled back into the **business** model. In this context, "design elements" are those things (eg. flags, codes, etc.) that have been introduced **specifically to make the system work**.

[16] The generation of a run-time system directly from the prototype may be necessitated by **performance requirements**.

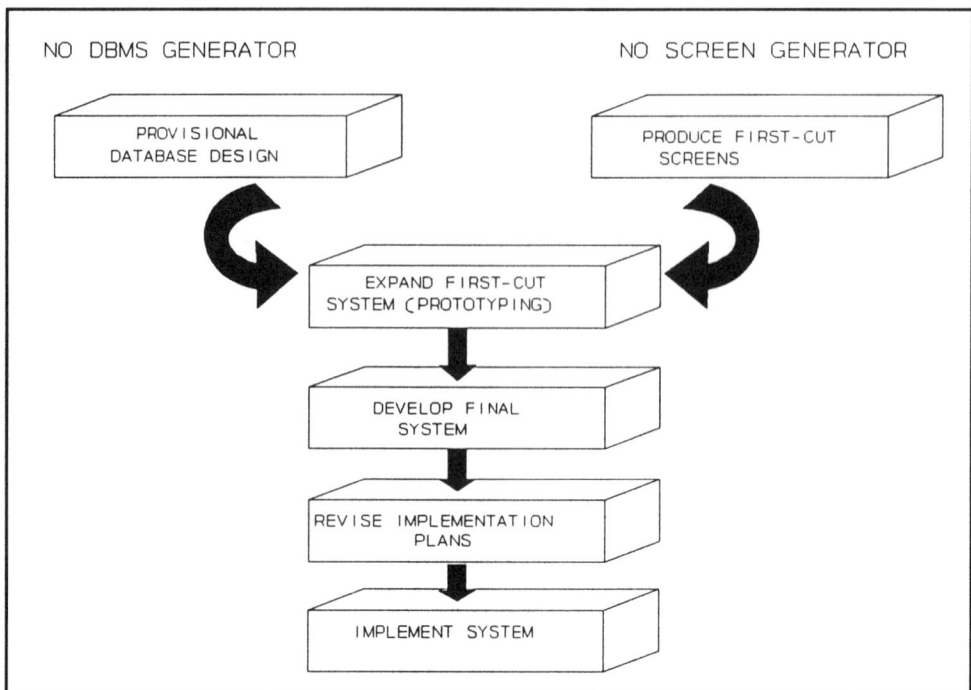

Figure 12.4 The Basic Issues Addressed in the BSD Phase

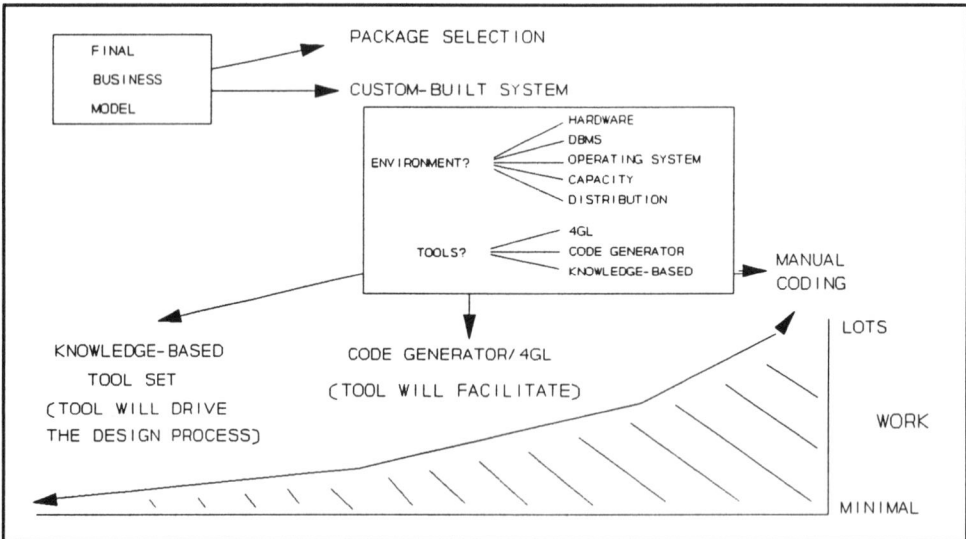

Figure 12.5 The Effect of Chosen Environment on the Design Process

around some intelligent engine will guide the design process and require minimum manual intervention.   Code generators and 4GLs fit somewhere between these extremes, as is shown in Figure 12.5.

In the past, what may be broadly classified as "environment decisions" have often been driven not by business considerations, but by the more technically-oriented data processing departments, who made decisions about hardware, DBMS, operating systems, development languages and environments, data communications, and the distribution or centralisation of computer services. Many of these decisions are, however, becoming more driven by business needs: the ISP technical architecture (see section 4.3.3) provides a business-driven framework for these decisions, while wider exposure to PC environments have created users with basic technical knowledge and keen, but not unrealistic, expectations from computer systems. In considering the issues to be addressed in the design process, the impact of such environment decisions should also be considered, and an IT professional should explain these to the overall decision makers, or demonstrate them via a simple prototype.

12.3.1 Preliminary Data Design

In undertaking the design of a system, it makes sense to begin with the data itself, for this forms the basic platform upon which any system runs. The main purpose behind preliminary design is to come up with a logical model of the data underlying the system. In order to this, the BAA data model that supports the whole business needs to undergo a number of small but significant transformations:

- All remaining many-to-many relationships are resolved into intersecting entities whose only purpose is to join one business entity with another. **These intersecting entities have no business meaning in their own right, and contain no independent attributes.**[17]
- All non-key entry points to the model are identified and annotated on it as is illustrated in Figure 12.6. This may require analysis of the logic underlying the relevant elementary processes (PAD), or may be performed automatically by the I-CASE tool's preliminary data design function.
- All paths through the model are annotated with the relevant volumetric data. These are required so that designers can begin to highlight those parts of the model where performance requirements may require compromises to be made from the default relational or "logical" model.

---

[17] Some IE practitioners advocate the resolution of all many-to-many relationships during the BAA phase. In practice, this results in the creation of an entity that is there only for technical reasons, and this tends to confuse the business users. Of course, where such a resolution does reveal an entity that has business meaning, but which has been concealed either through the operation of a current system, or because the business use of terminology is vague, the resolution **should** occur in the BAA. Such an entity will almost inevitably have attributes of interest to the business in its own right.

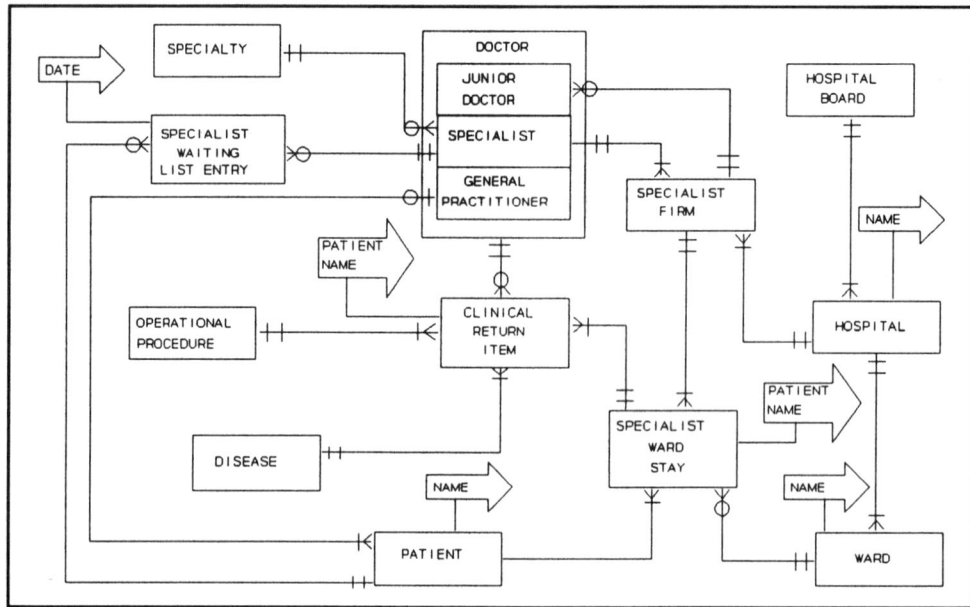

Figure 12.6 Annotating Non-key Entry Points

In more traditional IE theory, the Preliminary Data Structure takes no account of the target database or any of the constraints that this may impose upon the design itself - these are viewed to be aspects that are addressed as part of the Technical Design phase: the BSD data structure should be capable of implementation upon any technical environment. If the broader aim of the BSD project is the creation of a family of application packages which run on different hardware and software environments, then such a strict division between BSD and TD should be enforced; it should also be applied where there is no indication of what the target operational platform is. However, for the majority of design projects, the decision about an operational environment has been made. (Or even if it has not yet been finalised, it is currently likely to be Relational in concept.) Where this is the case, then there is a strong argument in favour of building the constraints and characteristics of the target DBMS into the design. A further impetus for this decision is if a decision has been made to use any form of prototyping as an integral part of the design process (see further section 12.2.3). In this case, a platform database needs to be created for the prototyping exercise, and the Preliminary Data Model will form the foundation for this database.

The main input required for Preliminary Data Design is the subset of the BAA ERM[18] that specifies the scope of the target system. This ERM comprises the Entity

---

[18] See section 8.2.1.

Types, Relationships, and Attributes identified, all fully named and defined, together with all relevant volumetric data that has been gathered. This will be transformed into a Preliminary Data Structure Diagram as is shown in Figure 12.7 which illustrates the

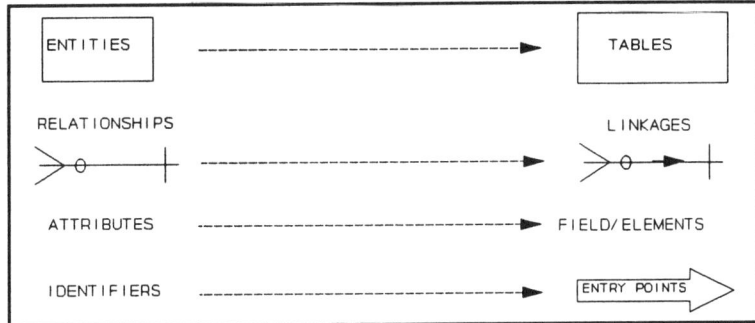

Figure 12.7 Transformation from ERM to Data Structure Diagram

transformation from entity to table, relationships to linkages, and contains attributes as fields or elements. Also annotated as entry points are identifiers to tables, and these are supplemented by alternative entry points. Figure 12.8 illustrates a convention for showing entry points.

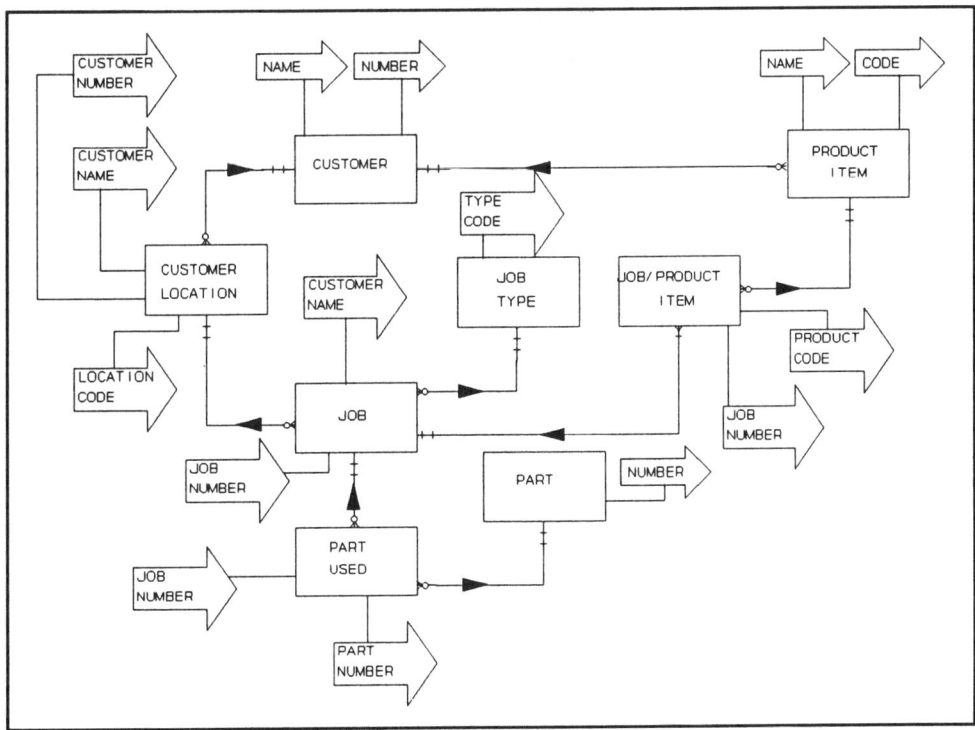

Figure 12.8 Data Structure Diagram Showing Alternative Entry Points

The Preliminary Data Structure Diagram shown in Figure 12.7 is a purely logical one in that it is still based on relation concepts, and has taken no account of any constraints that a target DBMS may impose upon it. It should be clear from the transformation from ERM to Preliminary Data Structure Diagram that the transformation would be far more radical if the target DBMS were one based on hierarchical or network principles.

Figure 12.9 shows a part of the same Data Structure Diagram (DSD) annotated with volumetric data.

The DSD will form the basic foundation for any further data design work, be it logical or physical.

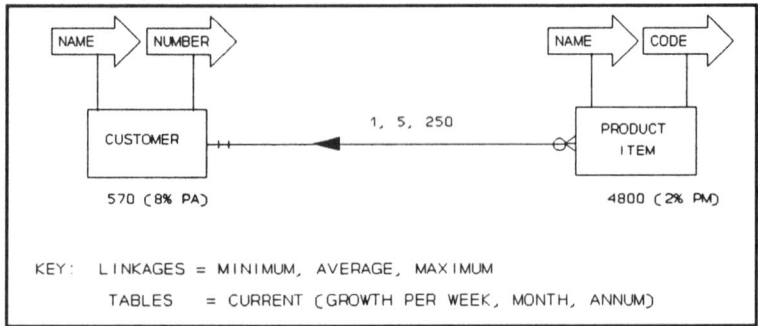

Figure 12.9   Data Structure Diagram Annotated with Volumetric Data

As procedures are identified and further refined and defined within the BSD phase (see section 12.3.2.1), they will be tested against the DSD in two ways:

- The Data Accesses required by the procedure will be traced against a subset of the data structure contained in the DSD to determine that no gaps exist in the access paths required to navigate from one table to another.[19] Where such gaps are identified, they need to be bridged, and the number of likely accesses to the new link for each execution of the procedure must be annotated on the DSD.
- The number of likely executions of the procedure per time period (hour, day, week, etc.) is used to form the basis for assessing whether the current data structure will support the system performance requirements. Possible bottle-necks should be highlighted so that compromises in the data structures can be made taking into account **all** system performance constraints.

The ways in which the activities of Preliminary Data Design, Procedure Design. and Data Access Design interrelate are shown in Figure 12.10. The mapping from the evolving DSD to the models of existing systems cannot be ignored, and the primary reference point for ensuring that such a mapping is traceable - especially where drastic changes are made in moving from an ERM to a DSD - is the mapping from the BAA

---

[19]   Initially, this procedure EMV should be either identical to, or a subset of the process EMV that the procedure maps to (see also section 12.3.3).

ERM to the model built up of the existing systems during current system analysis.[20] The Preliminary Data Structure, built up as part of the Preliminary Data Design task, will evolve as the business system procedures emerge, and will finally be changed - sometimes quite radically - as performance requirements are incorporated into it as part of the Data Access Design task. It is the final DSD that will be

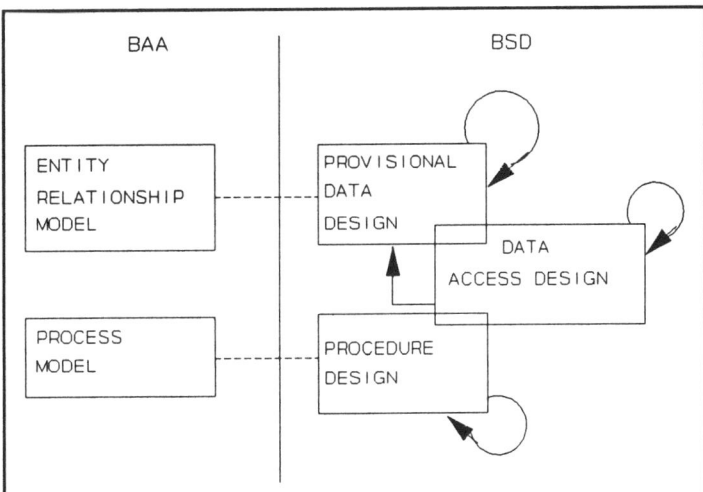

Figure 12.10 Interrelationship Between Preliminary Data Design, Procedure Design and Data Access Design

the input into the generation of the final database upon which the system will run.

It is not within the scope of this particular study to deal with the detailed principles underlying the design of databases. It is hoped though that this key task has been placed in an IE context, and that it will be better understood when we turn to the questions of system functionality that are addressed in the following section.

12.3.2 Structuring the System

In order for the envisaged computer system to meet business needs, it has to be structured in such a way that it both supports current business practises and procedures, and takes into account the broader context of computerisation within which the system will operate. The latter point highlights two key considerations:

● The strong need for the recognition of the constraints that a particular computer hardware and software environment will impose upon **how** a system will operate, particularly in the **sequence of the procedures** that can be undertaken by an operator.[21]
● The system itself will fit into the context of other already existing and planned computer systems. The BAA model that frames the design process may recognise, for example, that the creation of a key entity is **outside of the scope of the**

---

[20] This mapping is best stored in a spreadsheet.

[21] See discussion on pages 203 ff.

business area and hence of the system. The analysis should not only recognise this; it should also be able to state specifically in which other business area the entity is created. However, the reality of this may translate to the fact that although the "entity" does come into being as and where envisaged, that process **is not computerised and is unlikely to be computerised for some time yet**. The system being designed must take into account this reality, and should be augmented with a designer added procedure[22] (albeit a temporary one if computerisation of the offending external procedure is imminent). Similarly, where the information does exist in computerised format in another system, bridging procedures may need to be added to the system design in order to ensure that it enters the new system in the format required.

The first step in developing a sketch of the structure of the envisaged system is to determine how each elementary process within the system scope is going to be dealt with. This step is discussed in section 12.3.2.1.

Next, the gaps in that structure need to be filled, and the overall framing structure within which it will operate needs to be added to give it coherence. This process, discussed in section 12.3.2.2, may result in the identification of menus, fast path access conventions, and various overnight batch procedures.

12.3.2.1 Mapping Elementary Processes to Procedures

In the multi-processing environment that many state-of-the-art workstations are currently bringing into common usage, with a window-type interface between user and system, there is conceptually no need for the integrity of the business processing "unit" - the elementary process - to be compromised. As the computer operator interacts with the systems available, it is always possible to open a new window, thereby firing up a new procedure as and when needed. However, in a more conventional, mainframe-plus-dumb-terminal environment, it is essential for the program to have predetermined paths, and for its execution to be terminated or suspended **before** another program can be initiated. Let us examine what this can mean in business terms.

PROCESS CUSTOMER ORDER
APPROVE NEW CUSTOMER
PROVIDE PRODUCT INFORMATION

We have identified a number of elementary processes, perhaps from different related business areas, such as those illustrated in Figure 12.11. We are asked to design a system to process customer orders. A direct one-to-one mapping with the **Process Customer Order** elementary process would ensure that the single unit of work - taking the order - will be correctly performed

Figure 12.11
Some Elementary Processes

---

[22] See page 222.

as a result. The phone rings on the order clerk's table and the following dialogue takes place:

Clerk: **[Fires up *Take Order* procedure]** Good morning, XYZ Company, how may I help you?

Customer: This is ABC Enterprises, and I would like to place an order.

Clerk: Is that ABC Enterprises of 179 The Lane, London NW7?

Customer: That is correct.

Clerk: What would you like to order?

Customer: I would like 200 of your new widgets.

Clerk: Certainly. Do you need anything else?

Customer: No, that is all. When can I expect delivery?

Clerk: The day after tomorrow: your order number is CF197.

Customer: CF197? Thank you.

Clerk: Thank you, and good day. **[Ends *Take Order* procedure]**

Well, that is the way the business logic underlying the elementary process **Process Customer Order** works. But, unfortunately, the real world is a lot more complex than that. The dialogue could proceed as follows:

Clerk: [**Fires up** *Take Order* **procedure**] Good morning, XYZ Company, how may I help you?

Customer: This is ABC Enterprises, and I would like to place an order.

Clerk: We do not have a record of you on our computer, have you bought from us before?

Customer: No, this is the first time: I saw your advertisement in the Daily Blah.

Clerk: [**Ends** *Take Order* **procedure.** **Fires up** *Insert New Customer* **procedure**] May I take your details, please?...

...[**Ends** *Insert New Customer* **procedure. Fires up** *Take Order* **procedure**] What would you like to order?

Customer: Can you tell me about the specifications of your new widgets?

Clerk: Certainly. [**Ends** *Take Order* **procedure.** **Fires up** *Provide Product Information* **procedure**] I'm just waiting for the computer screen.... Right, ...

... [**Ends** *Provide Product Information* **procedure.** **Fires up** *Take Order* **procedure**] How many would you like to order?...

Of course the operator-computer interaction could be made much smoother **if the** "calls" to **Insert New Customer** and **Product Information** were "hard coded" into the original **Take Order** procedure, and that is precisely the point: in a conventional sequential processing environment, the calls have to be **designed in.** This requires either very structured dialogues, or very flexible systems with many calls to many procedures from many places. Is it possible to simplify the design of these calling patterns and to rationalise the overall system structure by doing so? We shall be examining the ways in which some of this can be facilitated both through the overall structuring of the system to meet the business requirements (section 12.3.2.2) and through the design of dialogues based on data structures (section 12.3.3).

Before turning to these topics, let us ask how the implemented **Take Order** procedure could be better mapped against relevant business processes to meet the real system needs. A designer needs to understand that a system to support the operation of a part of the business will reflect (and perhaps determine) **how the business operates or wishes to operate**. This can be **different** in substance from **what the business does**. The BAA model contains the business rules: the system needs to implement those rules in a combination that will allow it to operate. This requires that the elementary procedures within the scope of the system be mapped to business procedures: the mapping may be one-to-one - and often is - but it can also be one-to-many. The elementary process **Take Order** could be implemented as a batch procedure in a mail order firm in which a large number of orders are processed on a daily basis. The volume may dictate that the information is captured swiftly though a data entry front end, and the data captured is then processed overnight and transformed from requested orders into captured ones. Now if that mail order firm starts taking phone orders as well, then the logic of the elementary process is unlikely to change, but the procedure to do the work probably will: the new procedure may become implemented as an on-line interactive order capture dialogue. If, in the interests of providing a better service to customers, the firm now wishes to allow them to enter their orders themselves using a touch-tonetelephone, the logic behind the process remains the same, but a new procedure needs to be developed. By the time the firm described has the

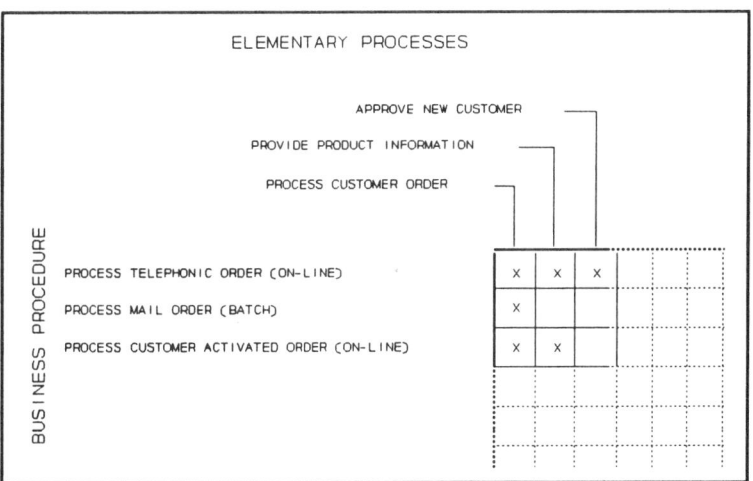

Figure 12.12 Recording Design Decisions in a Spreadsheet

three order capture procedures in place, it is clear that there is a one-to-many mapping from process to procedures. Effectively then, the first step of procedural design (determining exactly what the system will do) involves a chief designer and the business analyst confirming with the users exactly **how** each process will be implemented. Figure 12.12 shows ways of recording these decisions on a spreadsheet. The additional procedures identified need to be added to the (system) PHD which, in effect, becomes a Procedure Hierarchy Diagram such as the one shown in Figure 12.13.

Once this has been done, it will become necessary to determine how all these procedures will hang together as a system: this topic is discussed in section 12.3.2.2.

One slight complication that may arise at this stage is where it is determined to computerise only a part of an elementary process, the rest of it being implemented as

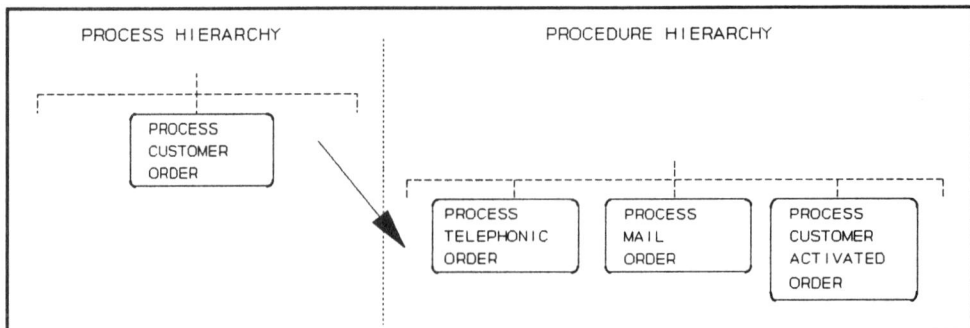

Figure 12.13 Procedure Hierarchy Diagram

a manual procedure. It is essential that such decisions are fully understood, and then carefully documented against the elementary process documentation so that no misunderstanding about the scope of such decisions can arise. Both the PAD and the EMV need to be annotated to reflect the impact of the decision: the portion of the business logic to be implemented in the PAD should be reviewed to ensure that logical coherence has been maintained, and that the "sub-PAD" conforms to the syntactic and integrity rules that apply.

12.3.2.2 Designing the System Structure

The business procedures that have so far been identified need to be joined together within the context of the system and the total integrity of the system needs to be checked and ensured.

Initially the checking will point the designers to those parts of the system that will require interfaces or **bridging procedures** to other systems.[23] Where such "systems" exist within the system architecture, but are, for the present, "conceptual systems" only, the designer may have to add procedures that supply the information that should be coming in from the yet-to-be-written system. For example, in a fictitious business, new customers are first approved by the customer service department for credit worthiness. This business process is fairly complex and is going to be automated. However, the order processing system has a much higher development priority and is currently being designed. The business rule does not allow new customers to place orders until their credit worthiness has been approved. Until the Customer Service System is in place a designer-added procedure **Enter New Customer** will have to be

---

[23] These will ensure that data is received from and/or be sent to other **existing** systems. It is possible to derive the structure for such a procedure from the EMV associated with the data flow to/from the procedure (see section 12.3.3), and the base logic for the data conversion from the spreadsheet that maps ERM Entity/Attribute to Current System File/Field (see section 5.2).

added to the new Order Processing System, and access to it may have to be restricted to the customer service department.

Once all the system procedures have been identified, work can begin on joining them to form the system structure. The starting point for this can be the BAA PHD to which have been added the business procedures identified in the process to procedure mapping process, the bridging procedures, and the designer-added procedures required to ensure the system functions as an integral unit. (The relevant subset of the BAA CRUD matrix should be updated to reflect these new procedures, and the matrix itself can be used in order to check that no remaining holes exist in the overall system design.) This Procedure Hierarchy Diagram gives the designer a first-cut at a system menu structure.[24] This menu structure can quickly be built and reviewed with users in order to determine whether the procedures as packaged reflect business practice, and whether parts of the menu structure need to be packaged together in order to meet security access restrictions.

The system structure developed in this way will be further refined as each procedure is developed in detail: dialogue flows will be built up for all on-line procedures (section 12.3.3), and these, in indicating the flow **between** procedures, will help to refine the system structure. Also, in understanding the various procedures identified and how they will be used, it may become necessary to build up fast-path access routes between all or some of the system.

Lastly, the place for batch procedures in the system structure will be reviewed, and, depending on their nature (eg. standard overnight runs versus user-initiated queries), front end parameter-driven menus may also have to be added to the system (section 12.3.4).

It is now time to turn to the procedures themselves, and the issues that need to be addressed in designing them within an IE context.

12.3.3 Data-Driven Dialogue Design

The starting points for designing the dialogue for each on-line procedure are the

---

[24]   Although by menu structure we are primarily here concerned with a multi-choice menu familiar from many "dumb terminal" contexts, this does not preclude the structure from being used as a basis for designing the menu options in a window environment. It should not be forgotten that the BAA PHD, from which the menu structure ultimately derives, reflects the **business**. In that context, if the PHD has been correctly decomposed , each "top branch" of the hierarchy will often be based upon one entity of central importance to the Business Area. Such an hierarchy is, conceptually, just a short step away from an Object-based system structure (see also section 14.1).

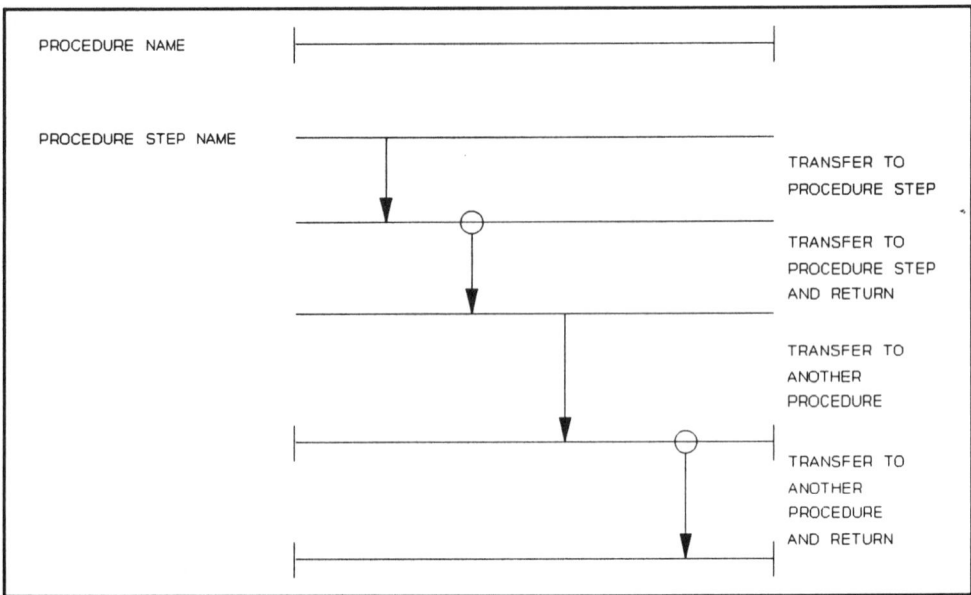

Figure 12.14 Dialogue Flow Diagram Conventions

elementary process PAD and the process EMV. Each of these deliverables should now be adjusted so as to reflect the realities imposed by the process to procedure mapping.[25] This is particularly important where a procedure implements part(s) of an elementary process.[26] The dialogue flow for each procedure is then depicted by means of a dialogue flow diagram. Many differing conventions are used for these in I-CASE tools, and the one illustrated in Figure 12.14 adopted here partly because it is relatively simple to understand.

One may tackle dialogue design from two ends: starting with the PAD, each logical step can be translated into a procedure step on the Dialogue Flow Diagram. So, for example, the on-line flow for the procedure **Take Order** is illustrated in Figure 12.15. Each procedure step then maps to a screen (or screen block) (Figure 12.16), and the business logic underlying the transition from screen to screen is mapped to the PAD logic. In this process, the PAD becomes transformed into a Procedure Action Diagram (PrAD) by the addition of the system logic required to handle the transition from screen to screen, and error conditions.

An alternative way in which to analyze and design the procedure dialogue flow is by examining the **structure** of the procedure EMV. This is always a sub-set of the BAA

---

[25] See also section 12.3.1, especially page 216.

[26] This is discussed on page 221.

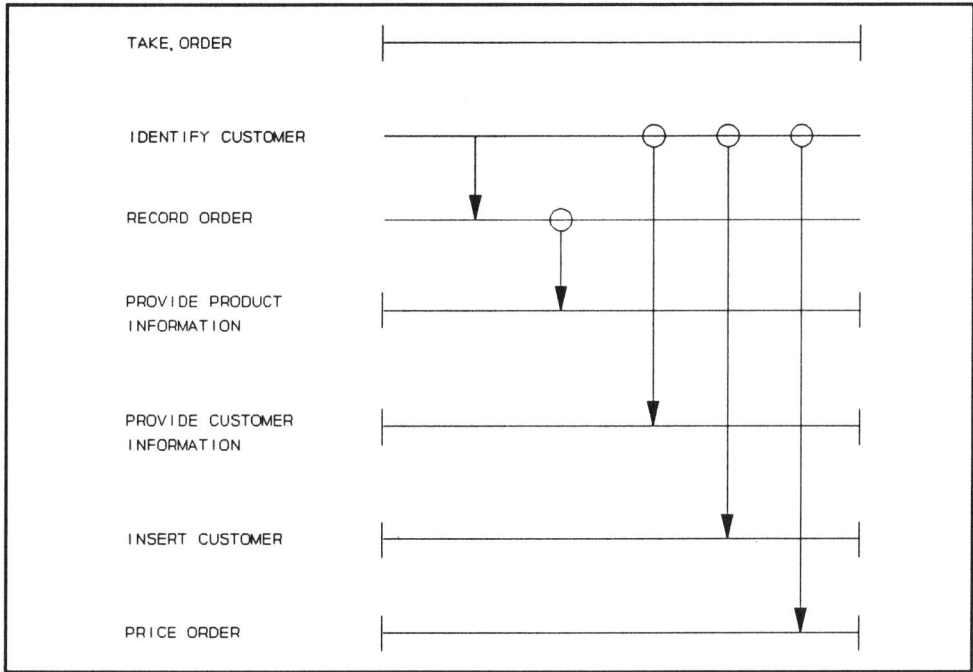

Figure 12.15 Dialogue Flow for **Take Order**

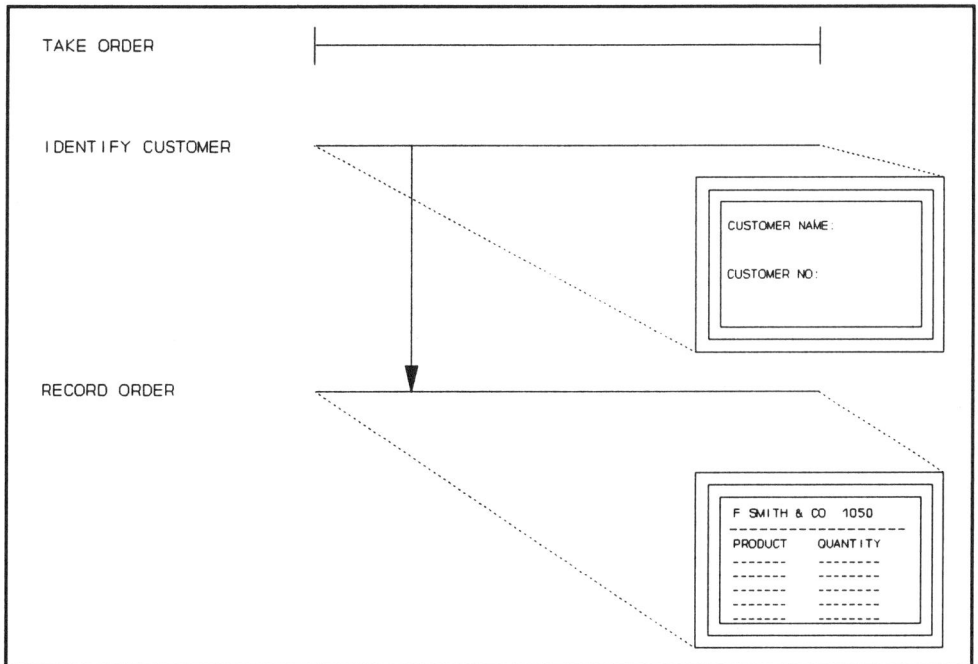

Figure 12.16 Procedure Step Mapping to Screen

ERM both in terms of the entities and relationships involved, **and in terms of their cardinalities**. This last point is important, for, as is shown in Figure 12.17, the **data** can drive the structure of the procedure, and hence of the design. Each procedure EMV "data unit" can map to a screen (or screen block), and the navigation along the relationship that joins one such "unit" with another represents the business rule (contained in the PAD) that determines the transition from one screen/procedure step to another. In some DBMS environments, this approach to dialogue design can have a significant impact on overall system performance considerations: the procedure EMV show potential table joins required, the complexity of such joins, and the likely traffic that these will encounter.

Whichever of these two approaches is adopted in getting a first-cut dialogue flow designed, it is clear that this needs to be reviewed with a user and adjusted, preferably using a prototyping approach. It is a rare user who can relate to paper-based dialogue flows and screen printouts!

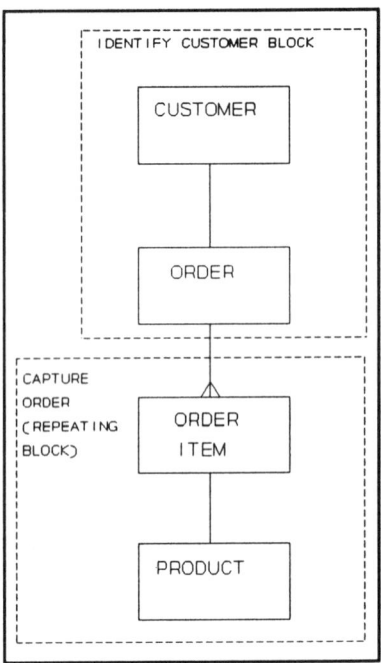

Figure 12.17   Data-Driven Dialogue Design

Once the internal procedure dialogue flow is acceptable to the reviewers, they will begin to point to the flows from the procedure into other procedures: an example of such a packaging of business procedures into complete business transactions is shown in Figure 12.18. What is meant by a business transaction in this context is the execution, or potential execution, of one or more processes in response to a triggering business event. Effectively, in system terms, this represents the combination of some of the system procedures (including designer-added ones) according to the sequential

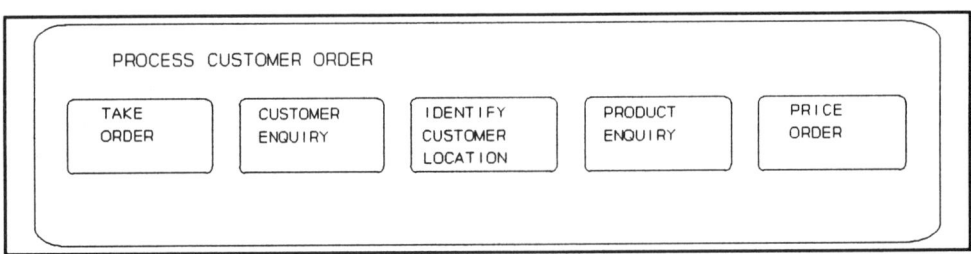

Figure 12.18 Business Transaction

processing requirements of the system.[27]

Again, the key structural element that underpins such an ostensibly procedural requirement is the data model - or more specifically, the common data elements between the two procedures. In Figure 12.19, the dialogue flow between two procedures is shown in data structure terms. The coupling between the two

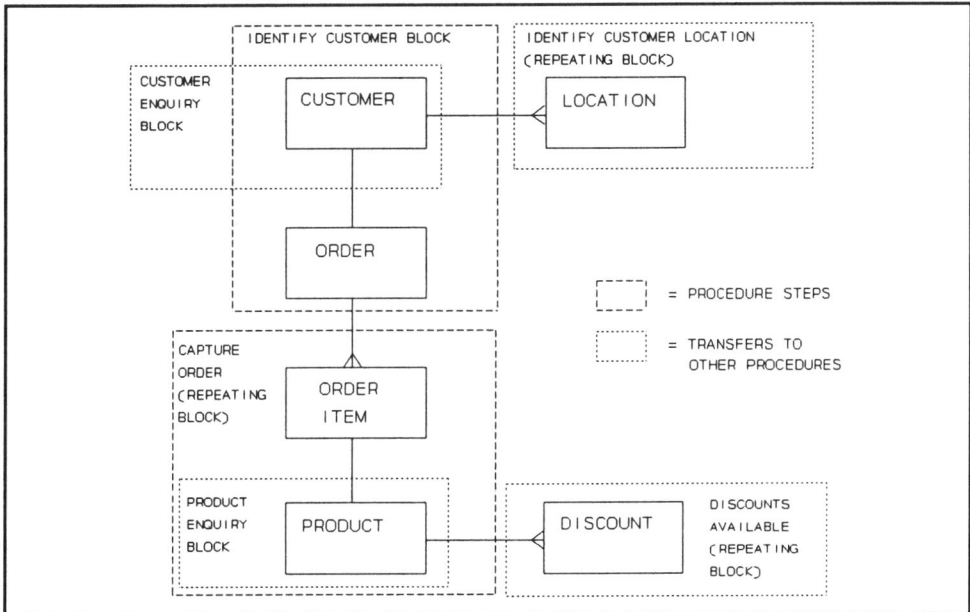

Figure 12.19 Combining Procedures Based on Data Structures

procedures, based as it is on shared data elements, is loose, and this will both facilitate system maintenance, and ensure that the designed system is robust enough to cope with potential business changes. (By definition, the elementary processes upon which the procedures are based are functionally cohesive.)

As the dialogue flow diagrams are amended to reflect the overall system data flows, a detailed picture of the overall system structure emerges which is more complex than the original Procedure Hierarchy Diagram described on page 223. This Procedure Hierarchy Diagram shows the system structure as seen from a business perspective. The expanded system dialogue flow diagram (as illustrated in Figure 12.20) shows the

---

[27] It is also possible to include within the context of a business transaction **actual system** procedures that exist and to which access is technically possible. (Where such access is not possible, then the logic of such procedures may have to be replicated, and an interface to the relevant existing system constructed.)

internal flow between procedures, and is of more relevance to the technical designers.

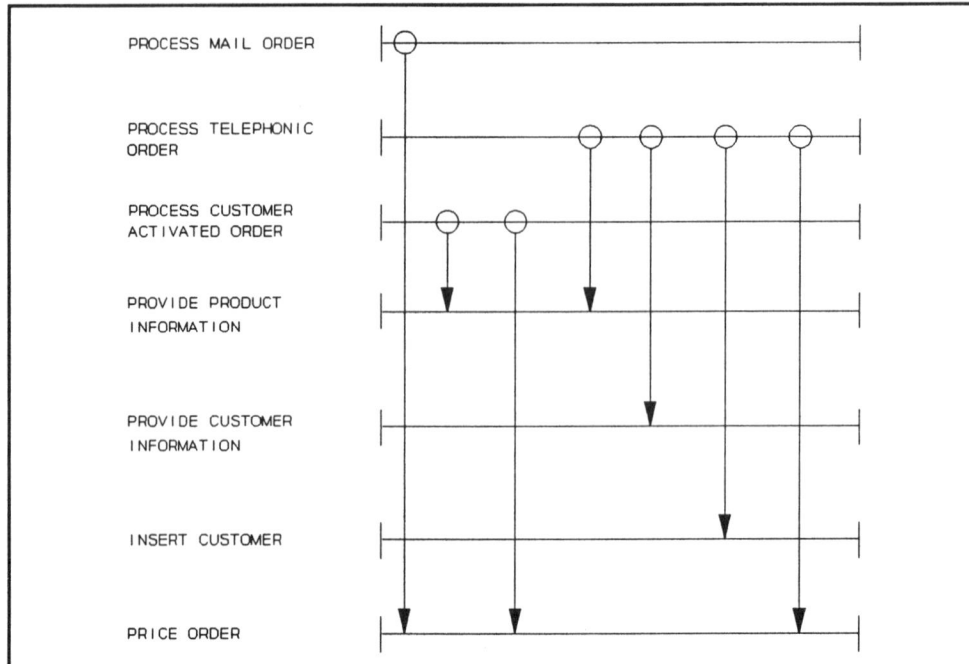

Figure 12.20 Expanded System Dialogue Flow Diagram

It is worth noting at this point that the common Process Action Blocks and business algorithms defined in the BAA, and which were made subject to change control (see section 10.1.3, page 167), can become the basis for reusable modules within (and even across) a group of systems. In some target environments, or where the system is going to be hand-

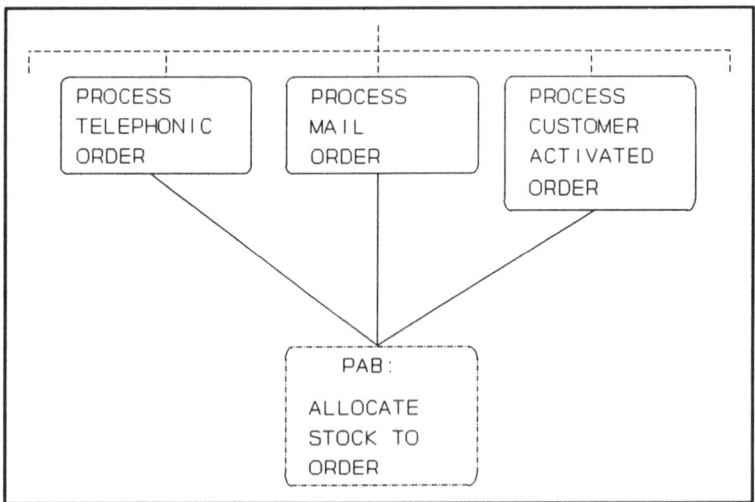

Figure 12.21 Reusability Shown by Fan-in

coded, it may be expedient to make this potential for reusability explicit by decomposing the Procedure Hierarchy Diagram to a Procedure Block level, where the fan-in to such reusable blocks will become visible. This is illustrated in Figure 12.21.

12.3.4 Batch Procedures

The existence of batch procedures will already have been identified in the Process to Procedure mapping exercise, and such procedures will appear in the Procedure Hierarchy Diagram. For each procedure so identified, the designer should determine from the PAD structure the sort of procedure being dealt with. Where the processing is clearly defined and regular (a bulk update, for example) then the menu entry may queue the procedure for later processing, or even perform it in low priority background mode. In some cases such a procedure may have different processing paths, for example where additional figures are gathered at month end as compared to the regular weekly information produced. In this case the menu entry is likely to evoke a small designer-added procedure in which the parameters driving the batch procedure are set up. Lastly, the procedure may be front-ended by a more complex dialogue flow setting up the parameters. This would, for example, be the case with unstructured queries.

In all these cases, the underlying data structures depicted in the procedure EMV can form the basis for the structuring and design of the procedure, much in the same way as data structures have been used in Jackson Structured Programming as the basis for driving the logical design of COBOL programs.

12.3.5 Additional Operational Considerations

Before the final design is agreed, it is essential for the data designers to do one last trawl through the final data structure to ensure that performance requirements will be met. Depending on the final operating environment, it may be necessary at this stage actively to consider additional system requirements such as audit, security, and recovery. These issues are never ignored in logical design, but there is no point in actually going ahead with the design **unless** it is clear that they are not adequately covered within the context of the target operating platform: there is little sense in designers detailing roll-back procedures when they are an integral part of the DBMS system. However, if, for example, the requisite levels of access security are not integrated into the operational environment **and** that environment has been identified, then these aspects of the system should be designed in as early as possible. This approach is, again, a pragmatic compromise of the strict divide between logical and physical, but unless tackled now, could result in a massive amount of redesign effort in the TD&C stage. Project managers should approach this with open eyes and make a positive decision to go one way or the other: the alternative could be a large time and cost overrun with the system operating as expected functionally, but still being unacceptable to the users.

***

We have now reached the familiar ground of a detailed system specification which could be hand-coded and brought into production following methods that are familiar to anyone who has ever been involved in the construction and implementation of a computerised system. In the next chapter, we will briefly consider some of the issues that IE may present when this familiar ground has been reached, particularly where CASE tools are used instead of programmers to complete the job.

Chapter 13 Reaching Familiar Ground

By the time we reach the point at which a detailed system specification can be written, we are on the familiar ground that system developers have traversed often with varied success since the advent of commercial computing. It is not ground that we wish to cover again.

What we need to consider are some of the familiar issues that arise when a system is being moved from its conception - the technical design specification, in conventional terms - to operational acceptance. If, following the BSD process, the intention is to take the data structure, screens, dialogues, and logic definitions, package them into a formal specification for hand-coding by an assembly line of programmers, then there is no need to read any further. The path ahead is well trodden. It can only be assumed that the rigour that has been applied thus far to designing a system based on a careful understanding of the business, and locating it within a business architectural context, is primarily in order to improve overall quality, and not, simultaneously, to address issues of productivity.

A basic tenet of the IE approach is that the rigour of the process can be used to specify systems so that the drudgery of coding can be done by the machines themselves. The BSD deliverable should not be reams of paper that need to be further studied and manually converted to code; it should be a working prototype that, in theory, needs only now to be constrained by the realities of its operational platform and environment in order to be brought into active operational use. We have argued in chapter 12 that, where possible, cognisance should be taken as early as possible of the hardware and software platform targeted for the eventual system in every aspect of the design. An ideal design environment would be one where the BSD prototype can either be compiled into a run time first release of the system, or converted **automatically**[1] into that first release. The system - already measured against user requirements by the users themselves, for they built it - can then be allowed to perform its function in "the real world" and enhancements to it become the next system release, with the required changes being put into place interactively by "growing the prototype". Two key factors need to have been addressed if this pipe dream is to approach anything resembling reality. Firstly, the system **must be capable of growth**. Secondly, each system release **must be able to function accurately in an operational environment**. The first of these issues has been addressed by the analysis and design process. The second will be addressed in section 13.1.

Once a system release has been accepted by the user community, how, in an IE

---

[1] Probably by means of a code generator or application generator.

context, do maintenance issues get addressed? Section 13.2 considers this question without becoming embroiled in the issues that are intrinsic to maintenance in general.

13.1   Bringing the System into an Operational Environment

In considering how to transform the designed system into an operational one, we need to make a number of assumptions about the nature of that designed system. A prototype should have been developed for each on-line system procedure to be covered by the BSD project. The whole approach adopted in design implies that operational users are actively engaged in developing the procedures that they themselves will have to use. In this context, whether the prototype that has been developed for each procedure is capable of direct translation into an operational environment needs to be considered.

The second assumption concerns batch procedures. Where these involve queries to the database, and the production of reports, prototyping can have occurred. It is still possible that some batch procedures (bulk overnight batch updates) are specified in more traditional terms for subsequent coding. In the latter case, the traditional approach to specifying and coding these procedures will still apply.[2] It is also possible that some batch procedures will contain PABs or algorithms that are, in effect, too complex to write in anything but a 3GL procedural language (or that performance constraints will force that decision upon the designers). Such "sub-routines" will have to be specified and tested in the traditional manner.

The question to be asked about those procedures that have been prototyped is whether the prototyping environment is capable of direct translation into an operational one. This is, of course, the most favoured position for it implies that the designer has built a procedure in complete cooperation with the users that fully meets their requirements. Now, that procedure can be transformed into a run time version by being pre-compiled. The situation is much more complex where the prototype is an approximation of the procedure, but requires further work. The project manager needs to understand clearly what is missing from the prototype. At the worst extreme, the prototype will represent a series of screens, loosely tied together. What will then be missing is the "glue". This may include all the detailed on-screen processing (validation checking of fields and cross-checking between fields, for example) as well as the rules for screen-to-screen dialogue flow. In such circumstances, the prototype, together with the missing information, serves as a "programming specification" that will require translation into an operational procedure. This remains the case even where the prototype itself will form the basis for such a "translation" - where the prototype will be built up into an

---

[2]   Realistically, for such batch procedures, traditional systems development practises will co-exist with those possibilities opened up by using IE and CASE. It will always be a case of choosing the most appropriate solution for each particular circumstance.

operational procedure in the back rooms, so to speak. This sort of approach is fraught with potential danger **unless** the users get regular sight of the evolving procedure: a designer left alone could easily, even at this late stage, lose touch with the business realities.

In all cases, the released procedure must still be subjected to rigorous operational testing. For that to occur, there must be a measurable set of acceptance criteria in place. Where these come from in an IE context is the concern of the next section.

13.1.1 Testing and Acceptance Criteria

The delivered system can be related back to those aspects of the business that motivated it in the first place. There should be a set of business objectives, problems, and critical success factors that are traceable back to the ISP whence they originate. Through the BAA the original matrices that mapped these factors to functions and data subject areas/entities are refined to apply to elementary processes and data entities. Then, in BSD, specific procedures (and the information they produce) become the focus of the mapping. So, at the highest possible level, it is these business objectives, problems, and critical success factors that the system must address **if it is to be acceptable to the business**. Further granularity of detail (for example, a functional requirement) is really a manifestation of business rules (BAA) and/or practice (BSD), the details of which are recorded at the appropriate IE phase, and confirmed with the users.[3] In a managed IE process, then, the acceptance criteria are built into the system as it evolves, and formal acceptance of a release of a system - particularly of the first such release - is really, on one level, a confirmation that those criteria are satisfied in an operational context.

It is in such a context that additional acceptance criteria relating to performance and throughput come into play; but these, too, were part of the volumetric data recorded, particularly in the BAA, and confirmed in the BSD.

How then can users develop a test plan for the system? The first item a quality controller from a non-IE context will ask for is a "specification". It is difficult to explain to such a person that **the system *is* the specification**. It is not sensible to test each procedure to ensure whether the code generated from a PrAD conforms to the PrAD, particularly if the PrAD generated the prototype in the first place. Clearly, however, there must be a point at which traditional system or integration testing takes place, and where the system is exercised in a controlled "operational" environment. The former **is still part of the Construction phase**; the latter part of the phase known in IE as Transition. It is in this phase that controlled parallel running of the system may occur to check that it does function correctly on a full set of operational

---

[3] This takes place either via a structured and/or informal review of the business model (BAA) or a review of the prototype (BSD).

data, and that it does meet the performance criteria required from it.

The overall correctness and acceptability of the delivered system (and of any subsequent releases of it) are not issues of quality that are tacked on at the end of the IE process: they are intrinsic to the process, and are an integral part of the constant user participation that is a key factor underlying the IE approach. Business knowledge is transformed into a system by the cooperative endeavour of business user and IT professional.

13.1.2 User Training

No system is ever successful unless it is used and understood by those it was intended for. During the Transition phase - the time when the system is being parallel tested against operational data -users can become familiar with the system operation.

The person(s) who is most familiar with the system from a user perspective is the user representative(s) who has been part of the design team. Throughout the BSD, each procedure has repeatedly been reviewed by this person who is, in effect, the operational expert of a particular part of the business. During the BSD, the User Liaison Committee has still continued to function, though its constituent members may have changed a little in make-up to reflect the shift in interest in this phase from business to system. At the very least, the committee should have had sight of each system procedure in its final state. Often, members would have had hands-on experience of the procedure in question.

It is the task of the team's user representative(s) to perform user training. Of course, the other team members will be available to provide technical back-up throughout this exercise. It is also the user representative's task to provide both business-oriented user guides, and the system help text as far as this is business oriented.[4] (These are, in effect, the users' back-up training in the system.)

By placing user training in the hand of the users, ownership of the system as a business system is transferred by the users to the wider user community. It is at this stage that the accountability of the user team members to their peers is most exposed, hence the need not to spring surprises on them, and to have kept them informed of the project throughout its progress - the real function of the User Liaison Committee.

13.2   Maintenance in an IE Context

A simplified version of the IE life cycle is illustrated in Figure 13.1. In it, the route from the Production phase does not lead into one called "Maintenance". This is

---

[4]   Technical help text (system error messages, etc.) and System Operational Manuals are the responsibility of the IT team members.

because the main function of the Production phase is ensuring that the system continues to meet business requirements by monitoring the system's performance against those requirements. The system will no longer meet the business requirements for one of two reasons: the system itself can no longer cope with them; or the requirements themselves can change.

In IE terms, any failure on the part of the system to meet the business needs for which it was intended can - and probably should - lead to an adjustment being made to the system... or what we traditionally call maintenance. The business requirements of the system have been fully and adequately documented in the analysis and design models (see also section 13.1.1), and may be expressed as a set of matrices that formally map the requirements to the data entities and system procedures that meet them.

If there is a gap between system and requirements, a reiteration of all or part of the IE cycle must take place, and it is part of the role of production monitoring to determine the nature of that particular iteration.

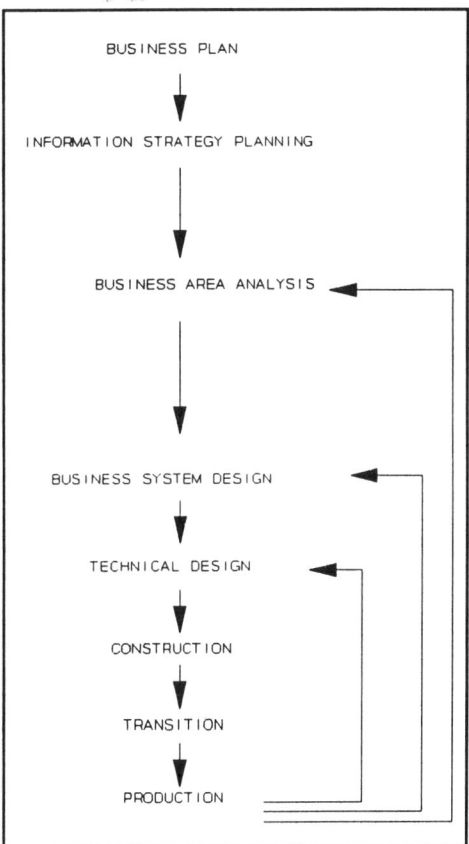

Figure 13.1 The IE Life Cycle

Where the system is no longer capable of meeting business needs (eg. response times are poor, or the system is running out of capacity), the cause of this is probably technical, and it is necessary to return to the Technical Design phase to sort the problem out. This may also be the starting point for maintenance when new releases of the DBMS or operating software take place. It is more likely though that these changes can be addressed at the Construction phase, requiring no more that a re-compile of generated code, or at worst, a regeneration of the code followed by a re-compile.[5]

The gap between system and business needs may, however, result from a change in

---

[5] Of course, in both of these circumstances, testing of the regenerated and/or re-compiled system will be necessary: the nature of such testing may vary depending on the extent and type of supporting software changes being addressed.

business procedure (perhaps made because of a change in business policy). For example, the rule may have been that no orders may be taken from a customer who has exceeded a pre-agreed credit limit: where this has occurred, the customer is immediately referred to the credit department who may, according to set criteria, increase the customer's credit limit either permanently or for this order only. Now, in order to improve on customer service, the order processors are given the same power as was previously exercised by the credit department within some clearly defined parameters. What the business does has not changed - the rules for credit extension are basically the same. However, how the rules are applied has been changed: in effect, the business procedure has been amended, and the system must be amended to reflect this change. Clearly, the cycle through the appropriate IE phases begins at BSD with **how** the business system needs to be changed: the business itself - the realm of BAA - remains unchanged.

The maintenance cycle would begin at BAA if the actual business rules - **what the business does** - change. For example, if the system deals with the issuing of private pension schemes and parliament decides to change the rules applying to such schemes, as well as introducing some new ones, the very nature of the business itself has been changed (on this occasion by an external factor). The business model itself would have to be changed and parts of it re-analysed in order to ensure that the new rules and principles are reflected in it. In such a case, maintenance would have to begin with an understanding of the business before the system design model can be adjusted (and augmented) to reflect those changes.

Does one ever return to ISP as part of a maintenance activity? Clearly if the nature of the business itself changed - we were selling fast food, but want to convert our outlets into launderettes - the system would no longer meet business needs. The information structure underpinning the new business is likely to differ fundamentally from the old information structure, and an entirely new ISP would have to be undertaken.[6] (This should not be confused with the annual revisiting and adjustment of the ISP that should be taking place as part of the business planning cycle.)

---

[6]   Arguably, common business areas in the two businesses (Accounting is the obvious example) could contain large areas of overlap notwithstanding our comments.

Chapter 14   Future Considerations

Like all developments in computing, the IE approach is not a static one. As it is being used and applied, theory gives way to reality, and, in this process, the theory is reconsidered and rewritten. Moreover, the CASE tools themselves respond to the technological changes occurring around them, and become more responsive to their users - the planners, analysts, designers, and constructors whose job it is to make them work.

The emphasis throughout this book so far has been on the here and now - on pragmatically applying IE theory to achieve results, even if those results in themselves represent some compromise on the theory and practice. A user will always be happier with a system that meets most of his needs rather than a set of models which, though perfectly correct, are, from the user's perspective, nothing more than a set of drawings.

For a moment, though, it is worth our while turning our attention, albeit briefly, to where IE is going, and to some of the factors that are already influencing IE both in theory and in practice.

The first of these, considered in section 14.1, is the question of Object-Oriented Analysis and Design (OOA/D) which currently exists outside of the IE framework. How, if at all, will the concepts encapsulated in OOA/D fit in with an IE approach? Or are we facing a totally new paradigm and do we have to go back to the (metaphorical) drawing board yet again?

Secondly, initiatives such as AD/Cycle® clearly relate in some way to an IE approach. What do such initiatives mean? What is the connection between them and IE? And how do the so-called Component CASE tools, or C-CASE, fit into the whole picture. These questions are considered briefly in section 14.2.

14.1   Object-Oriented Analysis and Design

It is impossible within the context of this book to tackle the concepts of Object-Orientation with anything approaching rigour. The intention is to consider, in a cursory way, what the key elements of an Object-Oriented approach are, and where these may fit in with the IE principles we have been examining.

The key concept in Object-Orientation is the Object itself. This may loosely be defined as **anything** that we may wish to know about and/or manipulate. In many senses, the object is very similar in concept to the Entity Type discussed in detail in section 8.2.1. In fact, it bears a lot of similarity to the concept of an Entity Supertype. What is a first essential difference in the OOA/D approach is that there is **no separation**

between data and process. The (business) processing rules that apply to an Object **are part of it**: they are intrinsic to the Object itself; part of its definition, and are stored with it. Thus any interaction at all between Objects takes place by means of Messages that are passed between them, and this traffic evokes the set of rules relevant to the object itself and the context within which the communication occurs.

The situation is, in reality, both more subtle and more complex though. Firstly there is the concept of Inheritance to come to grips with. In an OOA/D context, an Object may have a subtype in a manner completely analogous to the data modelling concept of an entity subtype. The object subtype inherits **all the characteristics of its supertype, including the processing rules**. So, for example, let us consider the

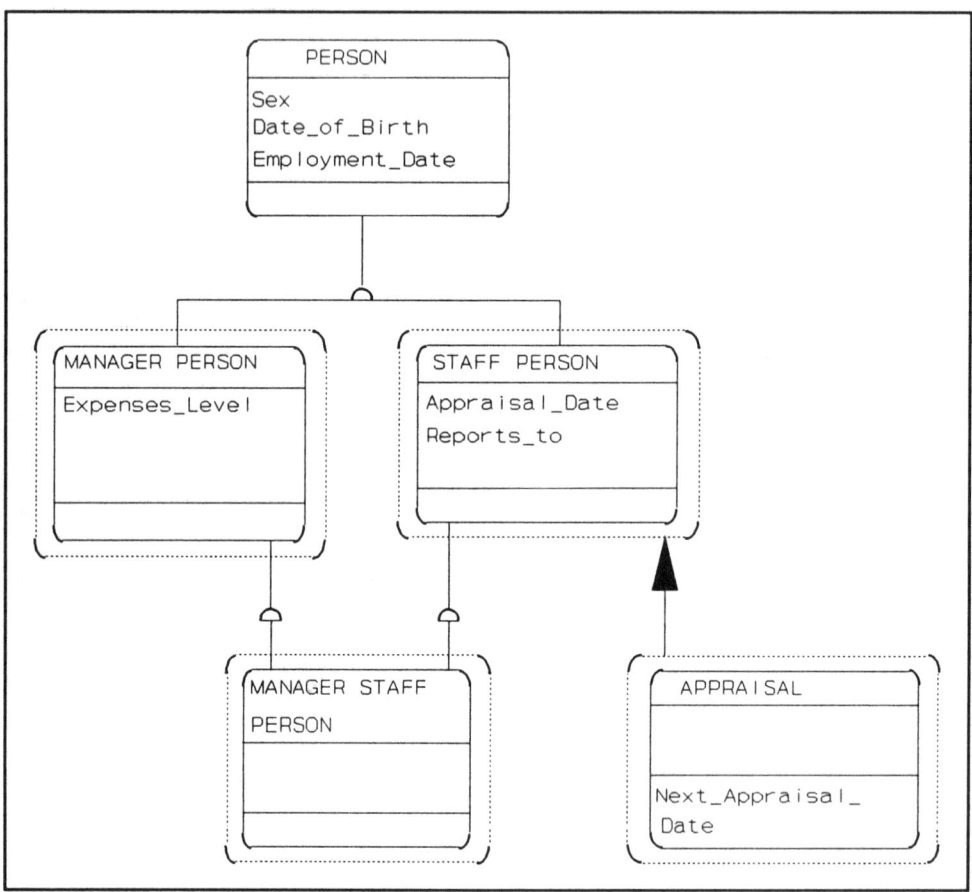

Figure 14.1 PERSON as an Object

simple Object illustrated in Figure 14.1[1]: a PERSON. In our business, the person is always either a MANAGER PERSON or a STAFF PERSON, and some people can be both (they manage people, **and** report to a manager). For each of these Objects and subtypes, there are things that we need to know about - attributes - some of which are unique to the subtype, but some of which **are inherited** from the supertype. Similarly there are processing rules that apply to all PERSONs in common - they must be either "Male" or "Female", must have a Date_of_Birth,[2] etc. There are also processing rules that are applicable to the subtype only. For example, a STAFF PERSON must report to one and only one MANAGER PERSON (the organisation is very hierarchical)[3], and each STAFF PERSON must be appraised for performance within six months of joining the company, and further staff appraisals must take place at least every six months.[4] (i.e. Appraisal_Date > (Employment_Date + 6 months) AND (TODAY + 6 months.))

These rules, which are part of the Object and, therefore, totally integral to it, only apply in certain contexts. For example, the rules relating to a PERSON's Sex and Date_of_Birth apply when a message is sent to the PERSON Object from another Object in an update/insert context, not in a read only one. The rules relating to the STAFF PERSON's Appraisal_Date apply when STAFF PERSON is called in the context of an APPRAISAL Object.

For the moment these ideas may seem quite remote from IE, but it is not difficult to understand how they might relate to an IE context. We have already seen a close analogy between Objects and Data Entity Types. These concepts are already coming into play in the ISP phase, but are developed more fully and extensively in BAA. OOA concepts will allow the rigid distinctions between data and process to become less, and the business rules, as they are identified, will be recorded with the appropriate aspect of the object they belong to. The context within which a rule or an aspect of it applies will also be recorded. The rather artificial analysis of sequential business logic represented in PADs will fall away. Instead, both business users and IT people will view things of interest to the business as a connection between the object, the rules applying to it, and the context within which the rules apply. In a seamless transition

---

[1] The conventions used follow those found in Coad, Peter and Yourdon, Edward, *Object-Oriented Analysis*, Second Edition, Yourdon Press, Englewood Cliffs, 1991.

[2] These are typical business rules that are captured in the BAA model: the permitted values for the attribute SEX are "Male" and "Female"; the DATE_OF_BIRTH attribute is compulsory.

[3] In an ERM, this business rule would be shown by means of a relationship between the entity subtypes MANAGER and STAFF.

[4] This business rule would be captured in the PAD during BAA if IE principles were being applied.

to design, OOD, **using the same principles,** will add a dimension of user interface rules to the Object-Oriented model. This model, containing the user interaction rules, will be the system: the analysis will become the design, and the context within which some of the user interaction rules will apply may be the system's operational platform.

So, OOA/D principles, in theory, could operate within a framing IE context, but they are likely to blur the distinction between the phases further, as is shown in Figure 14.2. This is not unlike the way in which Rapid Application Development principles have blurred the distinction between BSD and TD&C.

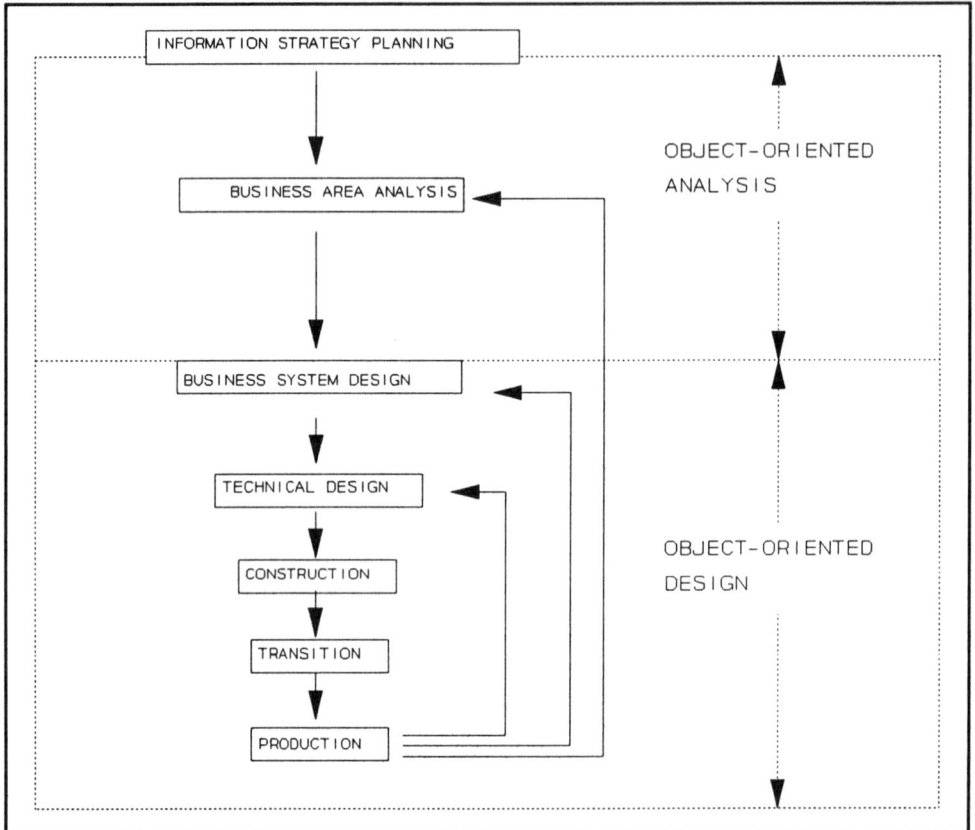

Figure 14.2 Object-Oriented Analysis/Design and Information Engineering

Clearly, new concepts affect the structures in which they operate, and this will be true too of applying IE principles to OOA/D. Again, though, IE could provide the solid framework - perhaps context is a better word - within which to operate. The evolution of OOA/D into a set of principles that can be used with practical consequences for the business will depend on the evolution of the tools to do the job. Object-Orientation grows out of concepts that are part of actual programming languages. These principles need to be elevated through the development life cycle, and the advantages they bring to the business need to be understood and communicated if Object-Orientation is not to be seen as just another technical innovation. One way of doing so could be a mapping of OOA/D to the phases and deliverables of IE.

14.2   AD/Cycle®, other Broad Frameworks, and C-CASE

A number of initiatives by IT manufacturers have brought the concepts of CASE tools and full life cycle management to the attention of the IT community in recent years. In doing so, they have given a tacit (and sometimes explicit) approval to the concepts that underlie IE, placing IE as a methodology in the spotlight of the attention of system developers.

Such initiatives, of which AD/Cycle®, illustrated in Figure 14.3, is but one,[5] in effect provide a particular IT manufacturer's framework for the use of CASE tools within the context of their product offerings. At the core of such a framework is the idea of a

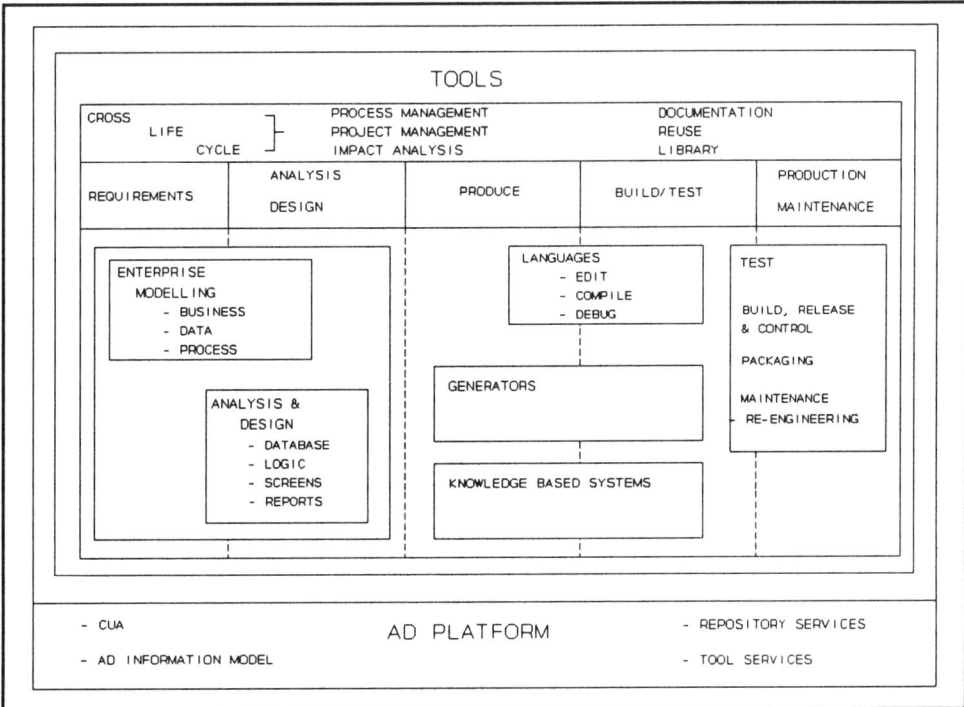

Figure 14.3 IBM's AD/Cycle®

---

[5] Digital's Cohesion Framework is another.

repository, which is an encyclopedia of information about information that also maintains the rules that govern relationships between the objects that are contained in it.   In the case of AD/Cycle®, products that are(/will be) AD/Cycle® compliant have/will have the ability to pass data to and from the mainframe encyclopedia that is the centrepiece of IBM®'s AD/Cycle® initiative.   The tools will also be CUA compliant, which means that they fit into IBM®'s SAA® architecture platform, and comply with the standards for interfacing with users.

Similar initiatives have been launched by other IT manufacturers, and what they share in concept is the idea of the repository as the means of exchanging modelling information between CASE tools across the complete systems life cycle, each of which may have its own internal standards and conventions for storing and depicting such information. The need then for Integrated CASE tools that provide complete life cycle coverage (I-CASE) disappears, and the user of CASE tools can choose a Component CASE product (C-CASE) that is best suited for the job at hand, mixing and matching different Upper CASE tools (used for planning and analysis) and Lower CASE tools (used for design, construction, and reverse engineering) from different suppliers.[6]

It is currently possible to mix and match in this way within the tight bounds that the CASE tool suppliers themselves operate in: bridges sometimes exist from a particular CASE tool to and/or from a predefined range of CASE tools. This is particularly useful when an I-CASE tool, or a powerful Upper CASE tool, does not move directly into the hardware and/or software environment that the envisaged system operates on. (The factors related to this particular issue have been discussed in section 12.1.) In such cases, bridging from one tool to another usually requires the purchase of additional conversion software and/or some "mopping up" work once the conversion has taken place.

There is no doubt that the broad CASE tool co-ordination platforms that major IT manufacturers have placed at the centre of their strategies for future systems development, together with the emergence of standards for the interchange of model information, will further encourage and facilitate the use of CASE tools in the future. Within such a context, the need for framing methodologies such as IE, supplemented by sound project management practices and predefined standards, will be more important even than now, if we, as IT professionals, are going to be able to "deliver the goods" to our users.

This book has been about getting the job done, and making the principles of IE work without becoming a slave to methodology or to a set of techniques. It is always difficult to keep the end goal - meeting user needs - in view when moving into a new theoretical and technical environment. The suspicion is that this task will become harder, not easier in the future, as both the tools and the concepts that they implement

---

[6] See also Chapter 3.

become more complex. But, immense opportunities open up to us as IT professionals together with such challenges **if we can make it work!**

Appendix A - Glossary of Abbreviations

The following abbreviations are used throughout the text. For further information, consult the relevant Index entry.

ADD	Activity Dependency Diagram
AHD	Activity Hierarchy Diagram
BSD	Business System Design
CICS	IBM®'s proprietary on-line transaction process monitor
CSA	Current Systems Analysis
CSF	Critical Success Factor
DBMS	Database Management System
DB2	IBM®'s proprietary relational database management system
DFD	Data Flow Diagram
DP	Data Processing
DSD	Data Structure Diagram
EHD	Entity Horizon Diagram
ELC	Entity Life Cycle Diagram
EMV	Entity Model View
ERM	Entity Relationship Model
ISP	Information Strategy Planning
OOA/D	Object-Oriented Analysis/Design
PAB	Process Action Block
PAD	Process Action Diagram
PC	Personal Computer
PDD	Process Dependency Diagram
PHD	Process Hierarchy Diagram
PrAD	Procedure Action Diagram
QA	Quality Assurance
RDBMS	Relational Database Management System
SAA	IBM®'s Systems Application Architecture
SQL	Standard Query Language, the standard relational database management system access language
TD&C	Technical Design and Construction
1NF	First Normal Form
2NF	Second Normal Form
3NF	Third Normal Form
3GL	Third Generation Language
4GL	Fourth Generation Language

Appendix B - Supplementary Reading

Readers who are interested in a more detailed discussion of some of the topics, and particularly of the techniques discussed in *Practical Information Engineering*, may wish to refer to a selection of the books listed below.

	A Guide to Information Engineering using the IEF™ Computer-Aided Planning, Analysis, and Design, Texas Instruments, 1988.
Barker, Richard	*CASE Method: Entity Relationship Modelling*, Addison Wesley, 1989.
Gane, Chris and Sarson, Trish	*Structured Systems Analysis: Tools and Techniques*, McAuto/IST Databooks, St. Louis, 1977. This book deals with Data Flow Diagrams from a process-driven analysis perspective.
Martin, James	*Information Engineering. A Trilogy*, Prentice-Hall, Englewood Cliffs, 1989.
Rock-Evans, Rosemary	*Analysis within the Systems Development Life Cycle*, (Four Volumes), Pergamon Infotech, Maidenhead, 1987.

Index